THE KANJI CODE

ABOUT THE AUTHOR

NATALIE HAMILTON is a writer, translator and lecturer in Translation Technology. She turned her focus to Japanese study while living and working in Japan's rural Oita Prefecture on the JET Programme. She was awarded a Master of Japanese Translation in 2014, which included a linguistics dissertation entitled Cracking the ON Yomi Code. She is NAATI-Certified in Australia for professional translation from Japanese to English and has translated academic papers in social science, and technical and corporate content for companies including Fujitsu, MUJI and Sony. She formerly wrote online content and elearning materials for global corporations. Natalie has taught English in Japan and Japanese at the Japan Foundation. Her Japanese was largely self-taught over four years living in Japan.

THE KANJI CODE

See the Sounds with Phonetic Components and Visual Patterns

加
机
検
請

Natalie Hamilton

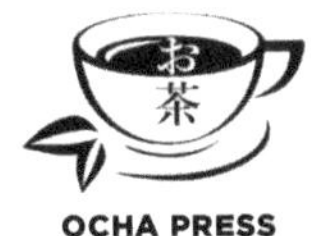

To my grandmother Leila Cumming,
and my parents,
Helen Cumming and Lachlan Cumming

First published in 2019 by Ocha Press
PO Box 3220
St Pauls Sydney NSW 2031
ochapress.com

The publisher and author thank Wikipedia author Pmx for providing reference images for some of the 'kanji kana' images. Image names: Katakana origin.svg, Hiragana origin.svg; Description: Table of hiragana and katakana characters, and the kanji from which they derive. Appearing in: Wikipedia article entitled Man'yōgana. Retrieved from: https://en.wikipedia.org/wiki/Man'yōgana. Source: Wikimedia Commons, the free media repository.

National Library of Australia Cataloguing-in-Publication Data:

Hamilton, Natalie, 1975 –

The Kanji Code: See the Sounds with Phonetic Components and Visual Patterns

2nd ed.

Includes index

ISBN: 978-0-6484886-0-6

ISBN: 978-0-6484886-1-3

1. Language and languages: study and teaching – Japanese – Textbook, reference.
2. Language arts – Japanese – calligraphy.

Cover design by Virginia Buckingham

Text layout by Virginia Buckingham

Printed in Australia by Ingram Spark

CONTENTS

INTRODUCTION 9

ABOUT THIS BOOK 15

CHAPTER 1 – THE SCRIPTS AND THEIR SOUNDS 27

CHAPTER 2 – THE KANA CODE 39

CHAPTER 3 – THE PHONETIC CODE 59

Standard Phonetics 74

Rhyming Phonetics 126

CHAPTER 4 – THE VISUAL CODE 137

APPENDICES 191

References 193

Acknowledgements 198

Glossary 199

1: Creative Component Stories 201

2: Radicals List 204

INDEXES 207

Components List/Index 208

Kanji Index 214

English Index 256

Radicals Index 264

INTRODUCTION

The Kanji Code teaches a systematic method for studying the readings or pronunciation of Japanese kanji characters – specifically, the Chinese or ON readings. A self-confessed kanji addict, I have been immersed in kanji for the past 14 years, either while living in Japan, studying Japanese translation or working as a translator. I have spent inordinate hours analysing the components of kanji and trying to break the 'kanji code' for the readings or pronunciations of hundreds of different kanji characters in relation to their visual appearance. I'll share with you some valuable tips and tricks to speed up your kanji reading, and make kanji learning less intimidating and a lot more fun.

This book is based on a Linguistics Dissertation I undertook at Macquarie University, Sydney, in 2011. I felt sure that the kanji ON readings could be learnt by more than rote memorisation, so I looked closely at the components and visual aspects such as shape, line and pattern for clues to help learn the readings.

I catalogued the 1,945 (at the time) daily-use kanji, or *Joyo Kanji*, and the relationship between their reading and visual look. The result is a list of phonetic components and a number of visual groups. In this text, I have also added a section which explains the historical link between hiragana, katakana and kanji, so you can use it as a way to learn their readings.

FOCUSED ON THE SOUNDS OR READINGS

While many kanji textbooks focus primarily on the *meaning* of kanji, this book focuses almost purely on how to read the *sounds* or *pronunciation* – in particular, the Chinese or ON readings. There are already many good books that explain kanji meaning using attractive illustrations, and I will touch on the radicals or meaning components, but that is not the main focus of this book. Clues to these Chinese readings can be found in the components and visual patterns of the characters, and can be traced back to their origins in the Chinese language where phonetics play a large role in indicating the readings of kanji characters – known in China as 'hanzi'.

REDUCE KANJI OVERWHELM

Memorising the long lists of kanji characters and their readings is one of the biggest challenges in learning the Japanese language. It's easy to feel overwhelmed when faced with hundreds upon hundreds of characters that look similar and have so many different readings to memorise. Unfortunately, while kanji is one of the most interesting aspects of the Japanese language, it is all too often the reason people quit learning it.

A SYSTEMATIC APPROACH

This book introduces systematic ways to learn common ON readings, and covers 585 useful kanji characters. It will help to reduce your reliance on rote learning by showing you how to identify the phonetic hints within kanji. By cutting the time needed to memorise the readings, you'll free up time for other important aspects of Japanese study, such as memorising kanji meanings and reading authentic texts.

UNDERSTAND THE PHONETIC ASPECTS OF KANJI

There is a common misconception that kanji are not phonetic; however, I will show that they do have phonetic aspects, they can be learnt and many can indeed be read for sound. The three aspects of the *Kanji Code* are outlined below.

THE KANA CODE

LEARN THE LINK BETWEEN KANJI AND KANA

A key piece of knowledge that every Japanese student should know is that each kana symbol is based on a kanji character. You can therefore leverage your existing knowledge of hiragana and katakana to learn the ON reading of 34 kanji characters that use the same readings today. I have also chosen 23 kanji characters that look like kana symbols to extend this idea.

THE PHONETIC CODE

LEARN THE PHONETIC COMPONENTS

This book provides a clear, easy-to-follow list of 150 phonetic components (also referred to as *phonetics*). These components each represent a particular ON reading. When you see one of these components within a kanji character, you will be able to make an educated guess about its likely ON reading. Just by learning the phonetics listed here, you will unlock the readings of 435 kanji characters and 737 compound words! Learning the phonetics allows you to 'read' kanji more like it was a phonetic alphabet.

THE VISUAL CODE

GROUP KANJI BY VISUAL FEATURES

Learn how visual features like shape and stripes can give a clue to the ON readings of 173 kanji characters. I have analysed a large number of kanji characters as if they were artistic works. Whether by design or coincidence, knowing that several kanji characters that feature thin horizontal stripes have the ON reading 'KEN' is useful to know. This novel approach will make your kanji learning more fun and seem less random. It should also appeal to people with an interest in art and design.

GAIN PHONEMIC AWARENESS

A welcome bonus from studying ON readings in this way is that you will become more familiar with the types of sounds that appear as kanji ON readings. You will notice sounds that are long, short, end in an inflection and end in the letter 'N'. You may start to notice which sounds tend to express certain ideas: positive, negative or neutral. You'll learn which kanji characters have rhyming ON readings and which have onomatopoeic readings. All of this information will feed into your overall understanding of the Japanese language and will improve your listening skills.

I would love to hear any insights you have into the look and reading of kanji in your own experience of studying kanji.

AUTHOR'S NOTE

Thank you very much for your interest in *The Kanji Code*. It is my sincere hope that this guide will make your kanji learning journey a little easier. I'd love to hear your feedback and suggestions about how it can be improved. I can be found on Twitter @ocha_natalie, and on Facebook at OchaTranslations. If you enjoy *The Kanji Code* and can find the time, I would really appreciate a short review online.

THE CHAPTERS IN THIS BOOK

ABOUT THIS BOOK

An extract from a Linguistics Dissertation I undertook at Macquarie University as part of a Master of Translation and Interpreting, this chapter introduces some recent research that supports the idea of teaching the phonetics and applying a visual approach to learning the ON readings.

CHAPTER 1 – THE SCRIPTS AND THEIR SOUNDS

An introduction to the Japanese scripts, and the common sounds of kanji ON readings.

CHAPTER 2 – THE KANA CODE

In this chapter, illustrations show the link between hiragana, katakana and the kanji characters that inspired them. Associating kanji readings with kana serves to reinforce your Japanese reading skills and phonetic awareness. It is also a great way to repurpose your existing knowledge of the kana symbols and will help you draw connections across the language as a whole.

CHAPTER 3 – THE PHONETIC CODE

Key phonetic components that appear in common kanji characters and Japanese vocabulary will be introduced in this chapter. Some of the phonetics are no more complex than a hiragana or katakana symbol, so you will be able to learn them just as quickly. A number of phonetics that indicate rhyming readings will also be presented, along with the idea of using onomatopoeia to group characters.

CHAPTER 4 – THE VISUAL CODE

In this chapter, I introduce 45 kanji groups, in which kanji characters share a visual feature and have the same or a similar ON reading. This section should be particularly inspiring to students who use visual clues when learning. You are invited to relax your eyes, activate your imagination and see a connection between the kanji in these groups that goes beyond their components. This original method for memorising kanji character readings has been very effective for myself; hopefully you'll find it so too.

WHICH KANJI FEATURE IN THIS BOOK

The *Joyo Kanji* or 'daily-use kanji' is a list of characters used in government documents and the media that the Japanese Ministry of Education expects Japanese school students to know by the time they graduate high school. In 2010, it was increased from 1,945 to 2,136 characters.

The first few hundred kanji characters you learn when you start studying roughly corresponds to Grades 1 and 2 of the *Joyo Kanji*. These characters tend to cover fundamental concepts like numbers, directions and elements, and are the building blocks for more advanced kanji. In fact, many lower grade characters also function as radicals, the components that indicate the meaning of kanji characters.

For example, the days of the week characters, which are usually taught at the beginner level are all common radicals that appear in a large number of characters. When 曜日 *youbi* is added to the ON reading of these characters, we get the days of the week. On their own, they represent a radical, as shown in the fourth column below.

Kanji + 曜日	English	Japanese	Radical
月	Monday	getsuyoubi	moon
火	Tuesday	kayoubi	fire
水	Wednesday	suiyoubi	water
木	Thursday	mokuyoubi	tree
金	Friday	kinyoubi	metal
土	Saturday	doyoubi	earth
日	Sunday	nichiyoubi	sun

It makes sense that these fundamental kanji characters are taught at the beginner level. However, for these radicals or characters with fewer strokes that don't contain a phonetic component, the system taught in this book is not at play yet. *The Kanji Code* therefore starts about halfway through Grade 2, when kanji become more complex and tend to have a phonetic component as well as a radical, and goes up to the secondary school level.

The Kanji Code doesn't follow the same order as the grades, because it is looking at patterns that occur across grades. If you've started this book with around 300 kanji, you will know 885 by the time you finish. This will put you well on the way to reading. Some estimates suggest that because many common kanji repeat a lot, you only need 800–1,000 kanji to be able to 'begin to make sense out of newspapers' (Pye, 1971).

Of course, while quantity is important, the *quality* of your understanding of the kanji *system* is what will set you apart from students trying to rote learn the ON readings. Once you are able to recognise which part of a kanji indicates its meaning, and which part indicates its sound, you will have a more sophisticated command of the written language that will continue to be useful as you move up the grades.

I believe that in order to learn to read Japanese efficiently, you should learn the following five elements in this order:

1. Hiragana
2. Katakana
3. Radicals
4. Phonetics
5. Kanji.

THE VALUE OF LEARNING IN ON READING ORDER

Kanji characters are usually listed in dictionary indexes in stroke order. The kanji below would appear in this order

Character	Meaning	Number of strokes
一	one	1
月	moon	4
緊	firm	15

Kanji characters tend to be taught along these lines too, starting with the simplest then moving up to the most complicated. However, Pye makes the good point that learning kanji in this order is a bit like a medical student lining up all the bones in the human body according to length and learning them in that order. It doesn't make sense, because there are more meaningful ways to group the bones.

Grouping kanji characters by sound connections and listing them in ON reading order, as in *The Phonetic Code* chapter, gives you a better chance of seeing patterns in the readings, which you can use to memorise key kanji information. As you become more familiar with the ON reading order, it makes it easier to look words up later.

ABOUT THIS BOOK

The idea for this book came about when I was studying kanji independently while living in Japan in 2006. At the time, a list of phonetic components was tantalisingly inaccessible and I was told 'You just have to learn them' one too many times. This is what prompted my own attempt to catalogue them, using coloured highlighter pens on a two-page printout of the *Joyo Kanji* listed in ON reading order. I later made this exercise formal by undertaking a linguistics dissertation at Macquarie University in 2011.

Although I first studied Japanese at high school in Sydney, it had been six years since I had picked up a Japanese textbook when I moved to Japan in 2004. From that point my study was done outside mainstream university channels, and my Japanese learning trajectory has therefore been unconventional. Stationed in a rural town, I relied on textbooks found on the shelves of bookshops in Osaka and Fukuoka and written in English. I had no knowledge of the two books written in English that listed the kanji in ON order: *The Study of Kanji* (Pye, 1971) and *Remembering the Kanji 2* (Heisig, 1987). These books were probably in university libraries but they weren't in the shops I went to. This meant that my research was conducted somewhat in a bubble, and the result is that I relied almost purely on my eyes; on the links I could see between the look of kanji and their ON readings.

Now that I have seen Pye and Heisig's books, I know I would have found them useful when I was struggling to learn those kanji. What I hope *The Kanji Code* does is take the same approach, of listing kanji in ON reading order, and take it another step further by explicitly stating which components are the phonetic and what sound they represent. I've tried to bring some of my technical writing and teaching background to the task to make it as user-friendly as possible. By using romaji for the readings, it should be accessible to students of all levels. And by using illustrations and tracing elements, I've tried to make it as visually engaging as possible.

Over the years I have continued to intermittently search online for a list of the phonetic components, mostly to no avail. In 2017, I stumbled upon a linguistics dissertation online, which included a list of the most useful phonetics (Townsend, 2011). Coincidentally, we had been working on our dissertations concurrently in Sydney and San Francisco, without knowledge of one another's work. There was some overlap in the phonetics we'd both identified. Some that I listed were not in Townsend's list, and some she had listed were not in mine. I have indicated in the References the ones that I obtained from Townsend's list. The discovery of her list was encouraging, and convinced me that my preoccupation with the phonetics and other visual clues wasn't a dead end, but was something in the zeitgeist and gaining momentum. This, teamed with other personal factors, gave me the impetus to push on with *The Kanji Code*.

Kanji learning and teaching is not making full use of the phonetic components (Toyoda, 2013). The question is not so much whether phonetics are useful, or which ones are useful, but can they be presented in a way that makes them easy to learn and practical to apply to kanji study?

I researched some diverse topics as part of the dissertation. An extract of the literature review with some more recent research included follows.

Learning kanji without adequate support and learning strategies can lead to feelings of helplessness and failure, and giving up

Usuki defines kanji learning problems as a sense of frustration or helplessness, or anxieties about the difficulty of learning kanji (Usuki, 2000). Respondents in this study reported quickly forgetting kanji even after writing them 50 times, and struggling with the different readings and pronunciation depending on the combinations of characters. A lack of confidence and feelings of failure lead students to consider giving up, and strips them of the enjoyment of learning. Many of the participants spoke of feeling like a failure as they studied hard but continued to get bad results in tests, unable to keep up with the hundreds of kanji they were expected to learn each week. On the other hand, some of the respondents who had persevered reported feelings of enjoyment at the challenge and a sense of accomplishment once they could see that kanji is a system (Usuki, 2000).

I was one of those students who eventually gave up studying because of kanji, dropping the subject for the higher school certificate, intimidated by the long list of kanji. So I am intimately acquainted with the feelings Usuki observed.

Look it up: dictionary issues and kanji

Getting better at guessing the ON readings provides the practical benefit of being able to look up new words more quickly.

Using a dictionary is rarely a straightforward process for kanji learners, who often face a 'chicken and egg' scenario when it comes to reading unknown kanji characters. That is to say, if they encounter a word written in kanji that they do not understand, they must look it up in a dictionary. Yet, if they do not know the pronunciation of the word, they cannot locate it in a standard Japanese-English dictionary, which lists words in their kana order, starting from あ [a] and finishing at ん [n].

Kanji dictionaries provide a workaround method that does not require knowledge of the reading, but is laborious and requires learners to follow complex steps to locate the kanji. For example, the standard kanji dictionary used by high school students requires users to first work out the kanji's radical, then count the number of strokes in that radical. They then turn to the radical index at the back of the dictionary, which lists radicals in order of the number of strokes. Once they have located the radical, they scan through a list of kanji containing that radical. When they find the kanji they are looking for, they use the page reference to find the kanji's entry. This entry is written in Japanese and the definition is likely to be incomprehensible to a Japanese as a Foreign Language (JFL) learner. Obviously, this method requires a detailed knowledge of radicals.

There are some English kanji dictionaries that allow JFL learners to locate kanji by different methods including categorising them by radical type and overall formation, for example, *Kanji Learner's Dictionary* (2001). These are certainly easier for JFL learners to use, but the time it takes to look up the meaning of a single kanji means that attempting to read a text made up of around half kanji is a painstaking task for learners. By the time you locate the meaning of the new word, you have lost the flow of the context around it.

Electronic dictionaries have made the process a little easier, but they can be difficult for beginner learners to use, as they require a learner to draw a kanji character using a stylus in the correct stroke order. If they draw the character too slowly or use the wrong stroke order, the electronic dictionary is unlikely to recognise the character and will instead return a series of seemingly random kanji characters that may be nothing to do with the kanji being looked up. Even now with 13 years of electronic dictionary use under my belt, and a good knowledge of the correct stroke order, I often find I am too slow and the results are far from what I was seeking.

Online dictionaries have made it faster for learners to look up the pronunciation of unknown characters. Various websites provide hints and learning aids, for example Pop Jisyo (meaning pop-up dictionary) allows users to hover their mouse over an unknown kanji, whereupon a pop-up window is displayed, indicating the meaning and all the ON and kun readings of the kanji character. The Google Translate website allows users to click a speaker icon and hear an automated voice reading a word out loud; it also shows the reading in text. While these are useful learning aids, they are dependent on the learner being connected to the internet, and rather than aiding learners to become self-sufficient in reading kanji, they simply provide an instant answer to the question of a kanji's reading.

As learners increase their proficiency, it is a desirable outcome that they will become less reliant on instant learning aids, and more reliant on their own memory and inferring skills when deducing the readings of unknown kanji in authentic texts such as newspapers and magazines. By learning the phonetics, they will get much better at guessing the readings, and therefore, will be able to look words up more quickly.

They will also be able to take advantage of predictive typing on a keyboard or phone, and start to type in the sound they think it might be, and then scroll through the options that are presented to check if their guess is correct.

What can we learn from character background learners?

A 2003 study compared the kanji learning strategies preferred by character background learners (CB) – that is, learners who have been schooled in Chinese characters, for example Chinese speakers – and alphabet background learners (AB) – those schooled using an alphabet-based language (Gamage, 2003). This study provides a rare insight into the impact of orthographic background on learning strategies.

The participants were beginner level Japanese language students at the undergraduate level in Australia. The strategies used most often were determined to be the ones that the students perceived to be the most helpful. The kanji learning strategies were separated into three categories: 'shape (visual strategies), meaning (semantic strategies) and pronunciation (phonological strategies)' (Gamage, 2003), noting that recent kanji textbooks emphasise the importance of contextual strategies.

Significantly, AB learners reported using 'repeated writing' strategies significantly more often than CB learners did, while CB learners made better use of the phonological aspects of kanji (Gamage, 2003). CB learners were significantly more likely to use phonetic strategies such as 'grouping kanji with similar pronunciations and phonetic [components]' and remembering both the ON reading and kun reading at the same time. In contrast, AB learners tended to use visual strategies including 'picture association to kanji'.

Gamage notes that while AB learners prefer to use cognitively less demanding strategies, CB learners tend to favour strategies that look at the internal structure of a kanji, such as grouping them by radical or stroke count. Gamage concludes that since CB learners are, to a certain extent, already familiar with the shape and meaning of kanji, they are likely to be able to bypass rote-learning strategies and instead, transfer their prior knowledge of kanji due to the wide exposure in their native language. Gamage recommends that cognitive processing strategies that are oriented to a learner's orthographic background be employed.

Rather than taking a fatalist view and saying, 'It's easier for Chinese students', and AB learners just have to learn by rote, a more positive approach is to ask the question: 'What can we learn from how CB learners approach learning Japanese kanji?' If Chinese learners group kanji with similar pronunciations and phonetic components, this method should be equally effective for non-Chinese learners, if they are taught the phonetic components and their associated pronunciations.

Phonetic components – an unknown quantity and hard to teach

Although the radicals and their role as indicators of kanji meaning are generally well known, the role of phonetic components is not easy to define (Miwa, 2012). This is partly because the roles of the two types of components are not mutually exclusive. For example, it is possible for the same component to play the role of the phonetic component in one kanji, and the semantic component in another (Toyoda, 2000). Furthermore, while semantic components are mostly on the left and phonetic components are mostly on the right, this is only a rule of thumb and there are many exceptions (Flores d'Arcais, Saito & Kawakami, 1995; Toyoda, 2000). For example, the character for 'knife' 刀 [katana] is used as a semantic component in about 80 complex characters and as a phonetic (dao) in around 12 (Flores d'Arcais et al., 1995).

Inexplicably, Japanese students are not introduced to the phonetic components in a structured form, and Japanese children learn kanji readings without these clues (Townsend, 2011). They have only recently become a topic of focus in Japan, with books released in 2012. The idea was definitely in the air while I was writing my dissertation.

Kanji is phonetic and reading it isn't that different from reading alphabets like English

Until recently, it was commonly believed that as a logographic script, kanji, and indeed Chinese, were only read for meaning, not sound. Most textbooks describe hiragana and katakana as the phonetic scripts, as if kanji was completely different.

Experimental evidence in 1991 supported the theory that reading Chinese characters involves phonological recoding not dissimilar to the process used when reading alphabetic scripts (Lam, Perfetti & Bell, 1991). This suggests that individual kanji characters have visual components which provide clear clues to their phonetic readings, and that native speakers and readers of logographic languages are equipped with knowledge of these phonological clues, whether consciously or not. Flores d'Arcais et al. (1995) concluded that readers of logographic scripts work out the pronunciation of unknown kanji characters, either via phonological information (post-lexically) or through the phonological information associated with the character. Furthermore, they state that the existence of phonetic radicals allows readers to follow a grapheme-to-phoneme route (Flores d'Arcais et al., 1995).

Bernhardt (1991) theorised that subvocalisation of some sort might be occurring during second language (L2) reading in Japanese or Chinese. Subvocalisation refers to the process of sounding words out in one's head while reading. In other words, JFL learners '*hear* when they read'

(Bernhardt, 1991, p. 76). This strengthens the case against the idea that kanji are not a phonetic script. The results of a study by Matsunaga & Crosby (1997) indicated that native Japanese participants perceive both sounds and meaning during the process of reading kanji, and the authors concluded that phonological coding is involved in kanji processing. If this were the case, it would be useful for JFL learners to be instructed on the phonological encoding inherent in kanji reading.

Sounding it out helps with inferring

Subvocalisation accounts for the preference of CB learners towards using phonetic strategies. One study by Kondo-Brown (2006) investigated how non-native learners of Japanese with English as their first language infer unknown kanji words in authentic texts. The participants were all advanced level Japanese language students in Hawaii, although some students were recorded as having higher proficiency than others. Some students had Japanese heritage, meaning that Japanese-speaking parents in an English country had raised them, while others were from a wholly English background, a factor that was taken into account in the discussion.

The results indicated that students were better at inferring the meanings of unknown characters when they were able to process the words phonologically, that is, correctly pronounce the kanji words. 'The more comprehensive a [student's] control of the phonological properties of a word, the greater the ability to inference' (Kondo-Brown, 2006, p. 144). This means that if you see a kanji compound that you don't know, but you are able to work out the pronunciation, you have a better chance of guessing the *meaning*.

Since students of advanced Japanese are expected to learn vocabulary from context while reading authentic texts (Kondo-Brown, 2006), the ability to correctly pronounce unknown kanji characters should therefore be a valuable skill for JFL learners.

Learning the phonetics and other visual clues to the ON reading therefore puts students in a better position to be able to guess the meaning of new words, and gives them a sense of confidence and control over their learning, countering the feelings of helplessness documented by Usuki.

The Chinese ON readings have more in common with modern Chinese readings than you may realise

Students from a Chinese background tend to be better at learning Japanese. This is partly because of the similarity in the readings and meanings, but also because they have already been trained in how to interpret the components of kanji.

The Chinese character script hanzi and kanji share the same etymological origin as well as the same semantic core (Lieh-Ting, 2008). In a study on two-character kanji compound words between Japanese and Chinese, Hong (2005) analysed 17,049 kanji compounds based on the similarities between Chinese and Japanese orthography and meaning, and found that 10,189 or 59.76% of all kanji compounds had either the same or overlapping orthography and meaning.

As well as the similarities in meaning, there are also regular and systematic correspondences between the phonetic elements of modern hanzi and kanji ON reading, which allow L1 Chinese learners to quickly establish phonetic associations, assisting in learning and inferring the pronunciation of unfamiliar kanji words (Lieh-Ting, 2008). Kanji words that originate from hanzi and are pronounced in the ON reading give Chinese learners of Japanese a sense of familiarity, which allows them to memorise the kanji much more easily through both visual representations (shapes) as well as the approximation of the sounds based on their Chinese counterparts (Lieh-Ting, 2008). For example, the kanji compound 安全 refers to 'safety' in both Japanese and Chinese, and its pronunciation is [anzen] in Japanese and [ānquán] in Chinese, making it very easy for Chinese learners to memorise both the meaning and the sounds based on their first language (L1) knowledge (Lieh-Ting, 2008).

Wang (2004) analysed vowel correspondences between hanzi and the ON reading of 2,136 kanji characters from the *Joyo Kanji* to find thirteen correspondence rules of Sino-Japanese vowels. Wan (1999) described the Sino-Japanese phonological correspondence between ancient hanzi and modern hanzi as an assonance relationship. Phonological similarities serve as an auxiliary tool for L1 Chinese learners to learn kanji through sound-spelling correspondences. A number of studies have suggested that this correspondence could be used to assist L1 Chinese learners in inferring Japanese kanji pronunciation (Lieh-Ting, 2008). Lieh-Ting proposed an instructional method to take advantage of these similarities, in which kanji were introduced to students in phonetic groups, through a web-based Sino-Japanese phonological correspondence system. The effectiveness of this method was tested by assigning two groups of participants kanji compound homework over a five-week period. One group was given access to the web-based system, while the other group were instructed to use hard-copy dictionaries to look up the meaning and pronunciation of kanji compounds.

The results of the five-week study were empirically examined to test the effect of the proposed method on learners' strategy use. The results showed that the participants who use Lieh-Ting's instructional method went from relying mainly on visual-based strategies to using both visual and phonological-based strategies. Furthermore, the participants who used Lieh-Ting's method performed significantly better than those who did not

(Lieh-Ting, 2008). While being careful to acknowledge that negative interference from hanzi knowledge sometimes results in problems, and hanzi and kanji are not identical, Lieh-Ting (2008) concludes that the benefits for Chinese background learners may still be greater than such interference problems and that knowledge of hanzi may allow L1 Chinese learners to gain an edge over alphabetical background learners.

These methods are useful to learners who know Chinese; a similar approach of teaching the phonetic clues in kanji could help students without prior knowledge of Chinese.

The natural advantage visualisers have in learning kanji

In recent years, the idea of learning styles has gained momentum and been used in teacher training. Learning style refers to an individual's natural and preferred method of absorbing and retaining new information and skills (Reid, 1995) and to their overall approach to the business of learning (Ehrman, 1996). Cognitive styles are defined as an individual's 'preferred and habitual modes of perceiving, remembering, organising, processing and representing information' (Dörnyei, 2005, p. 129) and relate more to style than to ability.

The Verbal-Imagery Style dimension divides individuals into those who are outgoing and tend to represent information while thinking aloud, and those who are more inward and tend to think in mental pictures (Dörnyei, 2005). Dörnyei states that *verbalisers* are better at working with verbal information, while *imagers*, also referred to in the literature as *visualisers*, are superior at working with visual or spatial information (Dörnyei, 2005). Verbalisers, tend to prefer a stimulating environment, whereas imagers are more content with a static environment.

When a visualiser is introduced to someone at a party, they often visualise the name written on the face of that person. When remembering information in an exam, they often picture their study notes exactly in the position they appeared on the page – for example, on the top right. Kanji was invented for visualisers, because they naturally think in images. If they like to draw and have a mind for art analysis, they will be in their element drawing kanji and analysing the meaning in relation to the radicals. They should also be able to memorise the phonetics and put them into practice with relative ease. They should also be able to see the same shapes and patterns that I have catalogued in Chapter 4, *The Visual Code*.

The way kanji are introduced doesn't necessarily make the best use of these tendencies. In my teaching experience, a key factor to help students learn is enjoyment. If they have fun while they are studying, they are more likely to remember the content, and self-motivation grows. Of course, what is enjoyable varies between learners.

The theory of cognitive profiles has been used to analyse how students prefer to write compositions (Tucker, 1995). While verbaliser students respond well when instructed to simply start writing in class, this approach did not work for the visualisers, who preferred to delay the moment when drafting began (Tucker, 1995). This delay is as important as the writing itself, and seems to work like an 'incubation' period (Tucker, 1995, p. 28). Flower and Hayes (1984) theorise that for visualisers, invention is not a logical or verbal process necessarily but instead involves imagery, analogy and schema (Flower & Hayes, 1984). They need to understand the associations between the parts in order to prepare the whole.

Tucker's attitude to teaching writing started to change once he saw it through the eyes of visualisers, whose minds seem to work better when given time to reflect quietly, group ideas and doodle. He also observes that visualisers have a better view of the 'big picture' and are able to visualise the rest of the document without seeing it in front of them. If kanji learning can be reframed with the visualiser learner in mind, it would keep all of these factors in mind; an approach which could be beneficial to visualisers and other learners.

For example, since OVs use imagery, analogy and schema, they are in a perfect position to memorise the radicals and learn the meaning of kanji words by considering the analogous connections and metaphorical combinations in creating the meaning of kanji and the words created from their combination. Their propensity for grouping ideas would work well with the approach listed here of grouping phonetics and kanji by visual similarity. If they like to see the 'big picture', then perhaps learning more kanji, while being shown the connections between them, will be more effective than the traditional 'drip feed' kanji teaching method, where students are exposed to small amounts of kanji at a time, depriving them of the opportunity to make connections between readings, meanings and visual form.

Object visualisers like still images, colour and shape

Recent literature in the field of behavioural and neuropsychology has looked at how different cognitive styles relate to working memory (WM). Li et al. (2011) proposed that the *visualiser* dimension be further subdivided into *object visualisers* (OV) and *spatial visualisers* (SV) (Li et al., 2011). OVs habitually use visual properties (e.g. colour and shape) to construct high-resolution objects and scenes, while SVs are more likely to use imagery to represent and transform spatial relations. Literature suggests that people with a particular type are more likely to work in certain professions. For example, visual artists are more likely to be OVs, and physics and engineering scientists tend to be SVs (Li et al., 2011). OVs were found to have higher neural efficiency than SVs in processing object tasks and were better able to memorise object information when the demands on memory were high (Li et al., 2011).

This could indicate that SVs prefer to learn with video games and animations within apps, while OVs prefer to have time to absorb visual information about kanji and their components in a static form such as a book or poster. By breaking down the elements of kanji into 'bite-size chunks', displaying them with different colours and drawing attention to their shapes, OVs will be able to use their natural visual processing abilities to learn kanji. By pointing out the similarities between kanji that contain the same phonetics and visual features like shapes and stripes, the OV's natural tendency to make associations between parts will be enhanced and supported.

As an OV, my learning style has a strong visual preference and relatively poor aural recollection. Learning a second language was therefore reliant on being able to visualise the words, and I intuitively knew that I would not make much progress with my Japanese until I had learnt a significant number of kanji and was able to visualise the words as I spoke and listened. Seeing learning framed in these two dimensions made sense to me. Rather than a 'one-size-fits-all' approach to kanji teaching, clearly different approaches will appeal to different learners.

A good ear: the need for visual aids

In second-language acquisition, phonological memory (PM) has been said to reflect a learner's ability to process the phonological aspects of language. PM is defined as one sub-component of WM, and is referred to in the various literature as verbal short-term memory, phonological working memory, phonological short-term memory and phonological loop. It refers to the memory of sound, and is used when remembering, processing and learning language. Individuals display varying levels of PM, with some people having good PM, which could be described as having 'a good ear', and others having low PM. Low PM has been associated with dyslexia and learning disabilities (Snowling, 2000).

One study found that Finnish children with a strong PM in non-word repetition tests were found to be better at learning English as a second language (Service, 1992) and PM can be a strong predictor of second-language achievement, in particular vocabulary acquisition (Hummel & French, 2010). While individuals might have an inherent potential for PM capacity, their processing efficiency could be improved through training (Hummel & French, 2010).

In language classroom, aural-input contexts, students rely heavily on PM (Hummel & French, 2010). This is a reflection of the fact that language classes are usually presented in spoken format, and students are required to learn on the go from the aural input. Students with weak PM may fall behind, as their ability to learn from simply listening is weaker than students with a good PM. However, providing more visual stimulus could reduce their reliance on PM and free up cognitive resources to process other elements of language, including syntactic patterns and semantic content (Hummel & French, 2010).

Other strategies suggested that may help students with poor PM include reducing the amount of material to be remembered, repeating key information, encouraging the use of memory aids and developing a child's own strategies to support memory (Gathercole and Alloway, 2008, p. 69). Phonological, lexical and semantic associations between a student's first and second languages also reduce the 'processing load' – that is, the mental strain taken to learn the new language – on PM because they rely more on long-term knowledge (Hummel & French, 2010).

Chun and Payne (2004) found that individuals with a low PM capacity looked up words three times as much as others, but performed much the same overall on the comprehension and vocabulary tasks, implying that compensation occurs. This prompted them to suggest the use of multimedia CD-ROMs for learning German, to allow learners with low PM to look up words and definitions. With the rise of the Internet and computer games, Japanese second-language teachers have investigated the efficacy of designing computer games that encourage the mastery of the semantic components of kanji (Harris, 2011). While computer games with moving objects may be an ideal learning aid for SVs, OVs may prefer images presented in a visually pleasing, quiet and static format.

The literature on PM adds another angle to the subject of kanji teaching. Because of the common belief that learning kanji is the most difficult aspect of learning Japanese, most kanji learning is delayed until students are at an advanced level. However, I would argue the value of teaching more kanji at an earlier stage, and providing useful clues to how to read them, could assist learners with a low PM to compensate by using kanji as an auxiliary visual aid. Rather than 'scaring learners off', showing them a lot of kanji at the start but pointing out the patterns will give them a sense that there is light at the end of the tunnel. They can see where they are and where they need to go, and they have been given plenty of clues for the journey.

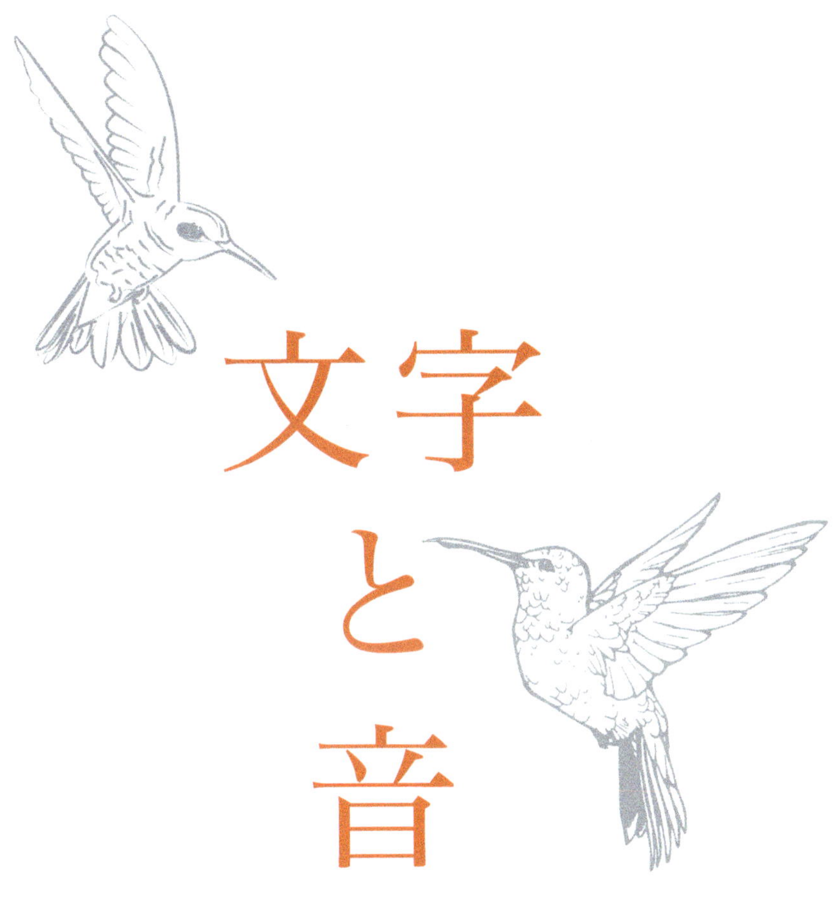

文字と音

CHAPTER 1 – THE SCRIPTS AND THEIR SOUNDS

CHAPTER 1 – THE SCRIPTS AND THEIR SOUNDS

Kanji was first introduced to Japan in the 5th century, when classical Chinese texts and Buddhist sutras were imported into the country. Before this there was no writing system in Japan, but there was a lively spoken language and culture. Hiragana and katakana were created later as a phonetic script. We will learn more about the surprising origin of hiragana and katakana in Chapter 2, *The Kana Code.*

Japanese is often referred to as having three types of scripts, but I think this description is misleading. I prefer to split it up into two scripts to reflect the different information they represent and function they perform.

1. Kana (Hiragana and Katakana)

Representing sound only

Hiragana and katakana (referred to collectively in this book as kana) are a purely phonetic script in which each symbol represents a single sound – much like the English alphabet. Each sound is only one syllable in length, for example, a, ka, sa, ta, ma. The only symbol that doesn't include a vowel sound is N. The 46 hiragana symbols and 46 katakana symbols can be learnt relatively quickly by associating one sound with each symbol.

2. Kanji

Representing sound & meaning

Kanji is a logographic script that represents both sound and meaning. There is a much broader range of sounds that can be applied to kanji characters, ranging from a one syllable sound like that of a kana (KA, MU) to two syllable sounds (KAKU, BETSU), right through to whole words with multiple syllables (katachi, hitsuji). Crucially, in addition to its sound, each kanji character carries a meaning. This could be a noun, verb or something more abstract. Moreover, this meaning is not completely fixed, but is somewhat mutable – that is, its meaning can change depending on how the kanji character is combined with kana or other kanji. Needless to say, memorising kanji characters and their associated sounds and meanings is a more mentally demanding task than learning the kana symbols and their sounds.

KANA

Hiragana ひらがな

平仮名

simplified script

The first character 平 means flat and level, and in this context means simple or simplified. The second and third characters 仮名 mean script.

Hiragana represent 46 unique sounds and are among the first things students learn when they study Japanese. They are used mainly for native Japanese words and grammatical features such as particles and verb endings. Visually, hiragana are rounded and fluid.

Hiragana	Reading
あ	a
か	ka
た	ta
ま	ma

Hiragana tend to appear as every third character or so in a Japanese sentence, so they also perform the purpose of breaking up the text and providing pauses between words written in kanji. For example, hiragana have been underlined in the sentence below.

私<u>は</u>日本人<u>です</u>。Watashi <u>wa</u> nihonjin <u>desu</u>. I am Japanese.

Historically, hiragana was used for personal notes, while kanji was used for official documents.

Hiragana's role in Japanese literature

During the Heian period from 794–1185, women were officially banned from learning kanji and could therefore only write in hiragana. The script was widely used among court women, and was known as women's writing 女手 (onnade) – a combination of the characters for woman and hand.

In fact, the world's first novel was written entirely in hiragana by a lady-in-waiting during the Heian period. Completed around 1021, The Tale of Genji 源氏物語 (Genji monogatari) is considered one of the great works of Japanese literature. It sheds light on court life at the time, and tells the story of the handsome and brilliant son of a Japanese emperor, Hikaru Genji. The author's real name is unknown but scholars have dubbed her Murasaki Shikibu, based on characters in the book.

Katakana カタカナ

片仮名

fragment script

The first kanji character 片 means fragment, which refers to the fact that each katakana symbol is a fragment taken from a kanji character. The second and third characters 仮名 mean script.

Visually, katakana symbols are more angular than hiragana. They represent the same 46 sounds as hiragana, and are in this sense an exact replica. You could almost go so far as to call them a different font, since in many cases the forms of hiragana and katakana look similar but for style.

Hiragana	Katakana	Reading
う	ウ	u
か	カ	ka
き	キ	ki
こ	コ	ko
も	モ	mo

Katakana was first used by Buddhist monks as a kind of crib note to show the readings of the kanji that appeared in Buddhist scriptures. In fact, they were used in much the same way that furigana is used today (tiny hiragana characters that sit on top of kanji characters when it is assumed that the reader might not know the reading).

Today, katakana is still used in dictionaries to show the readings of kanji characters. Its other main functions include writing 'loan' words from other languages, such as アカウント (akaunto) from the English 'account', writing onomatopoeia which features heavily in manga cartoons, and for visual emphasis in advertising and packaging.

KANJI

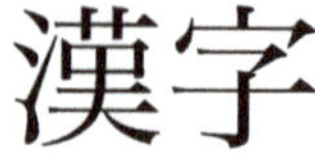

Chinese character

The first character 漢 means Chinese and also refers to the Han Dynasty. The second character 字 means character or letter.

As mentioned earlier, kanji are powerful characters jam-packed with sound and meaning information.

Take the following examples, which show the sound and meaning of four kanji characters.

Kanji	Sound		Meaning
	ON reading	Kun reading	
木	MOKU	ki	tree
彩	SAI	irodo(ru)	colouring
時	JI	toki	time
行	KOU, GYOU, AN	i(ku), yu(ku), okona(u)	go

Each character has a sound attached to it – an ON reading and a Kun reading. They also each represent a meaning. That is a lot of information contained in a single kanji character.

In terms of visual style, kanji characters can vary greatly. They can be simple or complex; angular or rounded; geometrical or fluid; symmetrical or asymmetrical; ordered or chaotic. They are generally more complex than kana, although it should be noted that some of the simplest kanji are even simpler than some kana. For example, the character for the number one is a single stroke, 一.

Kanji are used to write nouns, verbs and other key vocabulary. They can appear on their own, with hiragana to complete a word (okurigana) or with other kanji in compound words. The majority of compound words contain two kanji characters, but they can also contain three or four. *Yojijukugo* are set phrases such as proverbs and sayings comprised of four kanji characters.

Each kanji character can be broken down into smaller components, and the way these components work together to convey sound and meaning is quite logical. The more of these components you know, the less you need to rote learn the meanings and readings. You can learn them systematically, looking for clues within a kanji character, and using association as a key tool.

The kanji readings

There are two possible readings for each kanji character: the Chinese reading and the Japanese reading.

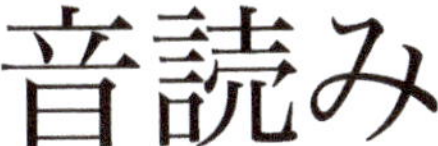

Chinese reading ***on yomi***

1. I refer to the **Chinese reading** as the ON reading, but its full Japanese name is *on yomi*. It is an adaptation of a kanji character's Chinese reading using Japanese pronunciation. For example, the Japanese reading for 明 is MEI, which is based on the Chinese reading MING (as in Ming Dynasty). It's a bit like how *akaunto* is an adaptation of the English word account.

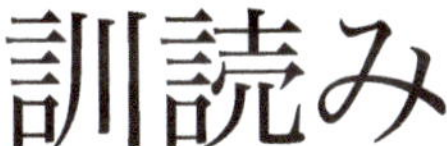

Japanese reading ***kun yomi***

2. I refer to the **Japanese reading** as the kun reading, but its full Japanese name is *kun yomi*. It is the existing Japanese word that corresponds to an imported kanji character. For example, *hitsuji* was the Japanese word for sheep 羊. Since the word already existed, when the kanji character was imported this reading was simply tacked onto the character.

   Another way to look at it is to see the kun reading as the Japanese translation. For example, when we say that 羊 means sheep, we are simply translating it into English. The same process was followed when applying the word *hitsuji*, the Japanese 'translation' of this kanji character.

Kanji character	English translation	Japanese translation & kun reading
羊	sheep	hitsuji
木	tree	ki
米	rice	kome
行	to go	iku
食	to eat	taberu

In some ways, rote learning is unavoidable with the kun readings. As you learn Japanese vocabulary, especially nouns and verbs, you simply have to learn the kanji that goes with it. Over time, you will come to associate the word with that kanji character.

The phonetic components that will be introduced in this book do not work for kun readings, because the native Japanese word existed before the kanji character was imported. Having developed in isolation and away from China, the relationship between a kanji character and its kun reading is therefore mostly random. The kun readings for each featured kanji can be found in its full entry in the index for you to study at your own pace, but the focus here is on the patterns of the ON readings.

The phonetics only help with words that use the ON or Chinese reading, because this system originated in China where it is still in use today. Even though the readings often changed in the process of importation from China to Japan, the correspondence of a certain ON reading to a certain phonetic component has been maintained. For example, the Japanese phonetic 甬 is read TSUU in Japanese and TONG in Chinese.

Why do some kanji have more than one ON reading?

In order to understand why one kanji character can have multiple readings, we need to learn a bit of history.

Kanji didn't arrive in Japan as a complete set in the 5th Century, but rather continued to trickle across the sea in dribs and drabs over hundreds of years. As the reigning powers in China changed, so did the language applied to certain kanji characters. This meant that some characters ended up with more than one ON reading. As a way of differentiating them, kanji dictionaries often list the era or Chinese Dynasty associated with a particular reading, although this is thankfully one thing you don't need to memorise!

ON Type	Reading	Era or Dynasty	Period
呉音	GO ON	Wu Dynasty	6–7th Century
漢音	KAN ON	Han Dynasty	7–8th Century
唐音	TOU ON	Chinese reading (closest to modern Chinese readings)	13th Edo period

Do any characters have only one ON reading?

Yes! The good news is that many kanji characters only have one ON reading. In fact, many kanji only have one reading, full stop – and no kun reading. Learning the readings for these characters is a much simpler process than for those with multiple readings. Just learn the meaning and one reading, and you're done.

The kanji characters with multiple readings tend to be those that express fundamental concepts such as to go 行 and to live 生. Being fundamental concepts, a large number of words contain them, words that were imported from China over hundreds of years. Also being fundamental, students tend to learn these characters when they start out, so it's easy to get the impression that all kanji characters are going to have 5–10 readings. It's enough to make you want to quit before your head explodes. Nevertheless, actually, the further you go along in your study and the closer you get to the advanced level, the fewer readings there are per kanji character.

ON readings: the long and the short of it

It's worth familiarising yourself with the kind of sounds that appear as ON readings. Doing so will not only assist with your memorisation of the readings, it will also help you recognise kanji when you are listening to spoken Japanese. I have divided the ON readings into two sound types:

1. **Short readings**

   These are ON readings that could be written with just one kana symbol. Accordingly, an alternative name would be 'kana readings'.

Character	Reading	Kana	No. kana
可	KA	か	1
士	SHI	し	1
皮	HI	ひ	1

2. **Long readings**

   These are ON readings that are written using more than one kana symbol. Since Chinese readings tend to be long, the majority of ON readings fall under this category.

Character	Reading	Kana	No. kana
小	SHOU	しょう	3
干	KAN	かん	2
昔	SHAKU	しゃく	3
令	REI	れい	2

First sounds

One thing that stood out when I was highlighting the two page list of the *Joyo Kanji* was that I was well down the second page before I got to a character with an ON reading that started with T. That is to say, most of the first page was taken up with kanji with an ON reading that started with the letters K (KA, KI, KYUU, KAN, KIN, KON) or S (SA, SHI, SHIN, SE, SO, SON). On page 2 there were quite a few kanji with T readings, including those that started with D and CH. In contrast, there were only a few readings that started with H, N, M or R, and hardly any that started with Y.

Interestingly, this frequency pattern reflects the order of the kana – with the exception of the first kana row of vowel only sounds (a, i, u, e, o).

A (e, i, o, u, etc.) K S T H N M R Y

The kana order is said to be based on the order of the Sanskrit alphabet, the language of the first Buddhist writings. Whether this is connected to this frequency pattern is a matter of speculation. On a practical level, knowing which first letters are the most prevalent will help with your ability to guess the ON reading of new kanji. You will have about a 50% chance of getting the first letter right if you guess that it starts with K or S.

Last sounds

In English, the first letters of words are often the way we remember them. You have probably found yourself searching for an English word and saying, 'I know it starts with a P'. With kanji, the last sound seems to be useful to jog the memory. You might find yourself saying, 'I know it ends with an N'. I have divided the last sounds into four main types:

1. **Long vowel** ends in UU or OU – e.g. SHUU, SHOU
2. **Inflected** ends in AI or EI – e.g. AI, KEI, MEI
3. **Rounded** ends in N – e.g. KAN, SHIN, NIN
4. **Double-barrelled** contains two distinct syllables – e.g. KAKU, SHITSU, RAKU.

The modification of H sounds

The reading of some characters that start with a sound from the H group (ha, hi, fu, he, ho) can harden if that character comes second in a compound. This usually occurs when it follows a character with the final sound N.

Kanji Compound	Incorrect Reading	Correct Reading	Meaning
昆布	KON FU	KON BU	konbu, kelp
添付	TEN FU	TEN PU	attach
多分	TA FUN	TA BUN	perhaps
寸法	SUN HOU	SUN POU	measurement

The usual hiragana rules for hardening K to G, and S to Z can also apply. However, many readings contain these sounds already (GA, GI, ZAI, etc.).

CHAPTER 2 – THE KANA CODE

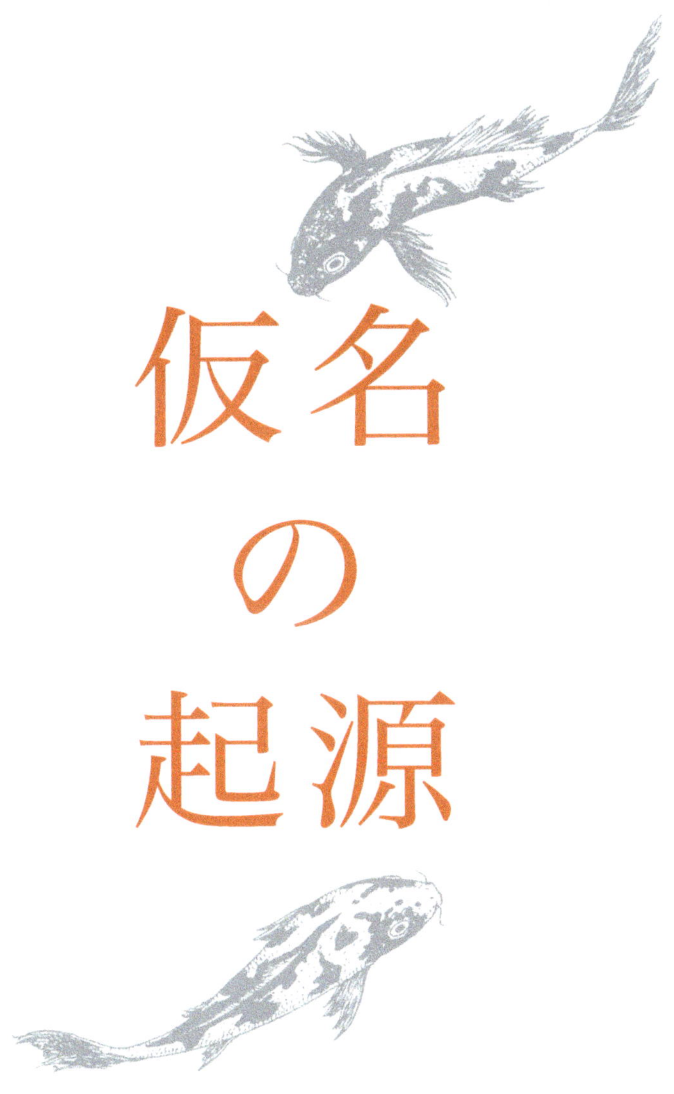

仮名の起源

CHAPTER 2 – THE KANA CODE

CHAPTER 2 – THE KANA CODE

THE GENESIS OF KANA

During the Heian period (794–1185 CE), certain kanji were selected for their phonetic features to create a purely phonetic script in order to write Japanese more fluently. This was the genesis of hiragana and katakana, and is one of the keys to understanding the language as a whole.

Generally speaking, the katakana symbols were created by taking a fragment or component from a kanji character and using it to represent that kanji character's sound. In contrast, the hiragana symbols are an artistic, impressionist version of a whole kanji character, based on the cursive script style of Chinese calligraphy. These different approaches can be seen in the following examples.

Example 1

The **katakana** symbol カ (ka) was created by taking a component from the character 加 (to add) which had the ON reading KA.

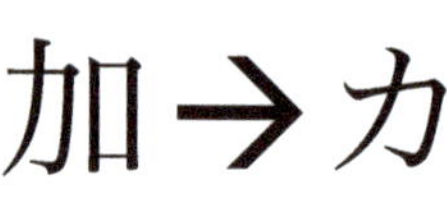

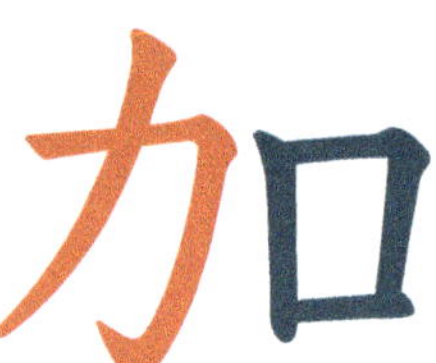

The **hiragana** symbol か (ka) is an artistic, impressionist reinterpretation of the same kanji character 加. The dash on the right represents the 口 on the right side of the kanji character 加.

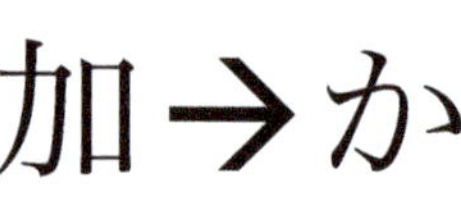

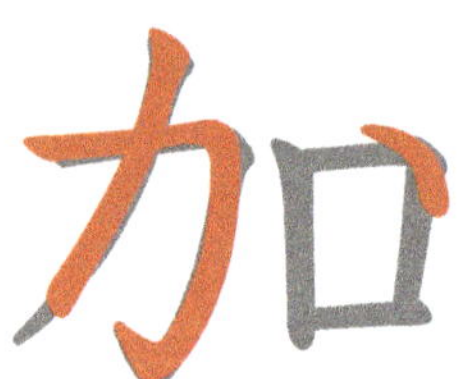

Example 2

The **katakana** symbol テ (te) was created by taking a component from the character 天 (heaven) which had the ON reading TEN.

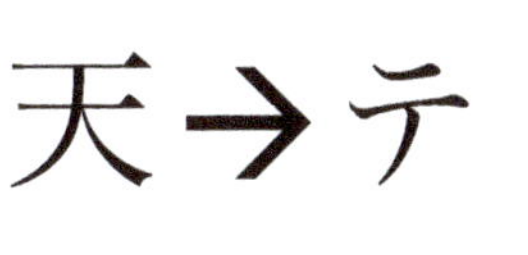

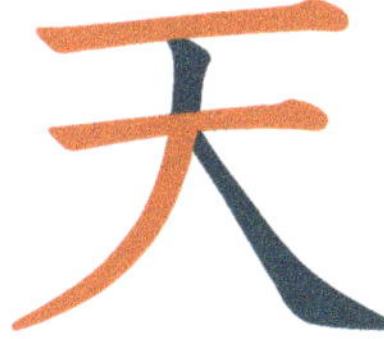

The **hiragana** symbol て (te) is an artistic version of the same kanji character 天. In this case, an aesthetic decision was made to keep the right-curving stroke, and discard the left-curving one.

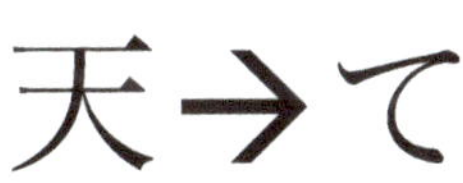

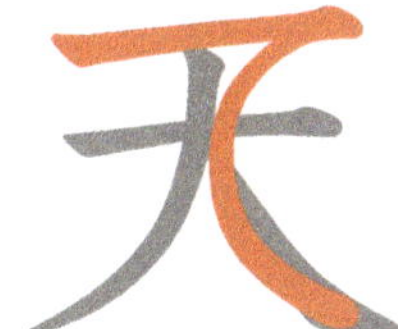

Example 3

The **katakana** symbol フ (fu) was created by taking a component from the character 不 (not/un-) which had the ON reading FU.

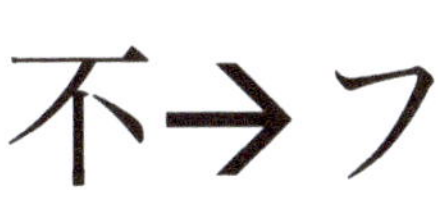

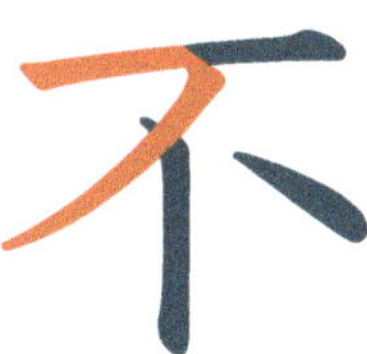

The **hiragana** symbol ふ (fu) is an artistic version of the same kanji character ふ.

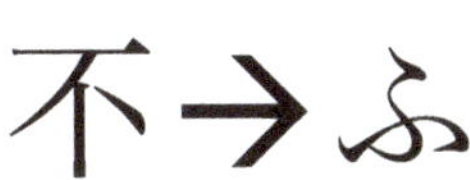

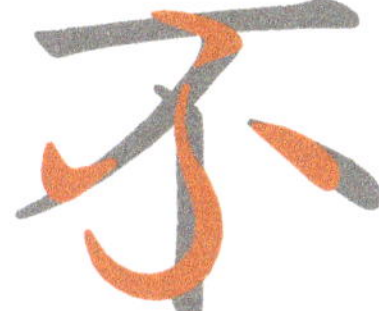

Understanding the link between kana and kanji sparked an 'aha' moment for me. Until then, I'd been under the impression that hiragana was a native Japanese script, katakana was for recently imported English words, and kanji was Chinese. In other words, they were three disparate scripts that reflected three different languages and cultures. It was a revelation to realise that all three scripts are kanji-based, and that the whole written language is connected. Four useful takeaways from this knowledge are outlined below.

1. Kanji and kana are closely connected, and work together as a set.

Source	Fragment	Artistic version
Kanji	**Katakana**	**Hiragana**
加	カ	か
天	テ	て
不	フ	ふ

2. You can sometimes 'see' the ON reading as a component within a kanji character, and use it as a mnemonic. For example, when you know that フ is based on 不 this can help you remember the character's ON reading, FU.

3. You can sometimes 'see' the ON reading of a kanji character as an artistic impression of the whole character. For example, when you know that ふ is based on 不 this can help you remember the character's ON reading, FU.

   In this section I introduce 57 kanji characters that were either the basis for kana symbols, or look like a kana symbol. By learning these, you will be able to memorise the ON readings of 57 kanji characters relatively easily, by leveraging your existing kana reading knowledge.

4. Understanding how the two styles of kana were created helps us find two ways to approach learning kanji readings.

   1. The Fragmenting Approach

   In Chapter 3, *The Phonetic Code*, we will use the fragmenting approach, drawing out the phonetic components, fragments of kanji that indicate the ON reading.

   2. The Artistic Approach

   In Chapter 4, *The Visual Code*, we will use the artistic approach, grouping kanji by visual features, and using these groups as a way to learn the ON readings.

K1 安 AN

安

relax, cheap

Basis for: A	hiragana あ	
安全	ANZEN	safety
不安	FUAN	anxiety, unease

K2 以 I

以

by means of, includes

Basis for: I	hiragana い	
以上	IJOU	... or more, that's all, above-mentioned
以後	IGO	hereafter, from now on
以内	INAI	within
以下	IKA	... or less, below-mentioned

K3 伊 I

伊

Italy

Basis for: I	katakana イ	
伊語	IGO	Italian (language)

K4 宇 U

宇

universe

Basis for: U	hiragana う	katakana ウ
宇宙	UCHUU	universe
宇佐	USA	city in Oita, Kyushu

K5 加 KA

add

Basis for: KA	hiragana か	katakana カ
追加	TSUIKA	add
参加	SANKA	participate

K6 機 KI

mechanism, chance

Basis for: KI	hiragana き	katakana キ
機会	KIKAI	opportunity, chance
機械	KIKAI	machine
危機	KIKI	danger, crisis

K7 久 KU, KYUU

a long time

Basis for: KU	hiragana く	katakana ク
KU		
久美	KUMI	girl's name
KYUU		
永久	EIKYUU	eternity, immortality
持久	JIKYUU	endurance, persistence

K8 計 KEI

plan

Basis for: KE	hiragana け	
計算	KEISAN	calculation
計画	KEIKAKU	plan

K9	己 KO			己
	self, oneself	Basis for: KO	hiragana こ	katakana コ
		自己紹介	JIKO SHOUKAI	self-introduction
K10	左 SA			左
	left, progressive	Basis for: SA	hiragana さ	
		左右	SAYUU	left and right
		左翼	SAYOKU	left-wing (politics), left flank
K11	散 SAN			散
	scatter	Basis for: SA	katakana サ	
		散歩	SANPO	stroll
		散文	SANBUN	prose
		解散	KAISAN	dissolve, break up
K12	寸 SUN			す
	unit of measurement, small	Basis for: SU	hiragana す	
		寸法	SUNPOU	measurement
		寸暇	SUNKA	a moment's leisure, free minute

K13 世 SE

世

world, generation

Basis for: SE	hiragana せ	katakana セ
世界	SEKAI	world
世代	SEDAI	generation
世間	SEKEN	world, society
出世	SHUSSE	successful career

K14 曽 SOU

曽

great-(grandmother etc), formerly

Basis for: SO	katakana ソ	
曽祖母	SOUSOBO	great-grandmother

K15 太 TA, TAI

太

thick, plump

Basis for: TA	hiragana た	
TA		
丸太	MARUTA	log
新太郎	SHINTAROU	boy's name
TAI		
太陽	TAIYOU	sun
太鼓	TAIKO	traditional Japanese drum
皇太子	KOUTAISHI	Crown Prince

K16 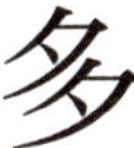 TA

many

Basis for: TA	katakana タ	
多分	TABUN	maybe, probably, perhaps
多数	TASUU	countless, majority

K17 知 CHI

wisdom, knowledge

Basis for: CHI	hiragana ち	
知識	CHISHIKI	knowledge
知人	CHIJIN	acquaintance

K18 天 TEN

heavens, natural

Basis for: TE	hiragana て	katakana テ
天然	TENNEN	natural
雨天	UTEN	rainy weather
天国	TENGOKU	heaven
露天風呂	ROTENBURO	outdoor hot spring bath, onsen

K19 止 to*

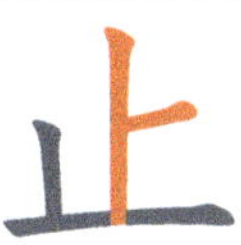

stop

Basis for: TO	hiragana と	katakana ト
止まる	tomaru	be stopped
痛み止め	itami dome	pain-killer (lit. stop pain)

* kun reading

K20 奈 NA

奈

phonetic NA

Basis for: NA	hiragana な	katakana ナ
奈良	NARA	Nara (Japan's ancient capital)
奈落	NARAKU	hell (Buddhism), worst possible circumstances

K21 波 HA

波

wave

Basis for: HA	hiragana は	
波浪注意報	HAROU CHUUIHOU	wave warning (for example, after an earthquake)
波及	HAKYUU	spread, ripple, after effect
電波	DENPA	radio wave

K22 比 HI

比

compare

Basis for: HI	hiragana ひ	katakana ヒ
比較的 に	HIKAKUTEKI ni	comparatively
比例	HIREI	proportion
無比	MUHI	unparalleled, peerless

K23 不 FU

not, un-

Basis for: FU	hiragana ふ	katakana フ
不明	FUMEI	unclear, unknown
行方不明	YUKUE FUMEI	whereabouts unknown, missing person
不満	FUMAN	unsatisfied
不完全	FUKANZEN	incomplete

K24 保 HO

preserve, protect

Basis for: HO	hiragana ほ	katakana ホ
保存	HOZON	save
保管	HOKAN	store, storage

K25 末 MATSU

end, last part

Basis for: MA	hiragana ま	katakana マ
月末	GETSUMATSU	month-end

K26 武 MU

military

Basis for: MU	hiragana む	
武者人形	MUSHA NINGYOU	samurai doll
荒武者	araMUSHA	rowdy, daredevil

K27 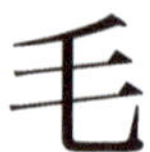 MOU

hair, fur

Basis for: MO	hiragana も	katakana モ
毛布	MOUFU	blanket
羊毛	YOUMOU	wool

K28 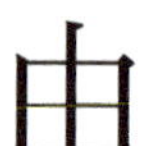 YU, YUU

reason

Basis for: YU	hiragana ゆ	katakana ユ
YU		
由来	YURAI	origin, reason
経由	KEIYU	through, via
YUU		
自由	JIYUU	freedom
理由	RIYUU	reason

K29 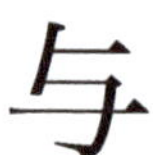 YO

give

Basis for: YO	hiragana よ	
与党	YOTOU	ruling party
関与	KAN YO	participation

K30 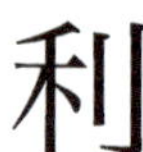 RI

profit, advantage

Basis for: RI	hiragana り	katakana リ
利益	RIEKI	profit
ご利用ください	goRIYOU kudasai	please use …
利子	RISHI	interest (banking)
権利	KENRI	right, privilege

K31 流 RU, RYUU

流

flow, current	Basis for: RU	katakana ル	
	RU		
	流布	RUFU	circulation, dissemination
	RYUU		
	流動的	RYUUDOUTEKI	changeable

K32 礼 REI

礼

etiquette, bow	Basis for: RE	hiragana れ	katakana レ
	礼儀	REIGI	manners, etiquette
	礼	REI	bow
	無礼	BUREI	rude

K33 呂 RO

呂

spine, phonetic RO	Basis for: RO	hiragana ろ	katakana ロ
	お風呂	oFURO	bath
	露天風呂	ROTEN BURO	outdoor hot spring bath, onsen

K34 和 WA

和

harmony, peace, Japanese-style	Basis for: WA	hiragana わ	katakana ワ
	和風	WAFUU	Japanese style (food, etc.)
	和室	WASHITSU	Japanese room (tatami mat flooring)
	平和	HEIWA	peace

KANA LOOKALIKES

This section builds on the previous section in using the connection between the look of kanji and kana to help remember the kanji's reading. These kanji are not the official basis for kana, I just think they look similar. It's a useful mnemonic to remember another 23 kanji readings.

KL1 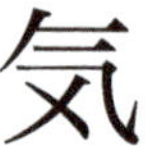 KI

spirit, air

Looks like: KI	hiragana き	katakana キ
気候	KIKOU	climate
元気	GENKI	in good spirits, energetic

KL2 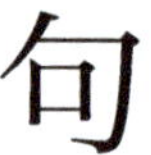 KU

phrase

Looks like: KU	katakana ク	
字句	JIKU	wording, way of expression
俳句	HAIKU	Japanese 17-mora poem
文句	MONKU	complaint

KL3 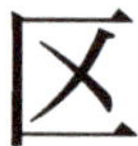 KU

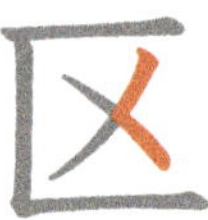

ward, district

Looks like: KU	hiragana く	
区別	KUBETSU	distinguish, differentiate
地区	CHIKU	district, section

KL4 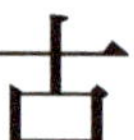 KO

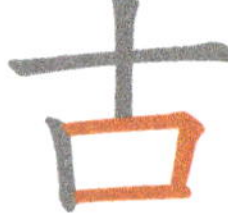

old

Looks like: KO	katakana コ	
古代	KODAI	ancient times
古文	KOBUN	classical (Japanese) literature (e.g. the school subject)

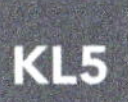

KL5 沙 SA

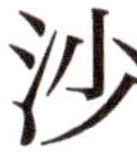

sand

Looks like: SA	katakana サ	
沙汰	SATA	matter, deed
沙織	SAori	girl's name

KL6 司 SHI

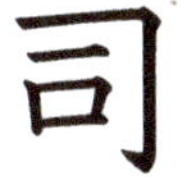 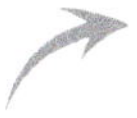 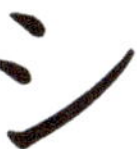

SHI

officiate, administrate, manage

Looks like: SHI	katakana シ	
寿司	SUSHI	sushi
司会	SHIKAI	chairman, host, presenter

KL7 寿 SU, JU

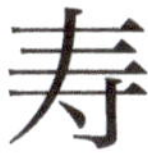

longevity, congratulations

Looks like: SU	katakana ス	
SU		
寿司	SUSHI	sushi
JU		
寿命	JU MYOU	lifespan
長寿	CHOUJU	longevity

KL8 祖 SO

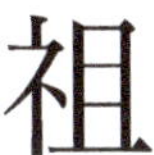

ancestor

Looks like: SO	hiragana そ	katakana ソ
祖先	SOSEN	ancestor
祖父	SOFU	grandfather, old man

KL9 地 CHI

ground, earth

Looks like: CHI	hiragana ち	
地区	CHIKU	district, section
地域	CHIIKI	community, district
地下鉄	CHIKATETSU	underground railway
現地	GENCHI	on-site, local
天地	TENCHI	heaven and earth

KL10 訂 TEI

revise, correct

Looks like: TE	hiragana て	
訂正	TEISEI	revision, correction
丁寧	TEINEI	polite, conscientious

KL11 定 TEI

decide, fix

Looks like: TE	hiragana て	
定食	TEISHOKU	set menu
設定	SETTEI	settings

KL12 低 TEI

low

Looks like: TE	hiragana て	
高低	KOUTEI	high and low, rise and fall
低ナトリウム	TEI natoriumu	low sodium

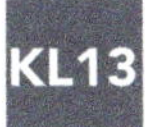
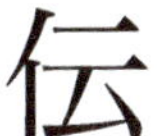

KL13 伝 DEN

transmit

Looks like: TE	katakana テ	
伝言	DENGON	verbal message, rumour
伝統	DENTOU	tradition
宣伝	SENDEN	publicity, advertising, propaganda

KL14 秘 HI

secret

Looks like: HI	katakana ヒ	
秘密	HIMITSU	secret
秘書	HISHO	secretary

KL15 非 HI

fault, non-

Looks like: HI	hiragana ひ	
非難	HINAN	criticism
非常 に	HIJOU ni	extraordinarily, extremely

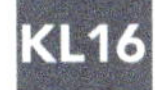
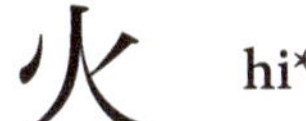

KL16 火 hi*

fire

Looks like: HI	katakana ヒ	
火	hi	fire
火花	hibana	spark
花火	hanabi	fireworks

* kun reading

KL17 付 **FU**

attach

Looks like: FU katakana フ

添付	TENPU	attachment (e.g. email)
付与	FUYO	grant, allowance

KL18 布 **FU**

cloth

Looks like: FU katakana フ

昆布	KONBU	kelp (often used as a soup base)
布団	FUTON	quilt, doona, futon mattress
綿布	MENPU	cotton cloth
分布	BUNPU	distribution

KL19 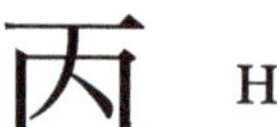 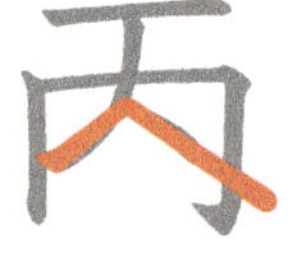

third in ranking

Looks like: HE hiragana へ

甲乙丙	KOU OTSU HEI	A, B and C

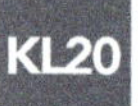 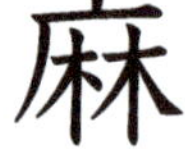 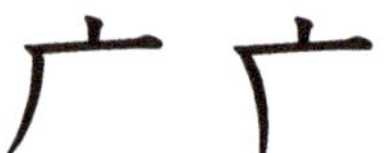 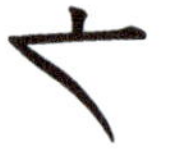 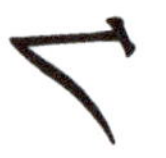  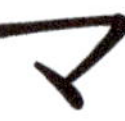

MA

hemp, numb

Looks like: MA katakana マ

胡麻	GOMA	sesame
麻酔	MASUI	anaesthetic
麻薬	MAYAKU	narcotic drugs

* The Japanese name for the 广 radical is madare, which means a MA enclosure in the top left position. The name is a direct reference to the ON reading of this kanji. The transformation to マ is my own interpretation.

KL21 理 RI

logic, science

Looks like: RI	hiragana り	
理科	RIKA	science
理解	RIKAI	understand, comprehend
理由	RIYUU	reason
論理	RONRI	logic
論理的	RONRITEKI	logical

KL22 令 REI

order, command

Looks like: RE	hiragana れ	
命令	MEIREI	order, command
法令	HOUREI	laws and ordinances

KL23 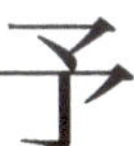 YO

prior, forecast

Looks like: YO	hiragana よ	
予定	YOTEI	plans, schedule
予防	YOBOU	prevention, precaution
天気予報	TENKI YOHOU	weather forecast

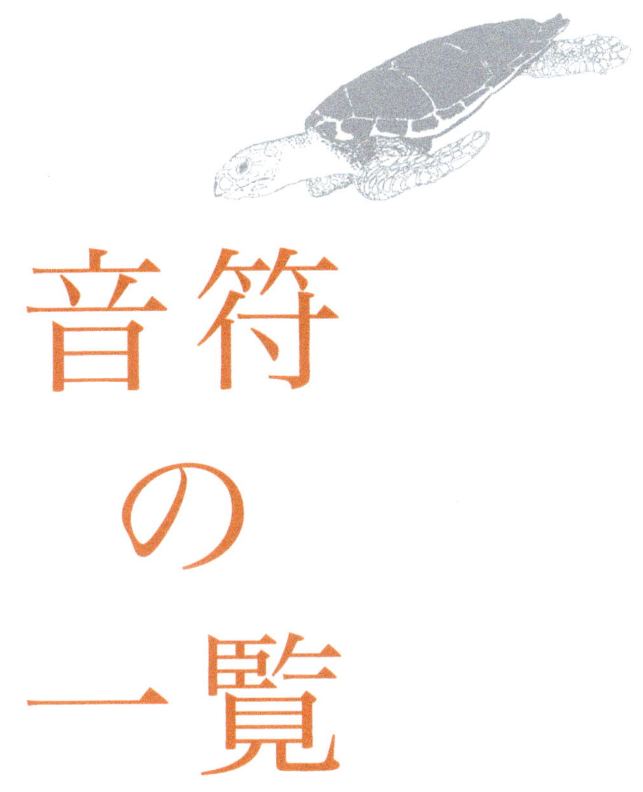

音符の一覧

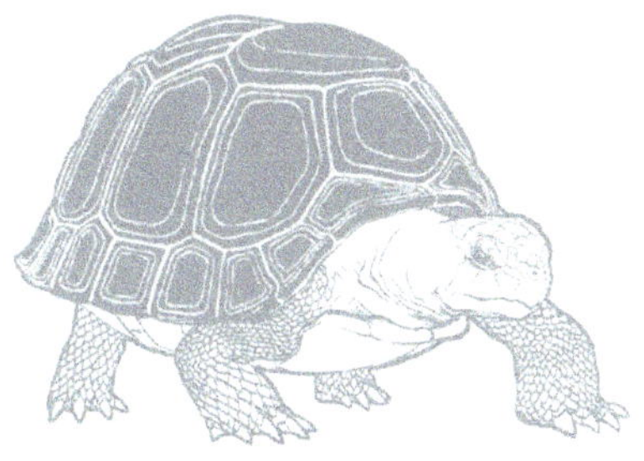

CHAPTER 3 – THE PHONETIC CODE

TWO TYPES OF COMPONENTS

A kanji character is not a cluster of randomly arranged strokes and squiggles, but rather it is composed of smaller components that work together in a systematic way.

While the focus of this chapter is the phonetic components, we need to learn about both types of components: radicals (meaning components) and phonetics (sound components).

Radicals – meaning components

Radicals are components within a kanji character that give a hint to its meaning. While the term *radical* is entrenched in Japanese language education, the term meaning component might be more useful for students. You will find a list of the 214 radicals in most kanji dictionaries.

All characters are comprised of at least one radical, though many have more than one. The radicals represent objects and ideas that were relevant to daily life when the characters were invented, including animals, weapons, elements, numbers and verbs. Several of these objects or concepts repeat in different forms, making the total number lower than 214. Some radicals look like the object they represent.

目	eye
木	tree
儿	human legs

With others, the original image has changed over time so it doesn't at first glance resemble what it represents. However, once learnt it is quite easy to associate the image with what it represents.

心	heart
水	water

Other radicals represent a concept rather than a physical object.

小	small

We can better understand why the radicals look the way we do if we learn some kanji history.

甲骨文字

Oracle bones script ***koukotsu moji***

The first known kanji characters appeared on turtle shells and animal bones. The majority that have been excavated are from the Shang Dynasty, from about 1200–1050 BCE. Kanji characters were carved onto the shell as part of a fortune telling ceremony for the Chinese emperor. A hot instrument was then applied to the shell, causing it to crack. The resulting lines were then interpreted, similar to the way tea-leaves are interpreted today. These ancient characters do not differ greatly from those we see today. The images appear simple because it was difficult to carve onto bone.

Below are examples of what mouth and sun looked like on the oracle bones, and the image they represent. Over time, the characters evolved as kanji characters were drawn on different materials. The names can vary but the historic phases are generally referred to as the Oracle Bone, Bronze, Great Seal and Traditional Scripts. Rounded objects like the sun were drawn square and over time became even more angular and geometric.

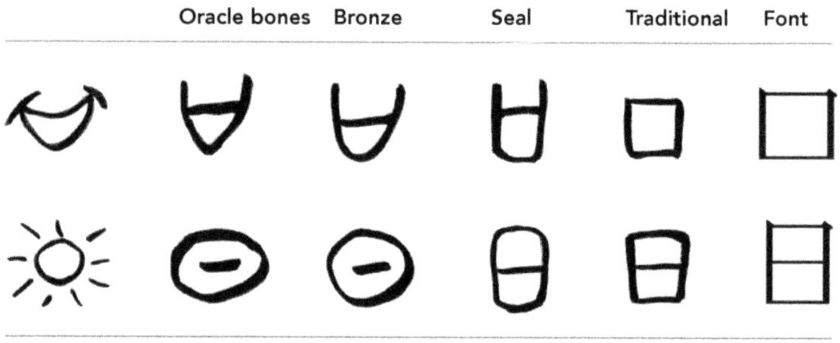

	Oracle bones	Bronze	Seal	Traditional	Font
					口
					日

氵 is the radical for water. While it doesn't look that much like water, the narrow version of the radical clearly represents three drops of water. This is simplified and narrowed so it can sit of the left side of a character.

水	water as a kanji
氵	water as a side radical

Put simply, the radical indicates the category or type of the kanji character. So those that contain the water radical could be read as water-related. Notice how it appears in all of these characters that are all water-related.

泳	swim
河	river
泡	bubble

Another radical that bears a helpful resemblance to the object it represents is the grass radical 艸 or 艹, in which two strands of grass poke up through the ground. When you see this radical on top of a character, you can be certain that the kanji relates to vegetation of some sort, or a quality of plants and flowers like fragrance.

花	flower
茎	stem
芳	fragrant
薬	medicine (think Chinese herbs)

Another way to think of radicals is as an abbreviation that appears after a word in a dictionary, for example n. for noun v. for verb. Except, the radical is a visual representation of the concept that appears within the word itself. You can find the radical of each kanji in the full index. Refer to the Radicals List to see the most common radicals and their meanings. While your eventual goal should be to learn the Japanese names, at first I think it is enough simply to memorise the meaning of each radical. Just think how many emojis you know. You know what each of those images stands for – learning radicals is a similar task. While radicals are traditionally listed in stroke order, I have categorised them into 13 groups by subject-matter. I think grouping them into smaller chunks like this makes them easier to learn. The groups are listed below with an example radical.

	Category	Example radical	
1	Nature	water	水 氵
2	Human Body	mouth	口
3	People	woman	女
4	Enclosures	cliff border	厂
5	Verbs & Language	speech	言
6	Natural Materials	bamboo	竹
7	Math & Measurement	one	一
8	Food	rice	米
9	Animals	horse	馬
10	Warfare	sword, knife	刀 刂
11	Man-made Tools	desk	几
12	Senses	sound	音
13	Supernatural	demon	鬼

Phonetics – sound components

Phonetic components are elements within a kanji character that give a hint to its ON reading. There is no official list of the phonetics, but this chapter suggests 150 as a useful starting point. If a kanji character contains the SEI phonetic 青 there is a good chance that its ON reading will be SEI. Take the following five characters, which all contain it and have an ON reading of SEI.

Kanji	Meaning	ON reading
青	blue	SEI
清	clear	SEI
精	spirit	SEI
請	ask	SEI
静	quiet	SEI

In cases like this, the phonetic is an incredibly helpful tool for remembering the ON reading. Learn that 青 is read as SEI and you will essentially be reading these kanji characters phonetically. It's not obvious at first viewing how the character for blue, spirit and quiet are linked, and in terms of meaning, these characters are all quite different. That is because they are linked by the phonetic and all have a different radical.

Do phonetics work all the time?

Unfortunately, no. They're not foolproof and there are many exceptions. There are kanji characters that contain a certain phonetic but have a different ON reading to the phonetic. Moreover, there are others with the same ON reading that don't contain that phonetic.

This aspect is what makes phonetics difficult to teach, and a little difficult to learn. People might have been put off by the fact that phonetics aren't 100% reliable. My view is that even though there are exceptions, there are enough that do follow the rule to make them worth learning.

English spelling and grammar rules are full of exceptions, but that doesn't mean we don't teach them. I learnt the rule 'I before E except after C' in about Year 3 and it became an internet meme because of all the other exceptions that exist. However, I still mentally check the rule when spelling words like 'receive'. Phonetics could be thought of as a similar kind of reading aid. If a character contains the SEI phonetic 青 it is likely to be read as SEI, except when it's read as SHOU. Nevertheless, the five times it is read as SEI surely make it worth your effort.

Not all phonetics appear in so many kanji, and 青 is a particularly consistent case. I call it a power phonetic since it unlocks the ON readings of so many characters and words – they are indicated with the 力 (power) symbol. With this knowledge, you can read one-half of the 10 example words provided. Many of the phonetics listed here only appear in two characters. Even so, at the very least you get two kanji readings for the price of one. Moreover, once you learn a few phonetics you will start to see them in all the texts you read, as well as on food products and street signs.

Your familiarity with the phonetics will make reading real Japanese texts like newspapers and magazines less intimidating, and the more at ease you feel with tackling authentic texts the quicker your reading will improve. Kanji will no longer seem a mass of unintelligible lines but, rather, a combination of recognisable components, each of which has a known purpose and function.

Sometimes, just being able to put a name on something makes it seem more familiar, and less overwhelming. When you can point to a component in a kanji character and know if it's a radical or a phonetic, you will feel more confident in your kanji reading abilities.

Learn phonetics like you learnt kana

The phonetic components allow us to bypass rote learning of ON readings for a large number of characters. By memorising them you will have a great tool for guessing the ON readings of new kanji you encounter. You will also have a useful way of memorising and associating kanji characters that share the same component. To better understand how phonetics work, we need an overview of the four types of kanji character.

The four types of kanji characters

1	象形	SHOUKEI	pictograph	Looks like what it signifies	木 人	tree person
2	指事	SHIJI	ideograph	Visual representation of a concept, often spatial	上 下	up down
3	会意	KEII	compound ideograph	Combination of pictographs or ideographs to create a third meaning	休	to rest a person sitting next to a tree
4	形声	KEISEI	semasio-phonetic/ form-sound character	Characters with a radical that denotes the meaning category, and a phonetic component that denotes the sound	訪 清	visit clear

The kanji characters that get the most attention in beginner textbooks are pictographs, ideographs and compound ideographs. So it might surprise you to learn that 80% of kanji fall under the fourth category, *keisei moji*. While Japanese school students are taught about *keisei moji*, non-native learners of Japanese are often unaware of them. The fact that there isn't even a clear English translation of the word *keisei* just serves to underline how obscure they are.

The dictionary definition of a *keisei moji* is a semasio-phonetic character. In other words, it is a combination of semantic (meaning) components and phonetic (sound) components. While this term may appeal to linguistics scholars, it doesn't exactly roll off the tongue. To find a plain English term, let's break the kanji compound down into its constituent characters:

形	声	文	字
KEI	SEI	MO	JI
form, shape, appearance	**sound, voice**	**character**	

The name tells you that these are characters in which the form, shape or appearance gives a clue to its sound. I call them form-sound characters.

How a form-sound character works

The **radical** tells you the meaning category.

Radical →	meaning category
氵	water
泳	swim
河	river
泡	bubble

And the **phonetic** tells you the pronunciation.

Phonetic → ON reading

Let's look at the phonetics of the three characters listed above and the ON sounds they represent.

Phonetic	ON reading
永	EI
可	KA
包	HOU

If we compare this with the kanji themselves, we can see how the phonetic is telling us the ON reading.

Kanji character	Phonetic it contains	Sound phonetic indicates	ON reading
泳	永	EI	EI
河	可	KA	KA
泡	包	HOU	HOU

When we put it all together, we can see that each of these characters has a clear meaning component, the radical, and a clear sound component, the phonetic.

Kanji	Radical	Meaning it indicates	Meaning	Phonetic	Sound phonetic indicates	ON reading
泳	氵	water-related	swim	永	EI	EI
河	氵	water-related	river	可	KA	KA
泡	氵	water-related	bubble	包	HOU	HOU

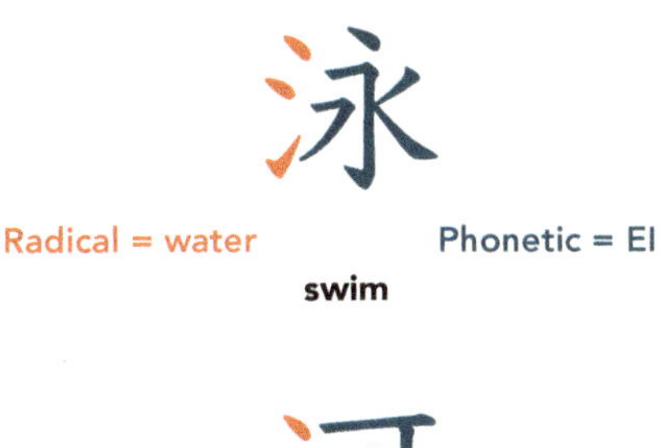

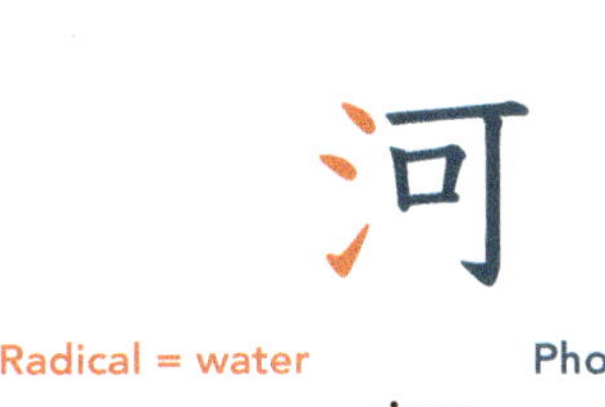

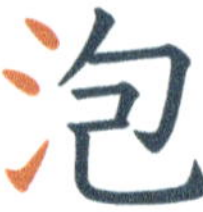

Radical = water Phonetic = HOU

bubble

The previous examples follow the classic form-sound character positioning, with the radical on the left and the phonetic on the right. It is also common to see the radical on the top and the phonetic on the bottom.

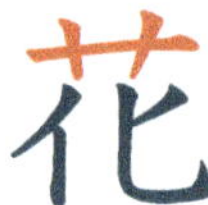

Radical = grass Phonetic = KA

flower

Or, the phonetic on the top and the radical on the bottom.

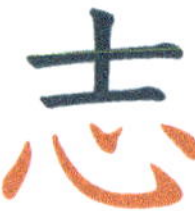

Radical = heart Phonetic = SHI

intention

The phonetic can also be on the left or within an enclosure. However, I don't think we should get too hung up on the position of the phonetic. If you learn the phonetics listed here, you will recognise them when you see them, regardless of their position.

The dual function of phonetics

Just because the phonetic indicates sound, doesn't mean that it does not contribute to the overall meaning of a kanji character. The phonetic often carries a meaning that relates to the meaning of the character as a whole. In addition, since the majority of the phonetics I have chosen to include in this book are also kanji characters in their own right, or radicals, most of them do carry a meaning.

For example, the phonetic HOU 包 is also a kanji character that means wrapping. An ideograph, the two outer strokes seem to be wrapping around one another. It looks like a stylised picture of a rolled-up scroll within a tube, in profile.

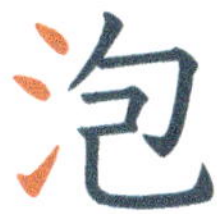

Radical = water　　　　　　Phonetic = HOU

Water + wrapping = bubble

When we combine the meanings of the radical and the phonetic, we get 'water wrapping'. Do you get it? A bubble is air wrapped in water. The phonetic here is clearly contributing to the overall meaning of the character, as well as giving a hint to its reading.

The centre phonetic – a good example

A good example to illustrate how the meaning of the radical and the phonetics can combine to create the meaning of the whole kanji character is the phonetic CHUU 中 which carries the meaning centre.

As a phonetic, it tells you that there is a good chance that the ON reading is CHUU. It also tells you that the meaning is related to the idea of centrality, whether figuratively or literally. Let's look at two characters that contain this phonetic.

Kanji	Phonetic's meaning	Phonetic's sound
仲	middle	CHUU
忠	centre	CHUU

By adding the information supplied by the radical to the table, we now have a category for each character. When we combine the meanings of the radical and the phonetic we get a little phrase or riddle that leads us to the meaning of the character.

Character	Phonetic's meaning	Radical	Meaning	Phonetic's sound	Combination of 2 meanings	Kanji's meaning	ON reading
仲	middle	person 人	a person of some kind	CHUU	middle person/ middle man	go-between, mediator	CHUU
忠	centre	heart 心	mental/ emotion-related	CHUU	centre of your heart	loyalty, devotion	CHUU

These are fantastic examples because the meanings of the radical and the phonetic clearly combine to create the character's meaning. The 'translation' from Japanese to English is almost literal. You could also read it left to right, or top to bottom, as in:

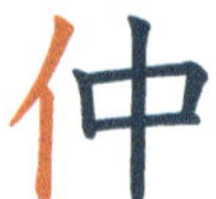

The person in the middle.

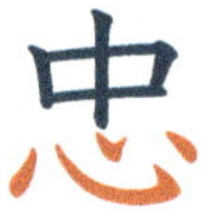

The middle of your heart.

The table had to get pretty wide to show all these hints. Rather than feeling overwhelmed by this large table, its width is cause for celebration. Once you learn the radicals and the phonetics, you realise that many characters are clearly telling you both their meaning and their ON reading.

Admittedly, radicals and phonetics do not always combine to create a kanji's meaning in such a literal way. Nevertheless, when you put together your radical and phonetic knowledge, you'll be able to use it to remember not only the meaning but also the sound of 435 kanji. Better still, you will understand how the components work together – and feel a lot more kanji-confident in the process.

Phonetic breakdown

Part 1: Standard phonetics

Key phonetic components that appear in common kanji characters and Japanese vocabulary will be introduced in this section. Some of the phonetics are not much more complex than a hiragana or katakana symbol, so you should be able to learn them just as quickly. And unlike with the kana symbols, you only need to recognise the phonetics as an initial step. For example, some common phonetics and the ON reading they represent are listed below.

可	KA
士	SHI
干	KAN
丁	TEI

Part 2: Rhyming phonetics

A number of phonetics that indicate rhyming readings will be listed in this section. These phonetics do not represent a specific ON reading, but kanji characters that contain them often have readings that rhyme. I'm calling this 'rhyming' for the sake of simplicity, although it doesn't strictly follow rhyme in the English sense. Rather, the last – and sometimes second last – sounds are the same. For example, in one group all the kanji have ON readings that end in OKU, and in another they all end in a vowel + I.

Kanji 1	ON reading	Kanji 2	ON reading	Final sound
浴	YOKU	俗	ZOKU	~OKU
米	BEI	迷	MAI	Vowel + I
因	IN	恩	ON	Vowel + N

I also introduce the idea of using sound effects or onomatopoeia to group kanji characters together by sound. For example, several kanji characters that contain the sword radical 刂 have a double-barrelled ON reading that ends in TSU (SATSU, BATSU, SETSU). This makes me think of the sound a sword might make when cutting through cloth. These are useful mnemonics that allow you to remember ON readings through associations with radicals.

Choice of phonetics

Many teachers of Japanese agree that phonetics have some use for learners (Toyoda, 2013). But which phonetics should be taught first? There are so many that students could feel just as overwhelmed by the phonetics as they do by kanji. To avoid this, I have carefully curated 150 phonetics based on my own experience as a non-native who learned to read Japanese mostly through self-study. The phonetics I think will be easiest for intermediate students to learn:

- are simple – starting with two and three stroke components like 几 and 干, and gradually increasing in complexity
- are visually distinct and therefore easier to remember
- have an ON reading connection that is strong and repeated, with few exceptions
- appear in kanji characters and kanji words that are relatively common
- are the ones that I have intuitively found to be the most reliable and the most useful.

Phonetic entries

Is it the only ON reading for that phonetic?

The ON reading assigned to each phonetic is not necessarily its only ON reading. For example, 生 can also be read as SHOU in addition to the reading listed here, SEI. However, to make it more learnable I've only listed one reading per phonetic. The full kanji index lists all the ON and kun readings for each kanji character in this book.

Order of the phonetics

The phonetics are presented in Japanese kana order as shown below.

A (e, i, o, u, etc.) K S T H N M R Y

Format of the readings

- ON readings are written in capital letters
- Kun readings are written in lower case letters
- Letters that appear after a kanji reading in brackets refer to additional sounds not included in the character's reading. These are usually written in hiragana to complete the word and are known as *okurigana*.

Names of phonetics

I believe things are easier to learn when you can put a name to them, so I have included a unique name for each phonetic, to make them a companion set with the radicals. You do not have to memorise these names, but doing so will help you identify the phonetics as you encounter them. While most names are based on kanji names and research, I have invented a few where a clear meaning could not be found. All invented component names are marked as *creative components*. If you can think of different names that are more meaningful to you, by all means use them.

To name the phonetics, I adhered to the following process:

- If it is a kanji character, one of the most memorable words that describes that character is used.
- If it is a radical, the radical's English name is used.
- If it is neither a kanji character nor a radical, it is referred to as a component. If a meaning can be readily found for this, that meaning has been used.
- If a component does not have a known meaning in Japanese but a relevant Chinese meaning exists, that is used. For example, 僉 means all/unanimous in Chinese and this idea can be related to the kanji characters it appears in: 検 means examine (examine all the parts); 験 means test (test all the elements).

Creative components

- I invented some names based on the radicals within the component – they are indicated with the 想 (idea) symbol. For example, 卓 is comprised of the 10 radical 十 and the early radical 早. I have combined the meaning to create the name 10 AM. The fact that this component appears in the morning character 朝 is an added bonus.
- I have 'reverse-engineered' the kanji that contain certain components to create a meaning that could work with the example characters and words. This way the phonetic should also help you remember the meaning of the character. For example, the phonetic 壬 appears in the characters for responsibility 任 and pregnancy 妊. I have therefore used creative licence, dubbing it a 'crying baby'. A person with a crying baby = responsibility, and a woman with a baby = pregnancy. 壬 could be seen as a baby with its arms outstretched and tipping its head back to cry.

In naming the phonetics, I have tried to make them memorable by fitting the following criteria where possible:

- One word.
- A unique word. If two components carry the same meaning, slightly different terms have been chosen to differentiate them. For example, I have named 良 'good' and 善 'kind', even though they can both mean good.
- The most literal word, rather than the figurative meaning, which may be at play in the compound words.
  - 青 I chose 'blue' rather than 'unripe' or 'young'.
- A simple word. For example:
  - 朱 I chose 'bright red' rather than vermilion.
  - 旬 I chose 'ten days' rather than 'ten-day period'.
  - 肖 I chose 'similar' rather than 'resemble'.
- A memorable, fun word.
  - 辰 I chose 'zodiac dragon' rather than other possible meanings like '5th sign of the zodiac'.
- An unambiguous word.
  - 正 I chose 'correct' rather than 'right', to avoid confusion with the directions left and right.

P1 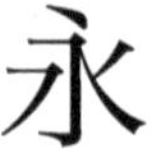 EI

eternal

Type: kanji

Kanji that contain this phonetic and use this ON reading:

永	eternal	永遠	EIEN	eternity, immortality
泳	swim	水泳	SUIEI	swimming
詠	compose	詠歌	EIKA	poem (esp. tanka), composition of a poem or song, read aloud a poem

P2 可 KA

possible

Type: kanji

Kanji that contain this phonetic and use this ON reading:

可	can	可能	KANOU	possible
河	river	河川	KASEN	river, stream
歌	song	歌舞	KABU	singing and dancing

P3 加 KA

add

Type: kanji

Kanji that contain this phonetic and use this ON reading:

加	add	追加	TSUIKA	add
架	hang up, stand	書架	SHOKA	bookshelf
賀	congratulate	年賀状	NENGAJOU*	New Year card (equivalent of a Christmas card)
嘉	excellent	嘉永 時代	KAEI JIDAI	Kaei era (February 1848 – November 1854) (rare)

* The ON reading for this kanji is GA, not KA. However, since the first kanji ends with N in this common compound word, it would probably be read GA anyway, so I have left it in.

P4 化 KA

change

Type: kanji

Kanji that contain this phonetic and use this ON reading:

化	change, convert	化学	KAGAKU	chemistry
花	flower	花壇	KADAN	flowerbed

P5 果 KA

fruit

Type: kanji

Kanji that contain this phonetic and use this ON reading:

果	fruit, result	果汁	KAJUU	fruit juice
課	lesson, section	学課	GAKKA	schoolwork
菓	candy	お菓子	oKASHI	sweets

P6 咼 KA

open mouth

Type: component

Kanji that contain this phonetic and use this ON reading:

過	pass through	通過	TSUUKA	pass through (train station, bill in parliament)
渦	whirlpool	過失	KASHITSU	error, blunder
		渦中	KACHUU	upheaval, trouble, vortex
禍	misfortune	災禍	SAIKA	disaster, catastrophe

P7 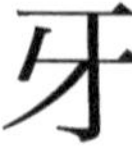 GA

tusk

Type: radical

Kanji that contain this phonetic and use this ON reading:

牙	tusk, tooth	牙城	GAJOU	stronghold, bastion
		歯牙にもかけない	SHIGA ni mo kakenai	take no notice of (lit. don't give a tooth)
雅	elegant	優雅	YUUGA	elegance, grace
芽	bud, sprout	発芽	HATSUGA	budding, sprouting

P8 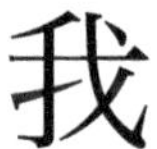 GA

myself, obstinate

Type: kanji

Kanji that contain this phonetic and use this ON reading:

我	myself, obstinate	自我	JIGA	ego
		我流	GARYUU	self-taught, one's own way
蛾	moth	蛾	GA	moth
餓	starve	飢餓	KIGA	famine, hunger

HINT: Can you see how the previous phonetic 牙 (tusk) can be found on the left of this one? It isn't exactly the same, but the shape is very similar. They both have the ON reading GA, and it can also be found in the next phonetic, GI (義) on the bottom left. 牙 therefore has a strong 'G' association. It even looks a bit like a lower case English letter g. g = 牙

P9

義 GI

morality

Type: kanji

Kanji that contain this phonetic and use this ON reading:

義	righteousness, morality	義理	GIRI	sense of duty
		義理のお母さん	GIRI no okaasan	mother-in-law
		正義	SEIGI	justice, righteousness
儀	ceremony	儀式	GISHIKI	ceremony, ritual
犠	sacrifice	犠牲	GISEI	victim, scapegoat

P10

各 KAKU

each

Type: kanji

Kanji that contain this phonetic and use this ON reading:

各	each, every	各種	KAKUSHU	every kind, all sorts
		各位	KAKUI	everyone, ladies and gentlemen
格	status	規格	KIKAKU	standard, norm
		性格	SEIKAKU	personality, disposition
閣	tall building, (government) cabinet	閣議	KAKUGI	cabinet meeting
		内閣	NAIKAKU	cabinet, ministry

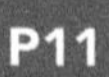 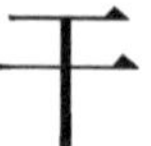 KAN

dry

Type: radical

Kanji that contain this phonetic and use this ON reading:

干	dry	干満	KANMAN	ebb and flow
		干渉	KANSHOU	interference, meddling
汗	sweat	汗顔	KANGAN	ashamed (lit. sweat face) (rare)
		発汗	HAKKAN	perspiration, sweating
肝	liver, courage	肝臓	KANZOU	liver
刊	publish	旬刊	JUNKAN	published every 10 days

P12 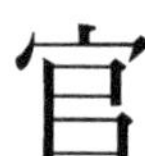 KAN

bureaucrat

Type: kanji

Kanji that contain this phonetic and use this ON reading:

官	government, bureaucrat	警官	KEIKAN	police officer
		官署	KANSHO	government office
館	building	館長	KANCHOU	director of library or museum
		館内	KANNAI	in the building
		映画館	EIGAKAN	cinema
管	pipe, control	管理	KANRI	management, administration

P13 門 KAN

gate

Type: radical

Kanji that contain this phonetic and use this ON reading:

間	space between, interval	時間	JIKAN	time, hour
		間奏	KANSOU	(musical) interlude
閑	leisure	閑静	KANSEI	quiet, tranquil (e.g. neighbourhood)
		繁閑	HANKAN	press and slack of business
関	connection, barrier	玄関	GENKAN	entrance, vestibule
		関係	KANKEI	relationship, connection
		関数	KANSUU	function (mathematics)
		関心	KANSHIN	concern, interest
簡	simple	簡単	KANTAN	simple, easy

P14 𠦝 KAN 想

10 AM

Type: creative component

Kanji that contain this phonetic and use this ON reading:

乾	dry	乾燥	KANSOU	dry, arid
		乾杯	KAMPAI	toast, cheers
		乾電池	KANDENCHI	battery
幹	trunk	新幹線	SHINKANSEN	bullet train
韓	Korea	韓国	KANKOKU	Korea

P15 几 KI

desk

Type: radical

Kanji that contain this phonetic and use this ON reading:

机	desk	机上	KIJOU	on the desk
飢	hunger, starve	飢餓	KIGA	starvation, famine

P16 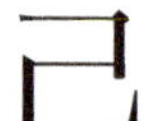 KI

oneself

Type: radical

Kanji that contain this phonetic and use this ON reading:

記	write down, account	記録	KIROKU	record
		暗記	ANKI	memorisation, rote learning
		記入	KI NYUU	enter, fill out (a form)
		記号	KIGOU	symbol
起	get up, occur	起立	KIRITSU	stand up

* On its own it is read KO.

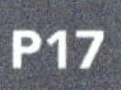 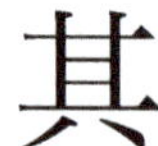 KI

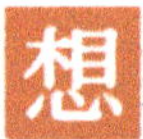

step ladder

Type: creative component

Kanji that contain this phonetic and use this ON reading:

棋	Japanese chess, shogi	棋士	KISHI	shogi, go player
		将棋	SHOUGI	shogi, Japanese chess
期	period of time	期待	KITAI	expectation, hope
		予期	YOKI	expectation, forecast
旗	flag, banner	国旗	KOKKI	national flag
基	foundation, base	基礎	KISO	basis, foundation
		基準	KIJUN	standard, basis
		基本的な	KIHONTEKI na	fundamental

P18 奇 KI

strange

Type: kanji

Kanji that contain this phonetic and use this ON reading:

奇	strange, unusual	奇数	KISUU	odd number
		珍奇	CHINKI	strange, novel
		奇妙	KI MYOU	bizarre, curious
騎	ride horses	騎士	KISHI	knight
		騎馬戦	KIBASEN	cavalry battle (on horseback)
寄	draw near	寄港	KIKOU	stop at a port

P19 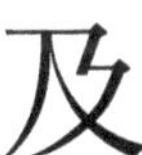 KYUU

reach

Type: kanji

Kanji that contain this phonetic and use this ON reading:

及	extend, reach	波及	HAKYUU	spread, ripple, after effect
吸	breathe in, inhale	吸気	KYUUKI	inhalation
		吸引	KYUUIN	absorption, suction
		呼吸	KOKYUU	breathing, respiration
級	level, grade	上級	JOUKYUU	advanced level
		二級	NIKYUU	level 2 (e.g. of the Japanese Language Proficiency Test)

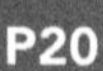

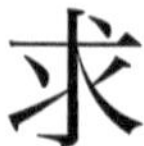

KYUU

want

Type: kanji

Kanji that contain this phonetic and use this ON reading:

求	want, request	要求	YOUKYUU	request, demand
球	ball, sphere	球体	KYUUTAI	sphere
		野球	YAKYUU	baseball
		球場	KYUUJOU	baseball stadium
救	save, rescue	救助	KYUUJO	relief, aid

P21

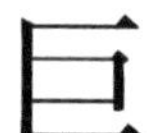

KYO

Enormous*

Type: kanji

Kanji that contain this phonetic and use this ON reading:

巨	Enormous, great	巨大	KYODAI	gigantic, enormous
		巨万	KYOMAN	huge fortune, millions
拒	refuse	拒絶	KYOZETSU	rejection, refusal
		拒否	KYOHI	refusal, denial, veto
距	distance	距離	KYORI	distance, range
		遠距離 恋愛	EN KYORI REN'AI	long distance relationship

* This capital E is deliberate – the kanji shape looks similar to a letter E.

P22

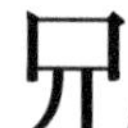

KYOU

older brother

Type: kanji

Kanji that contain this phonetic and use this ON reading:

兄	older brother	兄弟	KYOUDAI	siblings
況	condition, situation	状況	JOUKYOU	status, situation
競	compete	競争	KYOUSOU	competition, rivalry

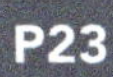

P23 竟 KYOU

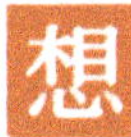

nosy neighbour

Type: creative component

Kanji that contain this phonetic and use this ON reading:

境	border, boundary	境界	KYOUKAI	boundary, border
		環境	KANKYOU	environment, circumstance
鏡	mirror, lens	鏡台	KYOUDAI	dressing table
		望遠鏡	BOUENKYOU	telescope

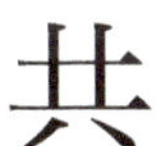

P24 共 KYOU

share

Type: kanji

Kanji that contain this phonetic and use this ON reading:

共	share, together with	共同	KYOUDOU	cooperation, collaboration
		共通	KYOUTSUU	common, shared
供	offer, present	提供	TEIKYOU	offer, provide
		供給	KYOUKYUU	supply, provide

P25 夾 KYOU

pinch

Type: kanji

Kanji that contain this phonetic and use this ON reading:

挟	pinch, hold between	挟撃	KYOUGEKI	pincer movement (technical)
狭	narrow	狭量	KYOURYOU	narrow-minded, petty
		偏狭	HENKYOU	intolerance, narrow-mindedness

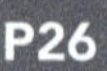

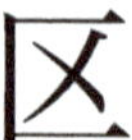

区 KU

ward

Type: kanji

Kanji that contain this phonetic and use this ON reading:

区	ward, district	区別	KUBETSU	distinction, classification
		地区	CHIKU	district, section
駆	drive	駆使	KUSHI	command of, use freely

P27

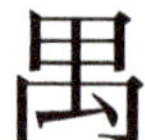

禺 GUU

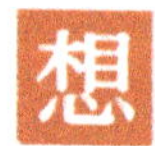

fasten together

Type: creative component

Kanji that contain this phonetic and use this ON reading:

偶	by chance, even number	偶然	GUUZEN	coincidence
		偶数	GUUSUU	even number
		配偶者	HAIGUUSHA	spouse
遇	encounter	境遇	KYOUGUU	environment, circumstances
隅	corner	一隅	ICHIGUU	corner, nook (technical)

P28

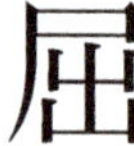

屈 KUTSU

bend

Type: kanji

Kanji that contain this phonetic and use this ON reading:

屈	bend, yield	不屈	FUKUTSU	persistence, fortitude
		理屈	RIKUTSU	theory, reason
掘	dig	掘削	KUSSAKU	excavation
		採掘	SAIKUTSU	mining
窟	cavern	巣窟	SOUKUTSU	den, hangout
		洞窟	DOUKUTSU	cave

P29

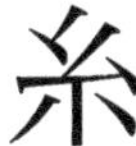

KEI

thread

Type: radical

Kanji that contain this phonetic and use this ON reading:

系	system	系統	KEITOU	system, lineage
		系列	KEIRETSU	series, sequence
係	duty, person in charge	関係	KANKEI	relationship
		係争	KEISOU	dispute, controversy

P30

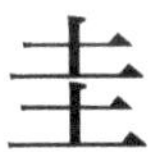

KEI

jade

Type: kanji

Kanji that contain this phonetic and use this ON reading:

圭	square jewel, jade	圭子	KEIKO	girl's name
桂	Japanese Judas tree	桂馬	KEIMA	knight (shogi)

P31

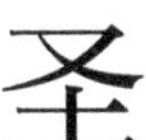

KEI

straight

Type: component

Kanji that contain this phonetic and use this ON reading:

径	diameter	直径	CHOKKEI	diameter
		直情径行	CHOKUJOU KEIKOU	impulsive and straightforward, guileless
経	pass through	経済	KEIZAI	economy
		経験	KEIKEN	experience
茎	stem	球茎	KYUUKEI	bulb (technical)

P32 敬 KEI

respect

Type: kanji

Kanji that contain this phonetic and use this ON reading:

敬	respect, reverence	敬服	KEIFUKU	great admiration
		敬老の日	KEIROU no hi	respect for the Aged Day holiday
		尊敬	SONKEI	respect, esteem
		尊敬語	SONKEIGO	honorific language
警	guard, alert	警告	KEIKOKU	warning
		警察	KEISATSU	police

P33 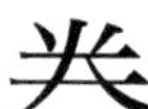 KEN

ticket

Type: component

Kanji that contain this phonetic and use this ON reading:

券	ticket	乗車券	JOUSHAKEN	passenger ticket
拳	fist	拳銃	KENJUU	pistol
圏	sphere	圏内	KENNAI	within range, within the sphere (of influence)
		成層圏	SEISOUKEN	stratosphere

P34 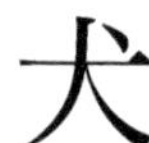 KEN

dog

Type: radical

Kanji that contain this phonetic and use this ON reading:

犬	dog	犬歯	KENSHI	canine tooth (lit. dog tooth)
献	present, offering	文献	BUNKEN	literature, books

P35   佥   KEN

everyone, all

Type: component

Kanji that contain this phonetic and use this ON reading:

検	check, examine	検査	KENSA	examination, inspection
		検討	KENTOU	consideration
険	precipitous, danger	危険	KIKEN	danger
験	test, verify	試験	SHIKEN	test, exam
		経験	KEIKEN	experience

P36   県   KEN

prefecture

Type: kanji

Kanji that contain this phonetic and use this ON reading:

県	prefecture	大分県	OOITA KEN	Oita Prefecture
懸	hang, suspend	一生懸命	ISSHOUKENMEI	with utmost effort

P37 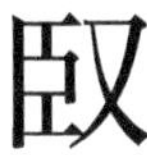 KEN

solid

Type: kanji

Kanji that contain this phonetic and use this ON reading:

堅	firm, strict	堅固	KENGO	solid, strong
賢	wisdom, clever	賢人	KENJIN	wise person
		賢明	KENMEI	wise, prudent

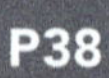

古 KO

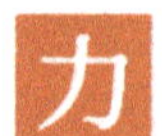

old

Type: kanji, power phonetic

Kanji that contain this phonetic and use this ON reading:

古	old	古代	KODAI	ancient times
		古文	KOBUN	ancient writing, classical Japanese literature
枯	wither, die	枯死	KOSHI	withering, dying (rare)
		栄枯	EIKO	vicissitudes, ups and downs
故	reason, happenstance	故郷	KOKYOU	hometown
		事故	JIKO	accident
固	solidify, set	固定	KOTEI	fixed, static
個	individual, counter for articles	個人	KOJIN	individual, personal
		一個	IKKO	one item
錮	confine, tie	禁錮	KINKO	imprisonment, confinement

P39

五 GO

five

Type: kanji

Kanji that contain this phonetic and use this ON reading:

五	five	五番	GOBAN	number five
		五色	GOSHIKI	variegated colours, five colours
		五十音	GOJUUON	order of hiragana (lit. 50 sounds – it is a 5 x 10 table)
悟	enlightenment, realise, perceive	悟性	GOSEI	wisdom, understanding
語	language, say	国語	KOKUGO	the national language, Japanese
		英語	EIGO	English language

P40 工 KOU

katakana E, work

Type: radical

Kanji that contain this phonetic and use this ON reading:

工	construct, manufacture	工場	KOUJOU	factory
		人工	JINKOU	artificial, man-made
紅	crimson, deep red	紅葉	KOUYOU	autumn leaves, red leaves
		紅茶	KOUCHA	black tea (lit. red tea – it looks red compared with green tea)

P41 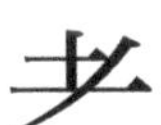 KOU

old age

Type: radical

Kanji that contain this phonetic and use this ON reading:

孝	filial piety, parental respect	親孝行	oya KOUKOU	filial piety, respect and care for one's parents
考	think	思考	SHIKOU	thought, consideration
		参考	SANKOU	reference, refer to

P42 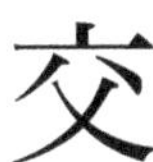 KOU

mix

Type: kanji

Kanji that contain this phonetic and use this ON reading:

交	interchange, mix	交通	KOUTSUU	traffic
校	school	学校	GAKKOU	school
		校閲	KOUETSU	proofreading, revision

P43 洪 KOU

flood

Type: kanji

Kanji that contain this phonetic and use this ON reading:

洪	flood, deluge	洪水	KOUZUI	flood
港	port, harbour	港湾	KOUWAN	harbour
		漁港	GYOKOU	fishing harbour

P44 冓 KOU

combine

Type: component

Kanji that contain this phonetic and use this ON reading:

構	build, construct	構造	KOUZOU	structure, framework
		結構	KEKKOU	splendid, enough (e.g. Would you like a second serving? いいえ、結構です Iie, kekkou desu = No thanks)
講	lecture	講義	KOUGI	lecture

P45 高 KOU

tall

Type: radical

Kanji that contain this phonetic and use this ON reading:

高	tall, high	高校	KOUKOU	senior high school
		高級	KOUKYUU	high class/grade
		最高	SAIKOU	the best, maximum
稿	manuscript, draft	原稿	GENKOU	manuscript, draft

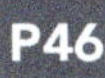

P46 艮 KON

力

boundary

Type: radical, power phonetic

Kanji that contain this phonetic and use this ON reading:

恨	bear a grudge, malice	遺恨	IKON	grudge, ill will
根	root	根拠	KONKYO	basis, foundation
墾	cultivate, reclaim	開墾	KAIKON	cultivating new land
懇	kind, cordial	懇切丁寧	KONSETSU TEINEI	kind and thorough (explanation, revision etc.)
痕	scar, trace	痕跡	KONSEKI	trace, vestige

P47 左 SA

left

Type: kanji

Kanji that contain this phonetic and use this ON reading:

左	left, progressive	左右	SAYUU	left and right
		左翼	SAYOKU	left-wing (politics), left flank
佐	assist, help	補佐	HOSA	aid, assistance
差	difference	段差あり	DANSA ari	speed hump
		時差ボケ	JISA boke	jetlag

P48 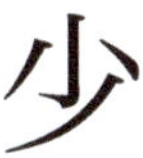 SA*

a few

Type: kanji

Kanji that contain this phonetic and use this ON reading:

沙	sand	沙汰	SATA	matter, deed
		ご無沙汰しております	Go BUSATA shite orimasu	I hope this finds you well (honorific letter starter; lit. no news)
砂	sand	砂丘	SAKYUU	sand dune
		砂糖	SATOU	sugar

* On its own it is read SHOU.

P49 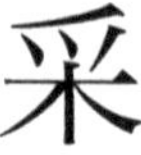 SAI

dice

Type: kanji

Kanji that contain this phonetic and use this ON reading:

采	dice, colouring	采配	SAIHAI	baton (of command), order
彩	colouring	彩色	SAISHIKI	colouring, painting
		色彩	SHIKISAI	colour, hue

P50 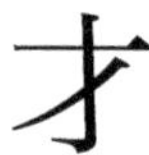 ZAI*

talent

Type: kanji

Kanji that contain this phonetic and use this ON reading:

材	timber, materials	材木	ZAIMOKU	timber, lumber
		材料	ZAIRYOU	ingredients, materials
		人材	JINZAI	human resources
財	wealth, assets	財産	ZAISAN	property, assets

* On its own it is read SAI.

P51 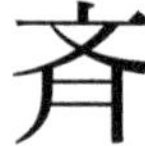 SAI

even

Type: radical

Kanji that contain this phonetic and use this ON reading:

斎	abstain, Buddhist vegetarian diet	斎場	SAIJOU	funeral hall
済	settle (debt), relieve (burden)	返済	HENSAI	repayment
		経済	KEIZAI	economy
剤	medicine	薬剤師	YAKUZAISHI*	pharmacist

* Although the ON reading is technically ZAI, this is very close to SAI and if the second kanji in a compound starts with S, it often changes to Z anyway. It's also a common word so I've included it here.

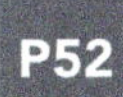 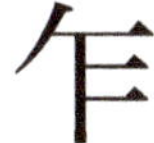 SAKU 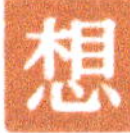

craft letter F

Type: creative component

Kanji that contain this phonetic and use this ON reading:

作	make, produce	著作	CHOSAKU	writing, book
昨	yesterday, past	昨年	SAKUNEN	last year
搾	squeeze	圧搾	ASSAKU	squeeze, compression

P53 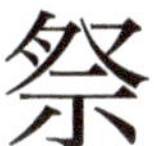 SATSU*

festival

Type: kanji

Kanji that contain this phonetic and use this ON reading:

察	investigate, judge	警察	KEISATSU	police
擦	rub	摩擦	MASATSU	friction

* On its own it is read SAI.

P54 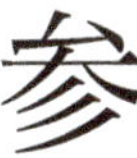 SAN

participate

Type: kanji

Kanji that contain this phonetic and use this ON reading:

参	participate	参考	SANKOU	reference, refer to
		参加	SANKA	participation
		参照	SANSHOU	bibliographic reference
惨	disaster, wretched	悲惨	HISAN	pitiful, tragic

P55 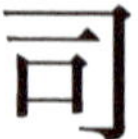 SHI 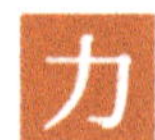

manage

Type: kanji, power phonetic

Kanji that contain this phonetic and use this ON reading:

司	officiate, administrate, manage	寿司	SUSHI	sushi
		司会	SHIKAI	chairman, presenter
		司令	SHIREI	command, commander
		上司	JOUSHI	supervisor, boss
伺	enquire, visit (formal)	伺候	SHIKOU	wait for someone
詞	part of speech, words	歌詞	KASHI	song lyrics
		品詞	HINSHI	part of speech (linguistics)
		動詞	DOUSHI	verb
		名詞	MEISHI	noun
嗣	succeed, heir	嗣子	SHISHI	heir
飼	raise animals	飼育	SHIIKU	breeding, rearing animals

P56 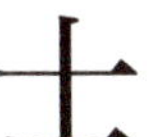 SHI

カ

scholar

Type: radical, power phonetic

Kanji that contain this phonetic and use this ON reading:

士	scholar, samurai	士官	SHIKAN	(military) officer
		武士	BUSHI	samurai, warrior
仕	official, serve	仕事	SHIGOTO	work
		仕様	SHIYOU	method, specification
志	intention	志望	SHIBOU	wish, desire
		意志	ISHI	will, intention
誌	document, magazine	雑誌	ZASSHI	magazine
支	support, branch	支持	SHIJI	support, endorsement
		支店	SHITEN	branch office
枝	branch, limb	枝葉	SHIYOU	leaves and branches, digression
肢	limbs (arm, leg)	肢体	SHITAI	limbs, body
		選択肢	SENTAKUSHI	choices, alternatives

P57 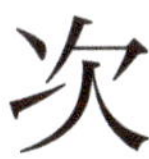 SHI*

next

Type: kanji

Kanji that contain this phonetic and use this ON reading:

姿	figure, appearance	姿勢	SHISEI	attitude, stance
		容姿	YOUSHI	physical appearance
		雄姿	YUUSHI	gallant figure
恣	selfish, arbitrary	恣意的	SHIITEKI	arbitrary
資	assets, capital	資本	SHIHON	funds, capital
		投資	TOUSHI	investment
		資格	SHIKAKU	qualifications
諮	consult	諮問	SHIMON	consultation

* On its own it is read JI.

P58 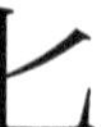 SHI

spoon

Type: radical

Kanji that contain this phonetic and use this ON reading:

死	death	死亡	SHIBOU	death
指	finger, indicate	指示	SHIJI	indication, designation
		指導	SHIDOU	leadership, guidance
脂	fat	脂肪	SHIBOU	fat

P59 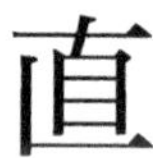 SHOKU*

direct

Type: kanji

Kanji that contain this phonetic and use this ON reading:

植	plant, grow	植物	SHOKUBUTSU	plant, vegetation
殖	increase, multiply	生殖	SEISHOKU	reproduction
		利殖	RISHOKU	money-making

* On its own it is read CHOKU.

P60 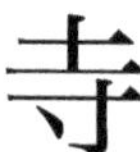 JI

temple

Type: kanji

Kanji that contain this phonetic and use this ON reading:

寺	Buddhist temple	社寺	SHAJI	shrines and temples
侍	warrior, attendant	侍女	JIJO	lady attendant, maid
		侍医	JII	court physician
時	time, hour	時間	JIKAN	time, hour
		当時	TOUJI	at the time, in those days

P61 昔 SHAKU

long ago

Type: kanji

Kanji that contain this phonetic and use this ON reading:

昔	old times	今昔	KONJAKU	past and present
借	borrow, rent	借家	SHAKUYA	rented house

P62 朱 SHU

bright red

Type: kanji

Kanji that contain this phonetic and use this ON reading:

朱	vermilion, bright red	朱筆	SHUHITSU	red ink brush
殊	special, particularly	特殊	TOKUSHU	special, particular

P63 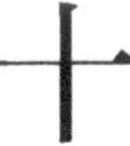 JUU

ten

Type: radical

Kanji that contain this phonetic and use this ON reading:

十	ten	二十	NIJUU	20
		十字架	JUUJIKA	cross (of Christ)
汁	juice, soup	果汁	KAJUU	fruit juice

P64 旬 JUN

ten days

Type: kanji

Kanji that contain this phonetic and use this ON reading:

旬	ten day period	旬刊	JUNKAN	published every 10 days
殉	martyrdom	殉難	JUNNAN	martyrdom

P65 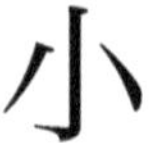 SHOU

small

Type: radical

Kanji that contain this phonetic and use this ON reading:

小	small	縮小	SHUKUSHOU	reduction
		小学校	SHOUGAKKOU	primary school
少	a few	少年	SHOUNEN	youth, young boy
		減少	GENSHOU	decrease, reduction
省	ministry	省	SHOU	ministry
		文部科学省	MONBU KAGAKUSHOU	Ministry of Education, Culture, Sports, Science and Technology

P66 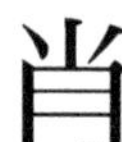 SHOU

similar

Type: kanji

Kanji that contain this phonetic and use this ON reading:

肖	resemble, look like	肖像	SHOUZOU	portrait
消	extinguish, cancel	消火器	SHOUKAKI	fire extinguisher
		消火栓	SHOUKASEN	fire hydrant
		消費税	SHOUHIZEI	consumption tax
		消防車	SHOUBOUSHA	fire engine
		消灯確認	SHOUTOU KAKUNIN	Confirm headlights are off (road sign at end of tunnel)
硝	saltpeter, nitrate	硝酸	SHOUSAN	nitric acid

P67 召 SHOU

summon

Type: kanji (honorific)

Kanji that contain this phonetic and use this ON reading:

招	summon, invite	招待	SHOUTAI	invitation
紹	introduce	紹介	SHOUKAI	introduction
照	illuminate, lighting	照明	SHOUMEI	lighting

P68 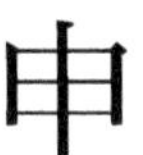 SHIN

say

Type: kanji (honorific)

Kanji that contain this phonetic and use this ON reading:

申	say (humbly)	申請	SHINSEI	application, request
伸	extend, stretch	屈伸	KUSSHIN	bending and stretching
		追伸	TSUISHIN	postscript (P.S.)
神	God, mind	精神	SEISHIN	mind, spirit, mental
		神聖	SHINSEI	sacredness
		神経	SHINKEI	nerve

P69 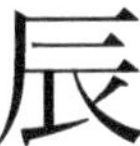 SHIN

zodiac dragon

Type: radical

Kanji that contain this phonetic and use this ON reading:

唇	lips	口唇	KOUSHIN	lips (medical)
娠	pregnancy	妊娠	NINSHIN	pregnancy
震	shake, quake	地震	JISHIN	earthquake

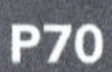

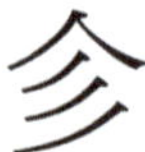

SHIN

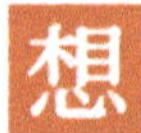

rash

Type: creative component

Kanji that contain this phonetic and use this ON reading:

診	diagnose, examine	診察	SHINSATSU	medical examination
		診療	SHINRYOU	medical treatment
疹	measles, sickness	麻疹	MASHIN	measles (medical)

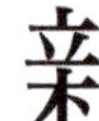

亲 SHIN

relative

Type: component

Kanji that contain this phonetic and use this ON reading:

新	new	新聞	SHINBUN	newspaper
		革新	KAKUSHIN	innovation
		新幹線	SHINKANSEN	bullet train
親	parent, intimacy	親族	SHINZOKU	relative, relation
		両親	RYOUSHIN	parents
		親切	SHINSETSU	kindness
		親友	SHIN YUU	close friend, buddy

P72

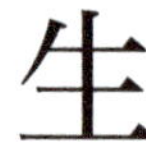

SEI

life

Type: radical

Kanji that contain this phonetic and use this ON reading:

生	birth, life, student	先生	SENSEI	teacher
		生産	SEISAN	production, manufacture
		生活	SEIKATSU	daily life, lifestyle
性	character, gender	性格	SEIKAKU	personality, disposition
		性別	SEIBETSU	gender
		女性	JOSEI	female, woman
		男性	DANSEI	male, man

P73 正 SEI

correct

Type: kanji

Kanji that contain this phonetic and use this ON reading:

正	correct, justice	正誤	SEIGO	right or wrong, correction
		正義	SEIGI	justice, righteousness
		訂正	TEISEI	correction, revision
政	government, politics	行政	GYOUSEI	administration
		政治	SEIJI	politics, government
		政府	SEIFU	government

P74 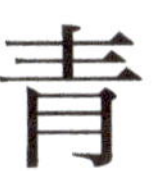 SEI

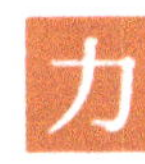

blue

Type: radical, power phonetic

Kanji that contain this phonetic and use this ON reading:

青	blue, green	青春	SEISHUN	youth
清	clear, pure	清算	SEISAN	settlement (accounts)
		清潔	SEIKETSU	clean, pure
精	spirit, energy	精神	SEISHIN	mind, spirit, mental
		精密	SEIMITSU	precise
		精力	SEIRYOKU	vitality, energy
請	ask, request	請求	SEIKYUU	request, claim
		申請	SHINSEI	application, request
静	quiet	閑静	KANSEI	quiet, tranquil (e.g. neighbourhood)
		静止	SEISHI	stillness, repose

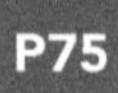

成 SEI

become

Type: kanji

Kanji that contain this phonetic and use this ON reading:

成	become, reach	成功	SEIKOU	success
		完成	KANSEI	completion
		賛成	SANSEI	support, approval
誠	sincerity	誠実	SEIJITSU	sincere, faithful
		誠忠	SEICHUU	loyalty
		誠心誠意	SEISHIN SEII	whole-hearted devotion
盛	prosper, flourish	全盛	ZENSEI	height of prosperity
		盛夏	SEIKA	midsummer

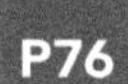

泉 SEN

fountain

Type: kanji

Kanji that contain this phonetic and use this ON reading:

泉	spring, fountain	温泉	ONSEN	onsen, hot spring baths
		源泉	GENSEN	source, origin
線	line, track	新幹線	SHINKANSEN	shinkansen, bullet train
		点線	TENSEN	dotted line
		光線	KOUSEN	ray of light, beam
		線路	SENRO	railway track, line
		国際線	KOKUSAISEN	international flight

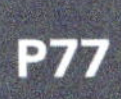
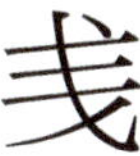

SEN

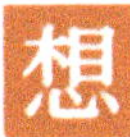

thinly sliced

Type: creative component

Kanji that contain this phonetic and use this ON reading:

浅	shallow, superficial	浅薄	SENPAKU	shallowness, superficiality
		深浅	SHINSEN	depth, shade (of colour)
銭	money, coin	金銭	KINSEN	cash, money
		銭湯	SENTOU	public bath-house

P78

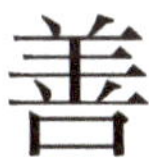

ZEN

kind

Type: kanji

Kanji that contain this phonetic and use this ON reading:

善	good, virtuous	慈善	JIZEN	charity, philanthropy
		善悪	ZENAKU	good and evil
		善悪不二	ZENAKU FUNI	good and evil are but two faces of the same coin (Buddhism, Lit. good & bad are not two different things)
膳	meals, table	配膳	HAIZEN	setting a place at the table

 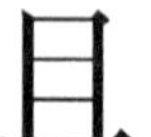 SO

moreover

Type: kanji (formal)

Kanji that contain this phonetic and use this ON reading:

祖	ancestor, founder	祖先	SOSEN	ancestor
		祖父	SOFU	grandfather, old man
		元祖	GANSO	founder, pioneer
租	crop tax, tariff	租税	SOZEI	taxes
		公租	KOUSO	public tax
組	organise, assemble	組成	SOSEI	composition
		組織	SOSHIKI	organisation (e.g. company), tissue (biology)
粗	rough, course	精粗	SEISO	fineness or coarseness

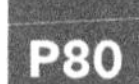 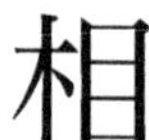 SOU

mutual

Type: kanji

Kanji that contain this phonetic and use this ON reading:

相	mutual, reciprocal	相談	SOUDAN	consultation, discussion
		相当	SOUTOU	corresponding to, suitable
想	think, idea	想像	SOUZOU	imagination
		予想	YOSOU	expectation, prediction
		感想	KANSOU	impression

P81 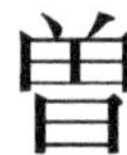 SOU

great grandma*

Type: kanji

Kanji that contain this phonetic and use this ON reading:

曽	great-(grandmother etc), formerly	曽孫母	SOUSOBO	great-grandmother
僧	Buddhist priest, monk	僧院	SOUIN	monastery, temple
		尼僧	NISOU	nun
層	layer, class	高層	KOUSOU	high-rise

* name simplified from great (grandmother, etc.)

P82 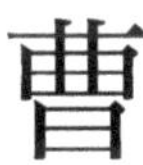 SOU

sergeant

Type: kanji

Kanji that contain this phonetic and use this ON reading:

曹	official, sergeant	法曹	HOUSOU	legal profession, lawyer
		法曹界	HOUSOUKAI	legal circles
漕	rowing, canal transportation	漕艇	SOUTEI	rowing, boating
槽	vat, tank	水槽	SUISOU	water tank, fish tank
		浴槽	YOKUSOU	bathtub

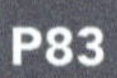 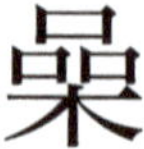 SOU 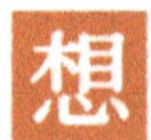

Christmas tree/pine cone

Type: creative component

Kanji that contain this phonetic and use this ON reading:

操	manipulate, operate	操作	SOUSA	operation, manipulation
燥	drying, dehydration	乾燥	KANSOU	dry, arid
		高燥	KOUSOU	high, dry ground

P84 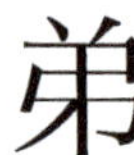 SOKU

rule

Type: kanji

Kanji that contain this phonetic and use this ON reading:

則	rule	規則	KISOKU	rules, regulations
		鉄則	TESSOKU	ironclad regulation
側	side	側面	SOKUMEN	side, profile
測	measure	測量	SOKURYOU	measurement
		目測	MOKUSOKU	measure with eye (lit. eye measure)

P85 弟 DAI

younger brother

Type: kanji

Kanji that contain this phonetic and use this ON reading:

弟	younger brother	兄弟	KYOUDAI	siblings
第	No., prefix for numbers	第一	DAIICHI	first, foremost
		第三者	DAISANSHA	third party
		第2章	DAINISHOU	Chapter 2

P86 旦 TAN

dawn

Type: kanji

Kanji that contain this phonetic and use this ON reading:

旦	dawn	一旦	ITTAN	once, temporarily
担	carry, bear	担当	TANTOU	being in charge
		負担	FUTAN	burden, responsibility
胆	gallbladder, courage	大胆	DAITAN	bold, daring (lit. big gall bladder – 'they've got gall')

P87 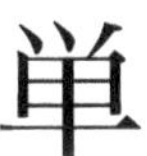 TAN

single

Type: kanji

Kanji that contain this phonetic and use this ON reading:

単	single	単位	TAN'I	unit
箪	bamboo basket	箪笥	TANSU	chest of drawers

P88 知 CHI

wisdom

Type: kanji

Kanji that contain this phonetic and use this ON reading:

知	wisdom, knowledge	知識	CHISHIKI	knowledge
		知人	CHIJIN	friend, acquaintance
智	wisdom, intellect	智能	CHINOU	intelligence, mental powers
		智者	CHISHA	sage, man of wisdom, Boddhisatva (Buddhism)

P89 竹 CHIKU

bamboo

Type: radical

Kanji that contain this phonetic and use this ON reading:

竹	bamboo	爆竹	BAKUCHIKU	firecracker
築	build	建築	KENCHIKU	construction, architecture
		改築	KAICHIKU	structural alteration of building

P90 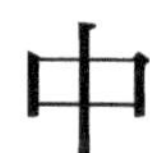 CHUU

centre

Type: kanji

Kanji that contain this phonetic and use this ON reading:

中	centre, middle	中央	CHUUOU	centre, middle
		中国	CHUUGOKU	China
仲	go-between, mediator	仲介	CHUUKAI	mediation
		仲介者	CHUUKAISHA	mediator, go-between
虫	insect	昆虫	KONCHUU	insect
忠	loyalty, devotion	忠実	CHUUJITSU	devoted, faithful
		誠忠	SEICHUU	loyalty

P91 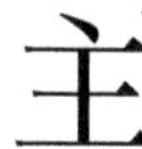 CHUU

main

Type: kanji

Kanji that contain this phonetic and use this ON reading:

注	pour	注意	CHUUI	caution, warning
		注入	CHUUNYUU	injection
		注文	CHUUMON	order
駐	stationed, stopover	駐車場	CHUUSHAJOU	parking lot

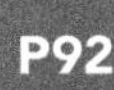

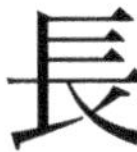

CHOU

long

Type: radical

Kanji that contain this phonetic and use this ON reading:

長	long, leader	成長	SEICHOU	growth, development
帳	notebook	帳簿	CHOUBO	register, ledger
		帳面	CHOUMEN	notebook, register
張	stretch, spread	拡張	KAKUCHOU	expansion, enlargement
		出張	SHUCCHOU	business trip

P93 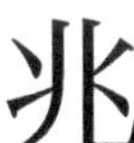

CHOU

omen

Type: kanji

Kanji that contain this phonetic and use this ON reading:

兆	omen, trillion	前兆	ZENCHOU	omen, portent
挑	challenge	挑戦	CHOUSEN	challenge, defiance
		挑発	CHOUHATSU	provocation, arousal
眺	look, gaze	眺望	CHOUBOU	prospect, outlook
跳	leap, prance	跳躍	CHOUYAKU	leap, bound

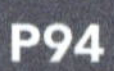

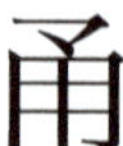

TSUU

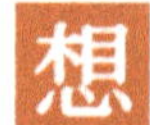

pack elephant

Type: creative component

Kanji that contain this phonetic and use this ON reading:

通	pass through, traffic	普通	FUTSUU	normal, general
		共通	KYOUTSUU	common, shared
		通常	TSUUJOU	usual
痛	pain	苦痛	KUTSUU	pain, agony
		悲痛	HITSUU	grief, sorrow

P95

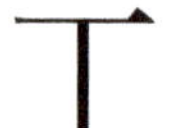

TEI*

nail

Type: kanji

Kanji that contain this phonetic and use this ON reading:

訂	revise, correct	訂正	TEISEI	correction, revision
		改訂	KAITEI	revision (of text)
亭	pavilion, restaurant	料亭	RYOUTEI	traditional Japanese restaurant
停	stop, halt	バス停	basu TEI	bus stop

* On its own it is also read CHOU, and can also mean a city block, or fourth in a list.

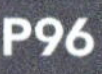

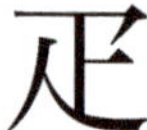

TEI

bolt of cloth

Type: radical

Kanji that contain this phonetic and use this ON reading:

定	decide, fix	定食	TEISHOKU	set menu
		安定	ANTEI	stability
		決定	KETTEI	decision, determination
堤	embankment	提案	TEIAN	proposal, suggestion
		提供	TEIKYOU	offer, provide

P97 氐 TEI

ancient tribe

Type: kanji (rare)

Kanji that contain this phonetic and use this ON reading:

低	low	低気圧	TEIKIATSU	low pressure system
		低脂肪	TEISHIBOU	low fat
抵	resist	抵抗	TEIKOU	resistance (human and electrical)
		大抵	TAITEI	usually, probably
邸	residence	私邸	SHITEI	private residence
		邸内	TEINAI	premises, grounds
底	bottom	海底	KAITEI	bottom of the ocean, sea floor
		到底	TOUTEI	cannot possibly (strong negative with a verb)

P98 廷 TEI

court

Type: kanji

Kanji that contain this phonetic and use this ON reading:

廷	court	宮廷	KYUUTEI	imperial court
		法廷	HOUTEI	courtroom
庭	courtyard, garden	庭園	TEIEN	garden, park

P99 啇 TEKI

stem

Type: component

Kanji that contain this phonetic and use this ON reading:

滴	drop, drip	水滴	SUITEKI	drop of water
摘	pick, pluck	指摘	SHITEKI	point out, indicate
適	suitable	適用	TEKIYOU	application
		適切	TEKISETSU	appropriate, suitable
敵	enemy	敵	TEKI	rival, opponent

P100 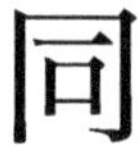 DOU

same

Type: kanji

Kanji that contain this phonetic and use this ON reading:

同	same	同情	DOUJOU	sympathy, compassion
		同上	DOUJOU	as above, ibid.
洞	cave	洞穴	DOUKETSU	cave, grotto
		洞察	DOUSATSU	insight, discernment
胴	trunk, torso	胴体	DOUTAI	body, torso

P101 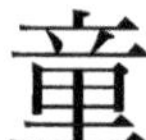 DOU

child

Type: kanji

Kanji that contain this phonetic and use this ON reading:

童	child	児童	JIDOU	children
撞	stab	撞着	DOUCHAKU	contradiction
瞳	pupil of eye	瞳孔	DOUKOU	pupil (of eye)

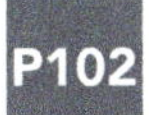 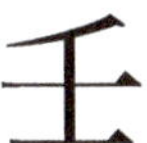 NIN 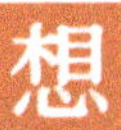

crying baby

Type: creative component

Kanji that contain this phonetic and use this ON reading:

任	responsibility	責任	SEKININ	responsibility
妊	be pregnant	妊娠	NINSHIN	pregnancy
		不妊	FUNIN	infertility

P103 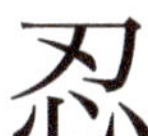 NIN

endure

Type: kanji

Kanji that contain this phonetic and use this ON reading:

忍	endure, bear	忍者	NINJA	ninja
		忍耐	NINTAI	endurance, perseverance
認	recognise	認識	NINSHIKI	recognition, awareness
		確認	KAKUNIN	confirmation, verification

P104 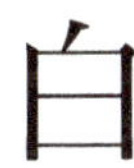 HAKU

white

Type: radical

Kanji that contain this phonetic and use this ON reading:

白	white	白髪	HAKUHATSU	white/grey hair
泊	stay overnight	一泊	IPPAKU	stay one night (e.g. at a hotel)
拍	beat, clap	拍手	HAKUSHU	clapping

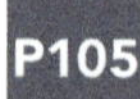 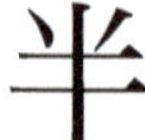 HAN

half

Type: kanji

Kanji that contain this phonetic and use this ON reading:

半	half	半分	HANBUN	half
		半年	HANTOSHI	half year
伴	accompany, companion	同伴	DOUHAN	accompany

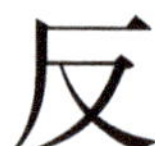 HAN 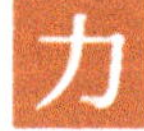

opposite

Type: kanji, power phonetic

Kanji that contain this phonetic and use this ON reading:

反	opposite, anti-	反映	HAN'EI	reflect, take on board
		反対	HANTAI	opposition, resistance
坂	slope, hill	急坂	KYUUHAN	steep slope
阪	heights, slope	阪急	HANKYUU	railway service connecting Osaka, Kyoto and other tourism spots
版	printing block, publishing	出版	SHUPPAN	publication
		版画	HANGA	woodblock print
販	sell, trade	販売	HANBAI	sales, marketing
飯	cooked rice, meal	ご飯	goHAN	cooked rice

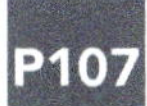
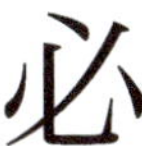

HI*

certainly, must

Type: kanji

Kanji that contain this phonetic and use this ON reading:

泌	seep out, ooze, secrete	分泌	BUNPI	secretion
秘	secret	神秘	SHINPI	mystery
		秘密	HIMITSU	secret
		秘書	HISHO	secretary

* On its own it is read HITSU.

Note: It's interesting that the words secretion, secret and secretary all contain the same component – they are also etymologically similar in English.

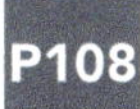
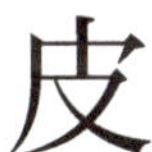

HI

力

skin

Type: radical, power phonetic

Kanji that contain this phonetic and use this ON reading:

皮	skin, hide	皮膚	HIFU	skin
		皮相	HISOU	superficial
披	open	披露	HIROU	announcement
彼	he, that	彼我	HIGA	self and others
		彼岸	HIGAN	Buddhist services during Equinoctial week
被	subject of an activity, receive	被服	HIFUKU	clothing
		被害者	HIGAISHA	victim
疲	tired	疲労	HIROU	fatigue

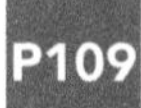

非 HI

non-

Type: radical

Kanji that contain this phonetic and use this ON reading:

非	fault, non-	非難	HINAN	blame
		非常	HIJOU	extraordinary, extreme
		是非	ZEHI	certainly, with pleasure
緋	scarlet	緋色	HISHOKU	brilliant red, scarlet
悲	sad, grief	悲痛	HITSUU	grief, sorrow
		悲劇	HIGEKI	tragedy
		慈悲	JIHI	compassion, mercy
扉	door	開扉	KAIHI	opening a door

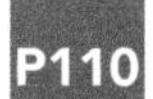
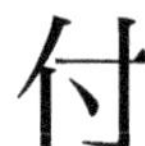

FU

attach

Type: kanji

Kanji that contain this phonetic and use this ON reading:

付	attach, adhere	添付	TENPU	attachment (e.g. email)
		付与	FUYO	grant, allowance
附	attach, append	寄附	KIFU	donation
符	sign, symbol	切符	KIPPU	ticket
		音符	ONPU	musical note, phonetic component
		声符	SEIFU	phonetic component – part of a kanji character that indicates its reading
府	urban prefecture	政府	SEIFU	government
		都道府県	TODOUFUKEN	prefectures

 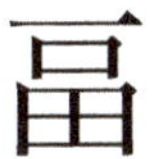 **FUKU** 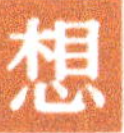

full box

Type: creative component

Kanji that contain this phonetic and use this ON reading:

幅	width	全幅	ZENPUKU	overall width
福	luck, (good) fortune	福祉	FUKUSHI	welfare, social security
		幸福	KOUFUKU	happiness, blessedness
		福岡	FUKUOKA	prefecture and city in Kyushu
副	deputy, vice-	副長	FUKUCHOU	deputy director, vice chief

P112 复 **FUKU**

lathe, repeat

Type: component

Kanji that contain this phonetic and use this ON reading:

復	return, repeat	往復	OUFUKU	return ticket
腹	stomach, abdomen	空腹	KUUFUKU	hunger
複	duplicate, compound	複数	FUKUSUU	several, multiple
		複雑	FUKUZATSU	complex, complicated
覆	cover, capsize	転覆	TENPUKU	capsize, turn over

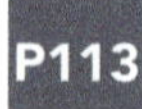

P113 分 FUN

minute

Type: kanji

Kanji that contain this phonetic and use this ON reading:

分	minute, part	自分	JIBUN	myself, oneself
		2分	NIFUN	2 minutes
		半分	HANBUN	half
		分解	BUNKAI	disassemble, analyse
粉	powder	粉末	FUNMATSU	fine powder
紛	disordered, scattered	紛争	FUNSOU	dispute, strife

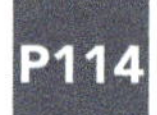

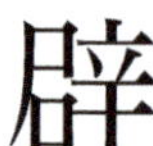

P114 辟 HEKI

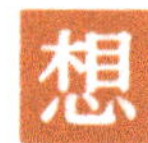

heckler, punish

Type: kanji/creative component

Kanji that contain this phonetic and use this ON reading:

壁	wall	壁画	HEKIGA	fresco, mural
癖	bad habit, weakness	習癖	SHUUHEKI	habit

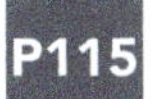

扁 HEN

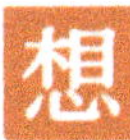

knitting

Type: creative component

Kanji that contain this phonetic and use this ON reading:

偏	inclining, leaning	偏向	HENKOU	propensity, inclination
遍	everywhere	普遍	FUHEN	universal, ubiquitous
		一遍	IPPEN	once, exclusively
編	knit, edit	編集	HENSHUU	editing
		編集者	HENSHUUSHA	editor

P116

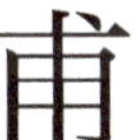

甫 HO

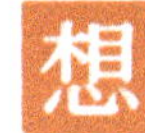

piercing sword/needle

Type: creative component

Kanji that contain this phonetic and use this ON reading:

捕	catch, seize	逮捕	TAIHO	to arrest
補	supplement, compensate	補欠	HOKETSU	fill a vacancy

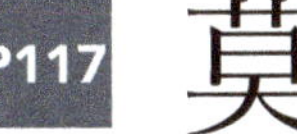

莫 BO

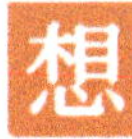

力

sundown

Type: creative component, power phonetic

Kanji that contain this phonetic and use this ON reading:

募	gather, recruit	募集	BOSHUU	recruitment
		募金	BOKIN	fund-raising
墓	grave, tomb	墓地	BOCHI	graveyard
暮	sunset, spend time	薄暮	HAKUBO	dusk, twilight
慕	long for, admire	慕情	BOJOU	longing, yearning
		敬慕	KEIBO	love and respect
模	model, pattern	規模	KIBO	scale, scope

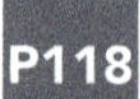

包 HOU

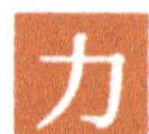

wrapping

Type: kanji, power phonetic

Kanji that contain this phonetic and use this ON reading:

包	wrapping, package	包囲	HOUI	siege, besiegement
		包容力	HOUYOURYOKU	broadmindedness
泡	bubble	気泡	KIHOU	air bubble
抱	hug, embrace	介抱	KAIHOU	nurse, look after
胞	womb, sac surrounding foetus	胞子	HOUSHI	spore
		細胞	SAIBOU	cell (biology)
砲	gun, cannon	鉄砲	TEPPOU	gun
		砲撃	HOUGEKI	shelling, bombardment
飽	tire of, satiate	飽食	HOUSHOKU	gluttony

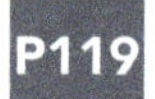

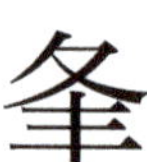

夆 HOU

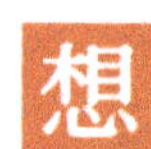

sewing needle/bee sting

Type: creative component

Kanji that contain this phonetic and use this ON reading:

縫	sew	縫製	HOUSEI	sewing
蜂	bee, wasp	蜂起	HOUKI	uprising

P120 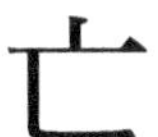 BOU

dead

Type: kanji

Kanji that contain this phonetic and use this ON reading:

亡	deceased, dying	亡命	BOUMEI	exile, seek asylum
		存亡	SONBOU	life or death, existence
忙	busy	多忙	TABOU	very busy
忘	forget	忘却	BOUKYAKU	lapse of memory
		忘年会	BOUNENKAI	end of year party
望	hope, expect	希望	KIBOU	hope, wish

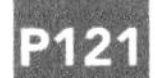 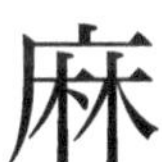 MA

hemp

Type: radical

Kanji that contain this phonetic and use this ON reading:

麻	hemp, numb	麻薬	MAYAKU	narcotic drugs
		麻酔	MASUI	anaesthetic
摩	rub, polish	摩擦	MASATSU	friction
		摩天楼	MATENROU	skyscraper
磨	grind, polish, brush (teeth)	研磨	KENMA	grinding, polishing, striving
魔	demon, witch	魔女	MAJO	witch
		悪魔	AKUMA	devil, demon, Māra (evil spirits or forces that hinder one's path to enlightenment (Buddhism))
		お邪魔します	O JAMA shimasu	set phrase said when entering another person's home (lit. I'm troubling you)

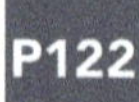
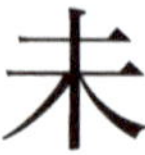

P122 未 MI

not yet

Type: kanji

Kanji that contain this phonetic and use this ON reading:

未	not yet (reached, achieved)	未来	MIRAI	future
		未満	MIMAN	less than
		前代未聞	ZENDAI MIMON	unprecedented
味	taste, flavour	意味	IMI	meaning
		興味	KYOUMI	interest (in something)
		趣味	SHUMI	hobby
		味噌	MISO	miso, soy bean paste
魅	charm, bewitch	魅力	MIRYOKU	attraction, appeal
		魅惑	MIWAKU	attraction, appeal

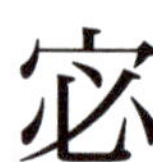
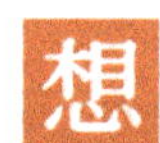

P123 宓 MITSU

hidden treasure

Type: creative component

Kanji that contain this phonetic and use this ON reading:

密	secret	秘密	HIMITSU	secret
		精密	SEIMITSU	precise
蜜	honey	蜂蜜	HACHIMITSU	honey

P124 名 MEI

name

Type: kanji

Kanji that contain this phonetic and use this ON reading:

名	name	氏名	SHIMEI	full name
		名刺	MEISHI	business card
		有名	YUUMEI	famous
		名作	MEISAKU	masterpiece
銘	inscription	銘柄	MEIGARA	brand

P125 明 MEI

bright

Type: kanji

Kanji that contain this phonetic and use this ON reading:

明	bright	説明	SETSUMEI	explanation
		不明	FUMEI	unclear, unknown (e.g. a person's whereabouts)
		証明書	SHOUMEISHO	certificate
		鮮明	SENMEI	vivid, distinct
盟	alliance	加盟	KAMEI	participation, affiliation
		同盟	DOUMEI	alliance, union

P126 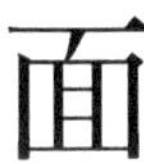 MEN

surface

Type: kanji

Kanji that contain this phonetic and use this ON reading:

面	face, surface	面会	MENKAI	meeting, interview
		方面	HOUMEN	aspect, field, direction
麺	noodles	麺類	MENRUI	noodles

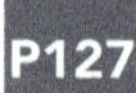

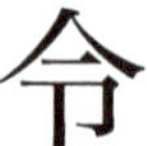

P127 令 REI

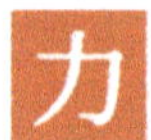

order

Type: kanji, power phonetic

Kanji that contain this phonetic and use this ON reading:

令	order, command	命令	MEIREI	command, order
		法令	HOUREI	laws and ordinances
冷	cold, cool	寒冷	KANREI	cold (weather report)
鈴	bell	振鈴	SHINREI	hand bell
		予鈴	YOREI	first bell (signalling that class or work will soon begin)
齢	age	年齢	NENREI	age, years
零	zero, nothing	零	REI	zero, 0, nought
		零下	REIKA	below zero, sub-zero

P128 良 ROU*

good

Type: kanji

Kanji that contain this phonetic and use this ON reading:

浪	wave, reckless	浪費	ROUHI	waste, extravagance
		波浪注意報	HAROU CHUUIHOU	wave, tsunami warning (news, weather report e.g. after an earthquake)
朗	clear, bright	朗読	ROUDOKU	reading aloud
		明朗	MEIROU	cheerful, clear
郎	young man, son	新郎	SHINROU	bridegroom
廊	corridor	廊下	ROUKA	corridor

* On its own it is read RYOU.

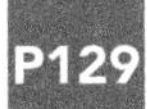

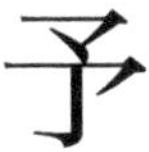

予 YO

look ahead

Type: kanji

Kanji that contain this phonetic and use this ON reading:

予	prior, forecast	予約	YOYAKU	reservation
		予定	YOTEI	plans, schedule
		予算	YOSAN	budget, estimate
預	deposit, custody	預金	YOKIN	deposit, bank account

P130 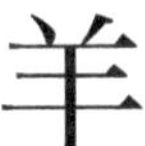

羊 YOU

sheep

Type: radical

Kanji that contain this phonetic and use this ON reading:

羊	sheep	羊毛	YOUMOU	wool
洋	ocean, foreign, Western	洋服	YOUFUKU	Western style clothes
		太平洋	TAIHEIYOU	Pacific Ocean
養	raise, nurture	養育	YOUIKU	bring up, raise

RHYMING PHONETICS

While the first letters of English words are often the way we remember them, with kanji reading, I have found that the final sound is equally important. In this section, a number of phonetics that indicate rhyming readings are presented. These phonetics do not represent a specific ON reading, but kanji characters that contain them often have readings that 'rhyme' or have the same final sound.

Long Vowel Sound

Ends in UU or OU. e.g. SHUU, SHOU

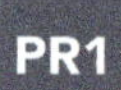

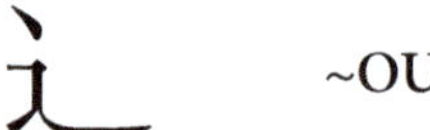

~OU

movement

Type: radical

Kanji that contain this phonetic and have the same final sound:

送	send	SOU	送信	SOUSHIN	send (email, etc.)
			転送	TENSOU	transmit, forward (email, etc.)
			放送	HOUSOU	broadcast (television, etc.)
道	road, way, teachings	DOU	道路	DOURO	road
			書道	SHODOU	calligraphy
導	guide, lead	DOU	指導	SHIDOU	leadership, guidance

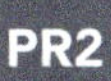

方 ~OU

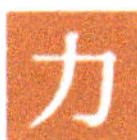

way

Type: radical, power phonetic

Kanji that contain this phonetic and have the same final sound:

方	direction, way	HOU	方法	HOUHOU	method, process
			地方	CHIHOU	district, region
訪	visit	HOU	訪問	HOUMON	visit
放	release, liberate	HOU	放送	HOUSOU	broadcast
			放棄	HOUKI	abandonment
芳	fragrant	HOU	芳香	HOUKOU	aroma
房	tassel, house	BOU	冷房	REIBOU	air-conditioning
			僧房	SOUBOU	priests' temple quarters
防	protect, defend	BOU	予防	YOBOU	prevention, precaution
肪	fat	BOU	脂肪	SHIBOU	fat

Inflected

Ends in EI or AI – e.g. AI, KEI, MAI

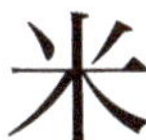

米 ~AI/EI

rice

Type: radical

Kanji that contain this phonetic and have the same final sound:

米	rice, United States	BEI/MAI	米国	BEIKOKU	USA, America
			米食	BEISHOKU	rice-based diet
			玄米茶	GENMAICHA	green tea with roasted rice
迷	be confused, lead astray	MEI/MAI	迷惑	MEIWAKU	trouble, bother
			迷子	MAIGO	lost child

Rounded/Soft

Ends in N – e.g. KAN, SHIN, NIN

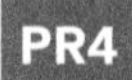
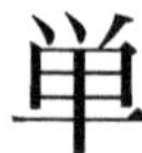 ~AN

single

Type: kanji

Kanji that contain this phonetic and have the same final sound:

単	single	TAN	単位	TAN'I	unit
			簡単	KANTAN	easy, simple
弾	bullet	DAN	爆弾	BAKUDAN	bomb

PR5
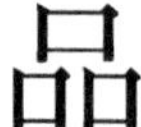 ~IN

goods

Type: kanji

Kanji that contain this phonetic and have the same final sound:

品	goods, article	HIN	作品	SAKUHIN	work (book, film, etc.)
			上品	JOUHIN	elegant, refined
			商品	SHOUHIN	product, commodity
			単品	TANPIN	single item, à la carte
			品質	HINSHITSU	quality
臨	attend, meet	RIN	臨時	RINJI	temporary, extraordinary

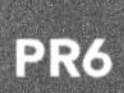
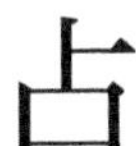

~EN

fortune-telling

Type: kanji

Kanji that contain this phonetic and have the same final sound:

占	fortune-telling, occupy	SEN	占拠	SENKYO	occupation (of territory)
			占星術	SENSEIJUTSU	astrology
店	shop	TEN	支店	SHITEN	branch office
点	dot, point, grade	TEN	欠点	KETTEN	fault, defect
			点検	TENKEN	inspection
粘	sticky	NEN	粘土	NENDO	clay
			粘着	NENCHAKU	coherence, adhesion
			粘膜	NENMAKU	mucous membrane

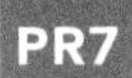
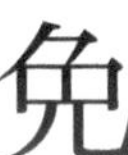

~EN

evade

Type: kanji

Kanji that contain this phonetic and have the same final sound:

免	evade, dismiss	MEN	免許	MENKYO	licence, permit
勉	study, make an effort	BEN	勉強	BENKYOU	study

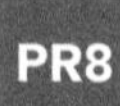 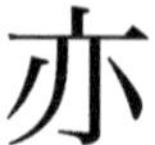 ~EN

also

Type: kanji

Kanji that contain this phonetic and have the same final sound:

変	change, strange	HEN	変更	HENKOU	change, modify
			変革	HENKAKU	transformation, evolution
恋	love	REN	恋愛	REN'AI	love
			遠距離恋愛	ENKYORI REN'AI	long distance relationship

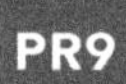 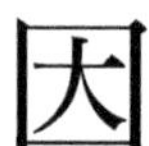 ~IN/ON

cause

Type: kanji

Kanji that contain this phonetic and have the same final sound:

因	cause	IN	原因	GEN'IN	cause, origin
			要因	YOUIN	primary factor, main cause
咽	throat	IN	咽喉	INKOU	throat (medical)
恩	kindness, mercy	ON	恩情	ONJOU	compassion, affection
			恩人	ONJIN	benefactor, patron

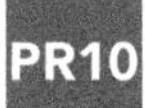

元 ~AN/EN

origin

Type: kanji

Kanji that contain this phonetic and have the same final sound:

完	complete, perfect	KAN	完璧	KANPEKI	perfect
			完全	KANZEN	perfect, complete
冠	crown	KAN	冠詞	KANSHI	article (linguistics)
			王冠	OUKAN	crown
玩	play with, enjoy	GAN	愛玩	AIGAN	care for, cherish (esp. pet, small object)
頑	stubborn	GAN	頑固	GANKO	stubborn
			頑強	GANKYOU	tenacious, dogged
			頑健	GANKEN	robust health
元	origin	GEN	元気	GENKI	in good spirits, energetic

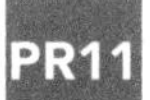

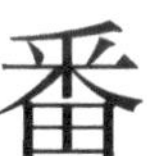

番 ~N

number

Type: kanji

Kanji that contain this phonetic and have the same final sound:

番	turn, number	BAN	一番	ICHIBAN	number one, best
			番号	BANGOU	number
審	investigation, hearing	SHIN	審議	SHINGI	deliberation
翻	turn over, waver	HON	翻訳	HONYAKU	translation

Double-barrelled

Contains two distinct syllables e.g. KAKU, SHITSU, RAKU

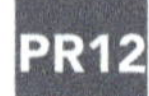

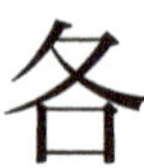

~AKU

each

Type: kanji

Kanji that contain this phonetic and have the same final sound:

各	each, every	KAKU	各種	KAKUSHU	every kind, all sorts
格	status	KAKU	規格	KIKAKU	standard, norm
落	fall	RAKU	落石注意	RAKUSEKI CHUUI	beware falling rocks
絡	entwine	RAKU	連絡	RENRAKU	contact

PR13

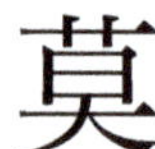

~AKU

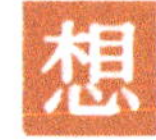

sundown

Type: creative component

Kanji that contain this phonetic and have the same final sound:

漠	desert, obscure	BAKU	砂漠	SABAKU	desert
膜	membrane	MAKU	粘膜	NENMAKU	mucous membrane
幕	curtain	MAKU	幕切れ	MAKUgire	curtain fall, end of act

PR14

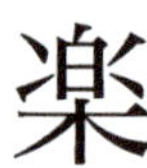

~AKU

fun

Type: kanji

Kanji that contain this phonetic and have the same final sound:

楽	music, comfort, fun	RAKU	楽天的	RAKUTENTEKI	optimistic
			楽	RAKU	comfort, ease
薬	drug, medicine	YAKU	薬品	YAKUHIN	medicine
			薬局	YAKKYOKU	pharmacy, drugstore
			薬剤師	YAKUZAISHI	pharmacist

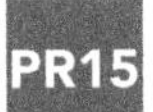

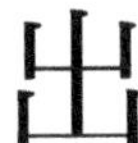

~UTSU

exit

Type: kanji

Kanji that contain this phonetic and have the same final sound:

出	exit, go out	SHUTSU	提出	TEISHUTSU	submission, handing in
			出張	SHUCCHOU	business trip
屈	bend, yield	KUTSU	理屈	RIKUTSU	theory, reason

PR16

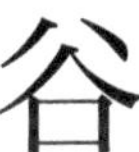

~OKU

valley

Type: radical

Kanji that contain this phonetic and have the same final sound:

谷	valley	KOKU	幽谷	YUUKOKU	deep ravine
俗	common, vulgar	ZOKU	俗事	ZOKUJI	worldly concerns, mundane events
			俗臭	ZOKUSHUU	vulgarity, worldliness
欲	desire, crave	YOKU	欲望	YOKUBOU	desire
			食欲	SHOKUYOKU	appetite (for food)
浴	bathe	YOKU	浴場	YOKUJOU	bathhouse, bathroom
			海水浴	KAISUIYOKU	sea bathing
			岩盤浴	GANBANYOKU	stone sauna

直 ~OKU

direct

Type: kanji

Kanji that contain this phonetic and have the same final sound:

植	plant (n.), plant, grow (v.)	SHOKU	植物	SHOKUBUTSU	plant, vegetation
殖	increase, multiply	SHOKU	生殖	SEISHOKU	reproduction
			利殖	RISHOKU	money-making
直	straight, direct, frank	CHOKU	直接	CHOKUSETSU	direct, face-to-face
			直感	CHOKKAN	intuition

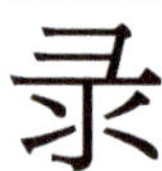

录 ~OKU

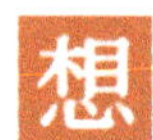

chisel/tea harvest (catch)

Type: creative component

Kanji that contain this phonetic and have the same final sound:

録	record	ROKU	登録	TOUROKU	registration
			録音	ROKUON	(audio) recording
			記録	KIROKU	record, document
緑	green	RYOKU	緑茶	RYOKUCHA	green tea
			新緑	SHINRYOKU	new green leaves

Onomatopoeia

The kanji characters that contain these rhyming phonetics are also linked by sound effects or onomatopoeia.

PR19 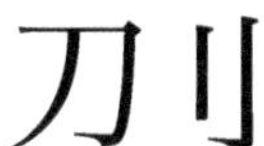 ~ATSU/ETSU

sword

Type: radical

These kanji contain the sword radical. Imagine that the sound made as a sword cuts through a piece of cloth is 'TSU'.

刷	print, brush	SATSU	印刷	INSATSU	printing
刹	temple	SATSU	古刹	KOSATSU	ancient temple
			名刹	MEISATSU	famous temple
罰	penalty, punishment	BATSU	罰金	BAKKIN	fine, penalty
			天罰	TENBATSU	divine retribution, karma
切	cut	SETSU	切断	SETSUDAN	disconnect, sever
			親切	SHINSETSU	kindness

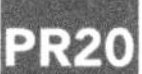 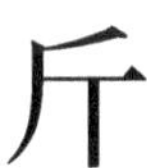 ~ITSU/ETSU

axe

Type: radical

These kanji contain the axe radical. Imagine that the sound made as an axe cuts through a piece of wood is 'TSU'.

質	substance, quality	SHITSU	質問	SHITSUMON	question
			本質	HONSHITSU	essence, substance
			品質	HINSHITSU	quality
折	fold, bend	SETSU	折衝	SESSHOU	negotiation
			屈折	KUSSETSU	bending, refraction

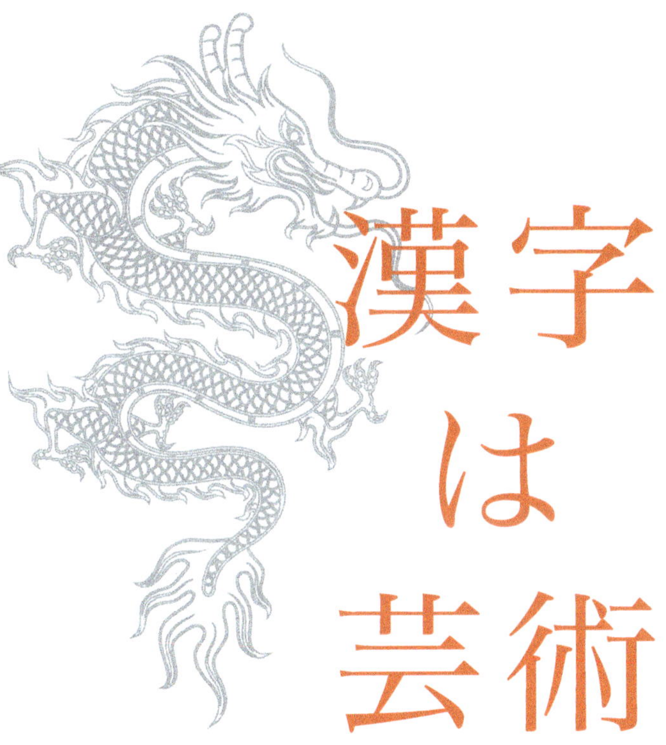
漢字
は
芸術

CHAPTER 4 – THE VISUAL CODE

THE ARTISTIC APPROACH

In this section, I have grouped kanji that share a visual style or feature and have the same or similar ON readings. I have described the similarity and provided images where necessary. If a mnemonic could easily be created based on the image and sound, it is included. If all the example words carry a certain connotation (for example, good or bad), it is included to help you associate the ON reading sound with the visual features.

Kanji grouped by visual style:

1	Trace elements – Not quite phonetic components	140
2	Trace elements with a rotation	145
3	Shape	147
4	Composition	151
5	Line	155
6	Series	176
7	Blur your eyes – Kanji that look similar from afar	185
8	Symbolic links	187

1

Trace elements – not quite phonetic components

In this section, I introduce some groups of kanji characters that are connected by a visual feature. They don't belong in the phonetic component section because they don't all contain an identical component. Rather, they each share a combination of strokes that may belong to the same or different components. The similarity between their visual look and ON sound is strong enough to call it a pattern. I have traced the part that unifies them and included a nickname and description to help you remember them.

V1 Protective arms YUU

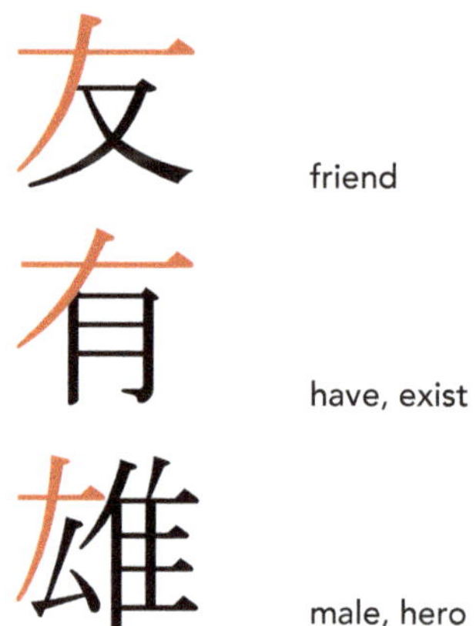

friend

have, exist

male, hero

These characters all feature two lines that cross in the top left corner. One line is horizontal and is crossed by a line that curves gently to the left. The shape resembles a katakana na ナ.

Mnemonic: A hero (eiYUU) stretches her arms out to protect YOU, a person in distress, who has collapsed on the ground below.

Connotation: Like all these examples, the sound YUU generally has a positive connotation, also appearing in words like excellent 優勝 (YUU SHOU) and elegant 優雅 (YUU GA). This helps explains why it is so common in both male and female names (Yuki, Yumi, etc.).

友好	YUUKOU	friendship
親友	SHIN YUU	close friend, buddy
有益	YUUEKI	beneficial, useful
有意義	YUUIGI	fruitful, meaningful
雄姿	YUUSHI	gallant figure
英雄	EIYUU	hero

V2 Fishtail SHUU

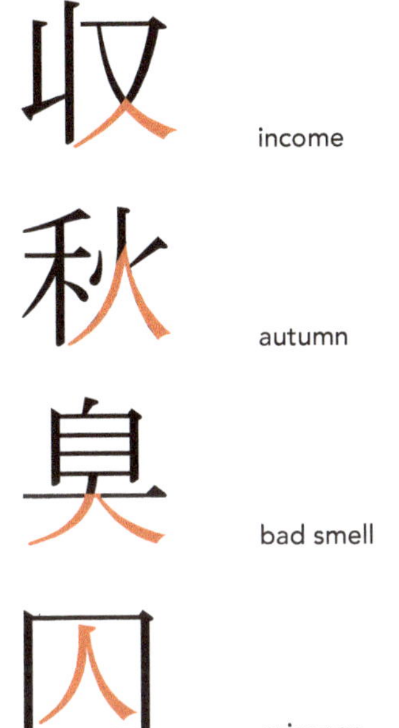

Each of these characters contain two strokes that flare down and out from their meeting point. The shape is usually at the bottom and resembles a fish tail.

Mnemonic: A fiSHUU tail.

収集	SHUUSHUU	collect, gather
秋分	SHUUBUN	autumn equinox
臭気	SHUUKI	bad smell, stink
囚人	SHUUJIN	prisoner

V3 Kicking leg SAI/ZAI

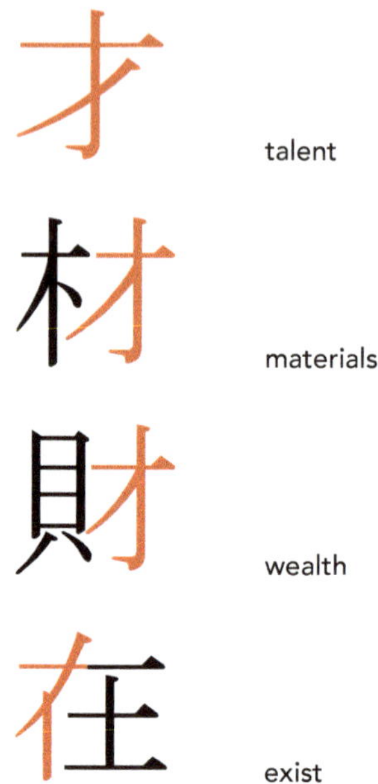

The first three characters contain the talent character 才, a cross with a small hook at the bottom of the vertical stroke and a diagonal stroke that moves from right to left. In the final character, the vertical line has been moved downward, creating a different component but leaving the shape impression.

天才	TENSAI	genius, prodigy
教材	KYOUZAI	educational materials
材料	ZAIRYOU	ingredients, material
財産	ZAISAN	property, assets
存在	SONZAI	existence
在宅	ZAITAKU	being at home

V4 Pot lid KAN

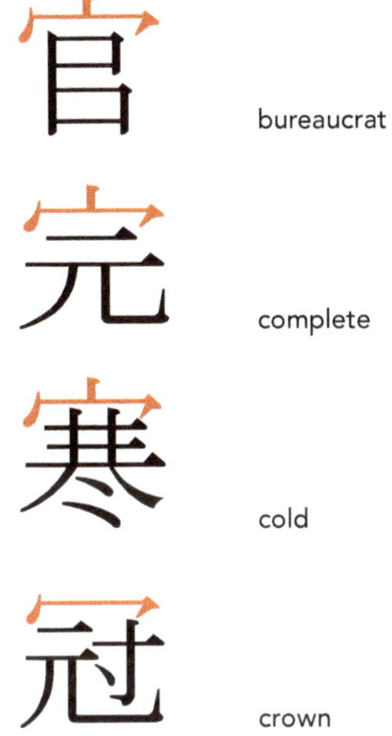

These characters all feature a 'lid' or flattened katakana wa ワ on top. In the first three this is the pot lid radical 宀, and in the last the crown radical 冖. Three of the characters also feature two strokes that flare down and outward. The overall impression is wide.

Mnemonic: When storing food, a CAN isn't much use without a lid.

Connotation: Apart from cold, they all represent the idea of officialdom and completeness. The rather orderly and authoritative look seems to echo this.

警官	KEIKAN	police offer
教官	KYOUKAN	instructor, professor
完璧	KANPEKI	perfection
寒暑	KANSHO	hot and cold
厳寒	GENKAN	intense cold
冠詞	KANSHI	article (linguistics)
栄冠	EIKAN	laurel, garland

Enclosures and the final N

Pay attention to characters that feature an enclosure, as they often end in a vowel + N. A mnemonic for this is an N-closure.

官	間	園	因
KAN	KAN	EN	IN
bureaucrat	interval	garden	cause

V5 The KEtsu curve KETSU

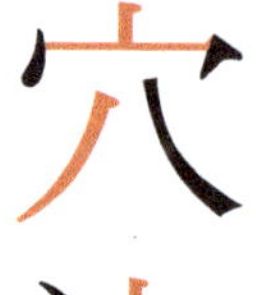

cave

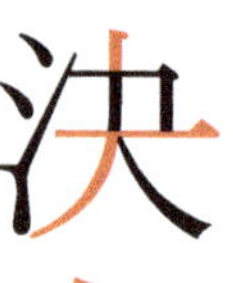

decide

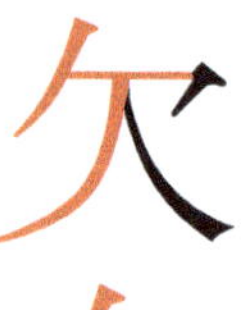

lack

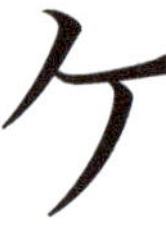

血

blood

These characters feature a short stroke that sticks out at the top, in most cases, in the centre. They also have a straight horizontal stroke near the top, and the first three have two curved strokes that flare out like legs below. Helpfully, the shape resembles a katakana ke ケ. You can trace a line across the horizontal and down the left curve on each of these, and a similar line can be drawn on the final character, 血.

Mnemonic: A katakana ke (TSU) ケ.

穴居	KEKKYO	cave dwelling
決定	KETTEI	decision, determination
決断	KETSUDAN	decision, determination
欠点	KETTEN	fault, defect
血圧	KETSUATSU	blood pressure

2 Trace elements with a rotation

In these groups, the first two characters contain the same component, and the final kanji contains a version of it that has been transformed or rotated sideways.

V6 Arrow KAI

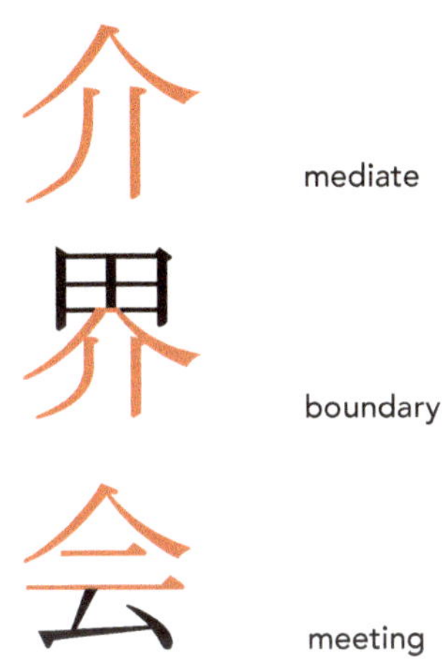

These characters all contain an upward arrow with two parallel lines directly underneath. In the third kanji the two parallel lines appear to have rotated to the right, and are horizontal rather than vertical.

Connotation: These characters all relate to the idea of mediation between two people or worlds.

紹介	SHOUKAI	introduction
介する	KAI suru	mediate
世界	SEKAI	world
境界	KYOUKAI	border, boundary
限界	GENKAI	limit
会話	KAIWA	conversation
会計	KAIKEI	account, bill
社会	SHAKAI	society

Upward inflections and an upward pointing arrow

Pay attention to characters that feature an upward pointing arrow shape within their lines. I have found that they often end in a vowel + I, creating an upward inflection. When I was making my original kanji cards and cataloguing ON readings, I intuitively used the symbol of an upside-down V or upward pointing arrow to indicate ON readings ending in AI or EI. It only occurred to me while completing this section that this is another visual-sound pattern.

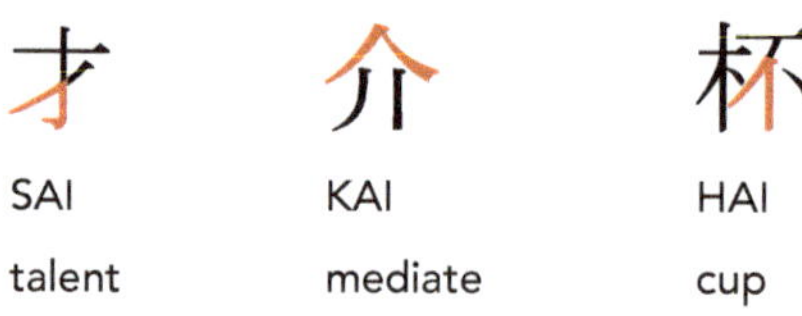

才	介	杯
SAI	KAI	HAI
talent	mediate	cup

V7 Old KO

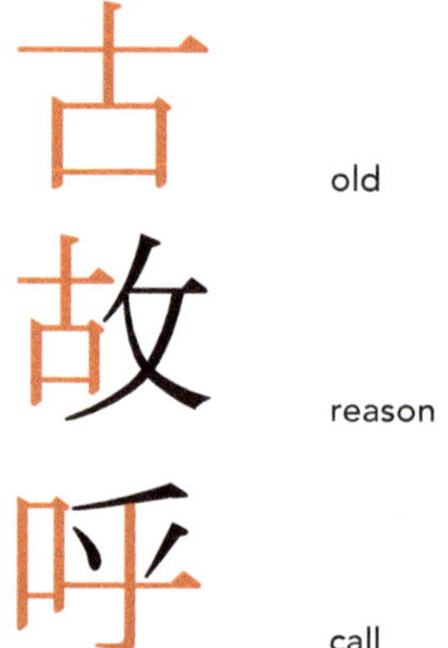

古 old

故 reason

呼 call

All of these characters contain a square with a cross on top, which in the first two characters is the character for old 古 (KO). In the final character, the cross has moved to the right position. You could imagine that the old character has rotated to the right.

古代	KODAI	ancient times
古文	KOBUN	ancient writing, Classical Japanese literature
事故	JIKO	accident
呼吸	KOKYUU	breathing, knack
点呼	TENKO	roll-call

3 Shape

The characters in this section are linked by a geometric shape that can be seen between the strokes. Mentally imagine that the outside shape is filled in, or join the dots in your head to see the shape.

V8 Square KOU

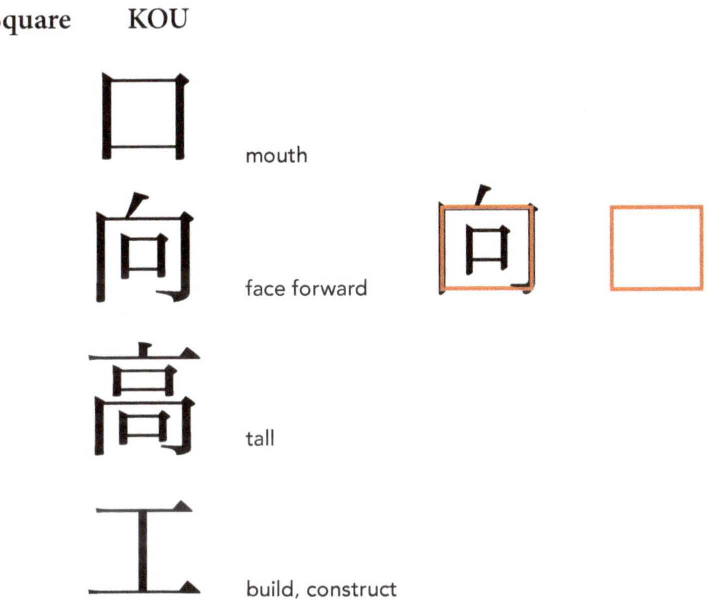

If you took a pencil and shaded in the area in between the square borders of the first three characters here they would look like squares. In addition, if you drew a dotted line to connect the top and bottom edges of 工 you'd get a square too. It looks like the centre beam holding up a building that is under construction, which links clearly to the idea of construction. A square is, by definition, balanced, and these characters all have a geometric look and authoritative feel that seems to suit the hard, long sound KOU.

河口	KAKOU	mouth of river	高低	KOUTEI	high and low, rise and fall
人口	JINKOU	population	最高	SAIKOU	highest, the best
向上	KOUJOU	improve, progress	工場	KOUJOU	factory
傾向	KEIKOU	trend, inclination	人工	JINKOU	man-made, artificial

V9 Chinese fan KA/KOU

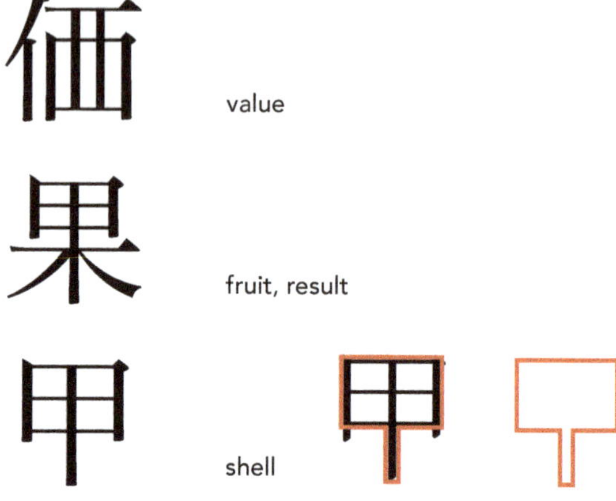

The characters in this group all contain a rectangle that is slightly wider than it is tall which is 'pierced' through the centre by one or two lines, which extend well beyond it. This makes me think of a traditional Chinese fan, with its square shape and handle. As with the previous group, the certain, geometric shape seems to be reflected in the hard sounds KA and KOU.

物価	BUKKA	cost of living
果汁	KAJUU	fruit juice
甲乙	KOUOTSU	Party A and Party B (i.e. in a legal document)
甲骨文字	KOUKOTSU MOJI	Oracle bone script

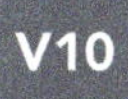

Triangle DO/TO/TOU

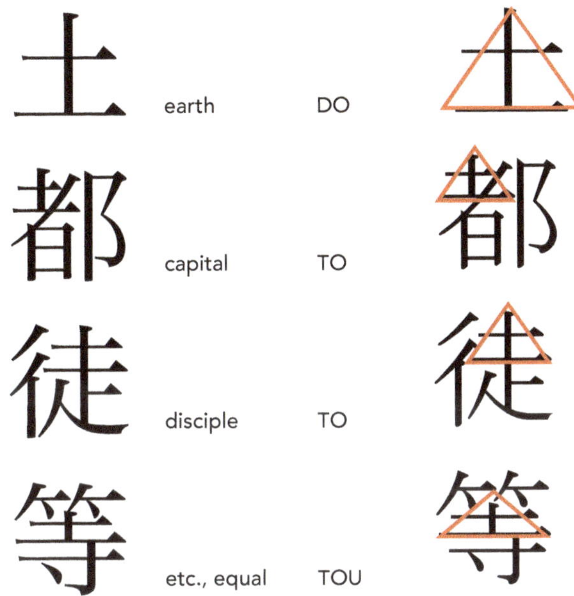

Each of the characters in this group feature the earth radical 土. If you were to roughly join the dots at the edges the resulting shape would be an upward pointing triangle. They all contain a variation of the TO sound: pure TO, hardened DO, or lengthened TOU.

土木	DOBOKU	civil engineering, public works	生徒	SEITO	student, pupil
粘土	NENDO	clay	等級	TOUKYUU	grade, class
都会	TOKAI	city	平等	BYOUDOU	equality
京都	KYOUTO	former capital, cultural capital of Japan			

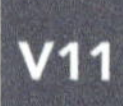

House TO/TOU

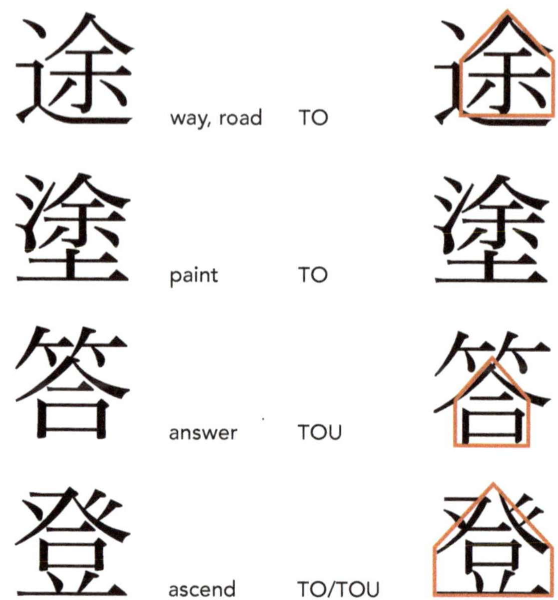

The first three characters here all have a clear upward pointing arrow or triangle on top. If you were to fill in the area below it to encompass the component below, it would resemble a house. The shape of 登 is slightly different but it still contains a definite triangular shape, the angle of the 'roof' is just steeper. This group combined with the previous one confirms a strong association between triangle shapes and the TO sound.

途上	TOJOU	on the way, en route	回答	KAITOU	answer, response
前途	ZENTO	future prospects, outlook	登山	TOZAN	mountain climbing
塗装	TOSOU	painting, coating	登場	TOUJOU	enter (on stage), appear (on screen)
塗料	TORYOU	painting material	登校	TOUKOU	attendance (at school)

4 Composition

The characters in these groups are united not by the same components, but rather by the composition of those components. It could be three components arranged together in a certain way, or a square component placed beside a cresent-shaped one. Either way, the fact that the composition aligns with the ON reading can be used as a mnemonic.

V12 Three elements (KEI)

型 type 啓 disclose

契 promise 警 guard, warn

Each of the characters in this group is composed of a larger base component in the bottom centre, and two smaller components balanced evenly on top. In each case, the top right component is either the knife radical 刀 or the activity/strike radical 攵 – in both cases the far right stroke hooks toward the centre of the character.

原型	GENKEI	prototype
模型	MOKEI	model
契約	KEIYAKU	contract
契機	KEIKI	opportunity, chance
啓発	KEIHATSU	enlightenment, development
啓示	KEIJI	(divine) revelation
拝啓	HAIKEI	dear … (formal salutation in a letter)
警告	KEIKOKU	warning
警察	KEISATSU	police

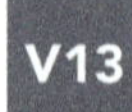

Three elements (KEN)

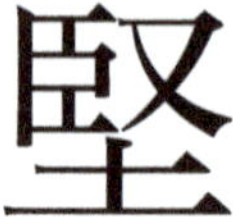

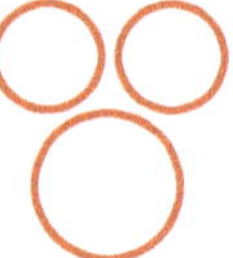

firm

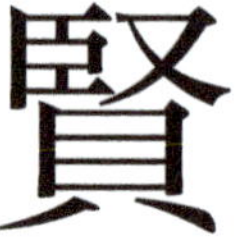

clever

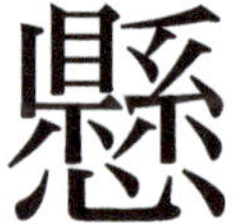

hang

As with the previous group, each of these characters is composed of two components on top, and one in the centre below. The first two kanji feature the KEN phonetic 臤 on the top. The last has a different component on top, but its top left component 県 is also stripy in appearance, like 臣.

堅固	KENGO	solid, strong
堅実	KENJITSU	reliable, sound
中堅	CHUUKEN	backbone, mainstay
賢人	KENJIN	wise man
賢明	KENMEI	wise, prudent
一生懸命	ISSHOUKENMEI	with utmost effort

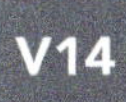

V14 Stack of books IN

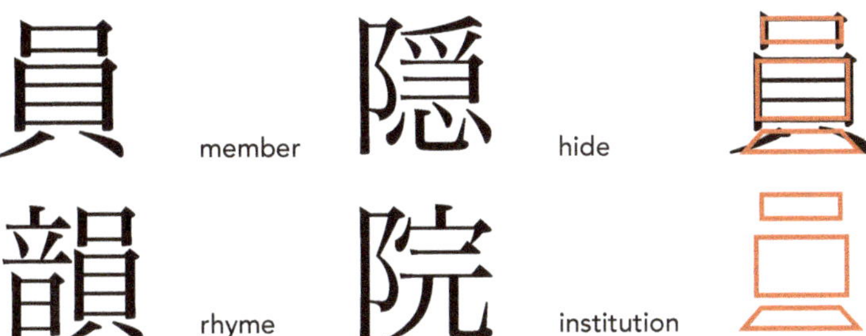

Apart from the first character, the focus of the visual connection of this group is on the right side of the characters – the side traditionally associated with phonetics. Each character (or the right part) contains a tall, narrow group of three components. The top element is wide and short or a horizontal line, and could be viewed as a book in profile. The middle element is stripy and could be seen as a stack of books. The bottom element contains two (or more) strokes that flare outward, which could be seen as the legs of a table. Together they account for nearly all the *Joyo Kanji* with the ON reading IN.

満員	MAN'IN	full house, no vacancy
社員	SHAIN	employee
職員室	SHOKUINSHITSU	school staff room
要員	YOUIN	personnel, essential person
韻律	INRITSU	rhythm, metre (poetry)
韻文	INBUN	verse, poetry
音韻	ON'IN	phoneme (linguistics)
隠語	INGO	jargon, secret language
隠居	INKYO	retirement, retired person
議院	GIIN	parliament, house, diet
病院	BYOUIN	hospital

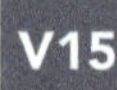

V15 Square and crescent MEI

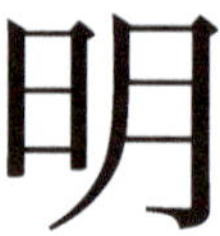

bright

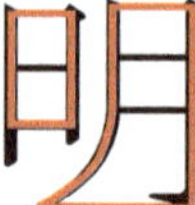

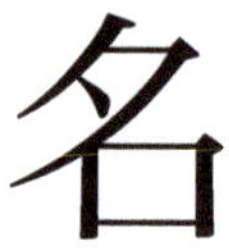

name

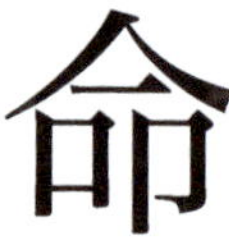

life, destiny

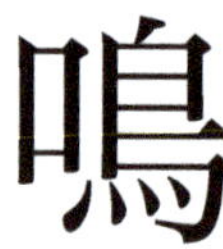

bird cry

The characters in this group feature two components that sit side by side: a square or rectangle and a slightly larger, crescent-shaped component. Rather than the component details, it is their consistent composition and proportional differences that make them visually similar. The first character features the sun radical 日, while the other three contain the mouth radical 口. The crescent-shaped component ranges from 月 and 夕 – both representations of the moon – to the stamp 卩 and bird 鳥 radicals. While far from identical, the crescent components all curve or hook slightly to the left. This group also covers off almost all the *Joyo Kanji* with the reading MEI, making it a reliable mnemonic.

説明	SETSUMEI	explanation	名刺	MEISHI	business card
証明書	SHOUMEISHO	certificate	亡命	BOUMEI	exile, seek asylum
鮮明	SENMEI	vivid, distinct	命令	MEIREI	command, order
氏名	SHIMEI	full name	運命	UNMEI	destiny, fate
有名	YUUMEI	famous	悲鳴	HIMEI	shriek, scream
名作	MEISAKU	masterpiece	雷鳴	RAIMEI	sound of thunder

5 Line

Line is perhaps the most obvious and important visual characteristic of kanji. The type of lines in a character can define its look and feel and give a hint to its ON reading.

Simple characters, simple sound

In these groups, simple characters with few strokes are matched with short, simple sounds: SHI, SHU and KA.

V16 Simple and centred SHI

士	scholar	止	stop
市	market, city	史	history
子	child	氏	clan

With a maximum of five strokes, these characters are all very simple. They are also visually balanced, tending to be as high as they are wide. There is generally one central vertical line, which is crossed by one straight perpendicular line. The lines of the last two characters are slightly curved, but they share the simplicity of the others.

武士	BUSHI	samurai, warrior	中止	CHUUSHI	suspend, interruption
市民	SHIMIN	citizen	禁止	KINSHI	prohibited
都市	TOSHI	city	歴史	REKISHI	history
子孫	SHISON	descendant, offspring	日本史	NIHONSHI	Japanese history
女子	JOSHI	girl, woman	氏名	SHIMEI	full name
			姓氏	SEISHI	full name, family name

V17 Simple and off-centre SHU

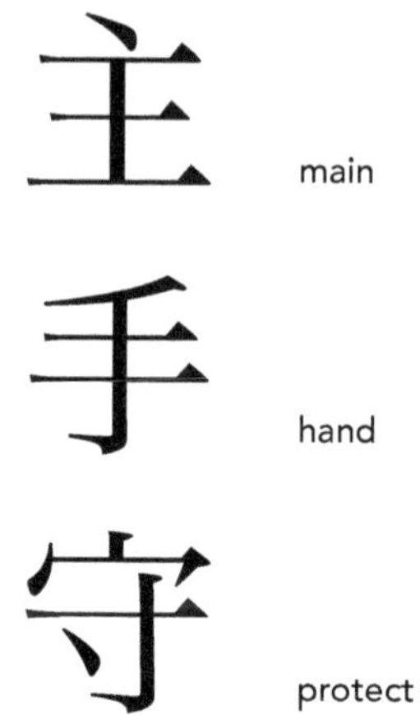

main

hand

protect

As with the SHI group above, these characters are all simple, with a maximum of six strokes. They also have a single vertical line, which is crossed by one, two or three horizontal strokes. However, while the SHI group are centred and symmetrical, the SHU group has an off-centre look. This can be seen in the diagonal stroke on the top of 主, which has the effect of tipping it slightly off balance and the diagonal stroke on top of the hand character 手 that has a similar effect. In 守, the fact that the vertical stroke of the inch radical 寸 is crossed about two-thirds across, rather than right in the centre, produces an aesthetically pleasing asymmetric look.

主人	SHUJIN	husband
主権	SHUKEN	sovereignty
手腕	SHUWAN	ability
選手	SENSHU	player (sport)
守備	SHUBI	defence
保守	HOSHU	maintenance, conservatism

V18 Simple and angular KA

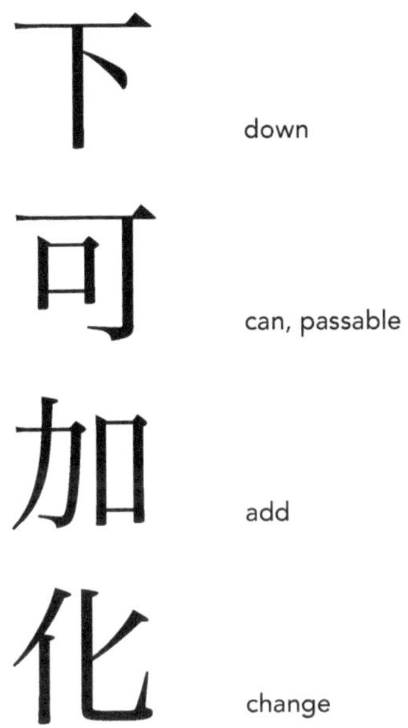

With five or less strokes, the characters in this group are also very simple. They also all have an angular look. The first two characters contain perpendicular lines, and the last two contain a stroke that bends halfway to create a shape that could be the corner of a square or a set square. As with the square and fan shapes above, the angular shape seems to fit the hard sound KA.

下流	KARYUU	downstream
下降	KAKOU	descent, decline
可能	KANOU	possible
追加	TSUIKA	add
化学	KAGAKU	chemistry

Long look, long sound

In this group, long looking characters are matched with a long vowel sound: SHOU, SHUU and JOU.

V19

Long and centred SHOU

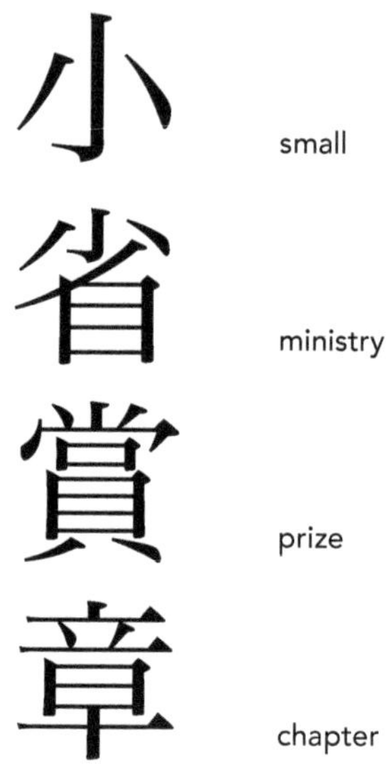

The characters in this group all have a long look, which matches their long vowel sounds. Like the shorter sounding SHI above, the look is symmetrical. The first three characters feature a central line with two symmetrically placed short strokes on either side. The last three contain a vertical stripy rectangle that elongates the overall shape.

Connotation: With the exception of small (which lacks the stripy rectangle element), they all have an official connotation, from government ministry to being awarded a prize by the authorities, to the official chapters in a book.

縮小	SHUKUSHOU	reduce
省略	SHOURYAKU	abbreviation, omission
賞与	SHOUYO	reward, bonus
文章	BUNSHOU	sentence, writing
第一章	DAIISSHOU	Chapter 1

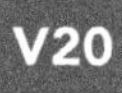

V20 Long and off-centre SHUU

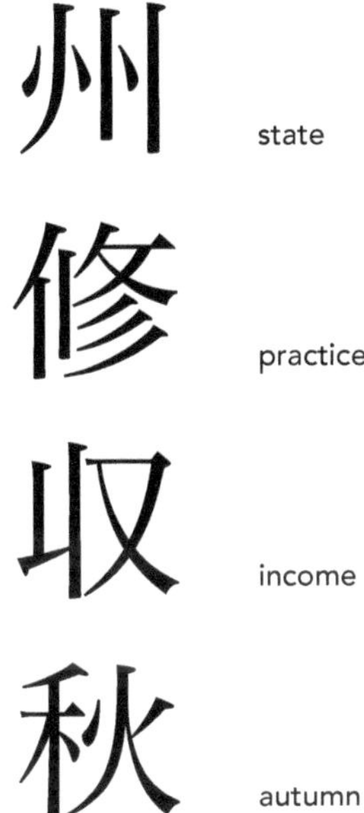

Like the previous group, these characters all appear long, which matches their long vowel sound. Each contains at least two vertical parallel lines. In all but 収, the longer lines are set against two or three short, diagonal strokes. This juxtaposition of long and short strokes makes the long strokes appear even longer. Like the shorter sounding SHU, the look is slightly off-centre.

九州	KYUUSHUU	Southern Japanese island
州議会	SHUUGIKAI	state legislature
改修	KAISHUU	repair, improvement
修理	SHUURI	repair
収集	SHUUSHUU	collect, gather
秋分	SHUUBUN	autumn equinox

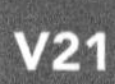

V21 Long with short strokes JOU

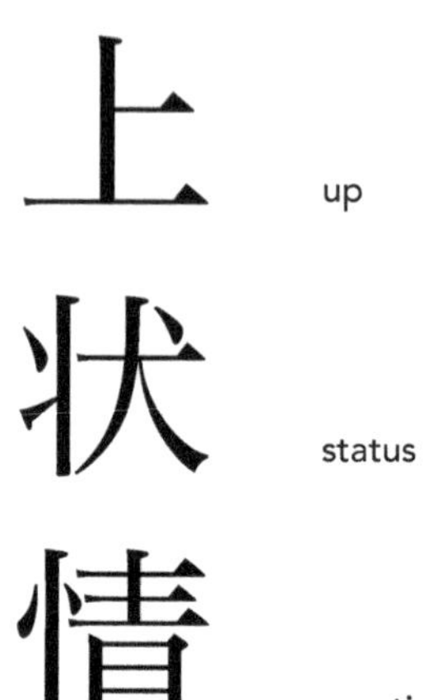

As with the 州 group, these characters all suggest height or length, which matches their long vowel sound. They each have one straight, vertical stroke that stretches the length of the character. This stroke has one or two smaller strokes around or extending from it. This juxtaposition makes the vertical line appear even longer.

上昇	JOUSHOU	rise, ascend
地上	CHIJOU	above ground
状況	JOUKYOU	situation, circumstances
状態	JOUTAI	status, condition
情報	JOUHOU	information
愛情	AIJOU	love

Balanced

The lines of these characters are well balanced, identical (or nearly identical) on the left and right side.

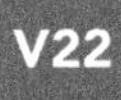

V22 Inkblot painting MI/BI

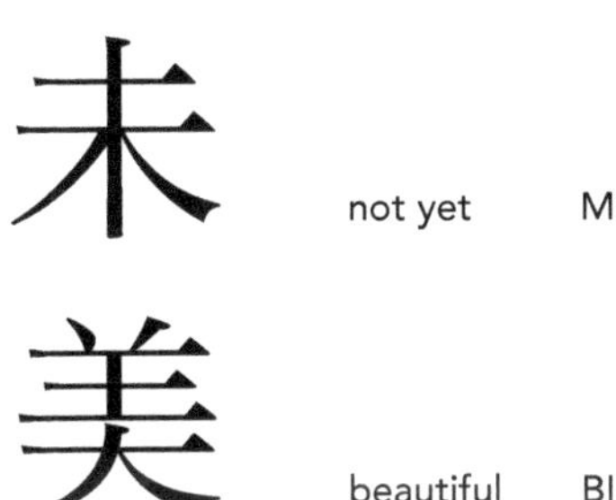

The characters in this group remind me of an inkblot painting in the way they have a central line, then flare out in a symmetrical pattern, as if a piece of paper has been folded in half to create the design. The readings also rhyme (MI/BI), and M and B tend to be 'sister sounds' in kanji (refer to The wool series). Since 未 also appears as a phonetic in taste 味, this group has a sensory connotation, tending to describe things that are beautiful to taste, or look at.

未満	MIMAN	less than
前代未聞	ZENDAI MIMON	unprecedented
未完	MIKAN	incomplete
味噌	MISO	miso, soy bean paste
美術	BIJUTSU	art
美術館	BIJUTSUKAN	art gallery
美容師	BIYOUSHI	hairdresser, beautician (person)
美容院	BIYOUIN	beauty parlour, hair salon (place)
美人	BIJIN	beautiful woman

V23 Clothes stand HAI

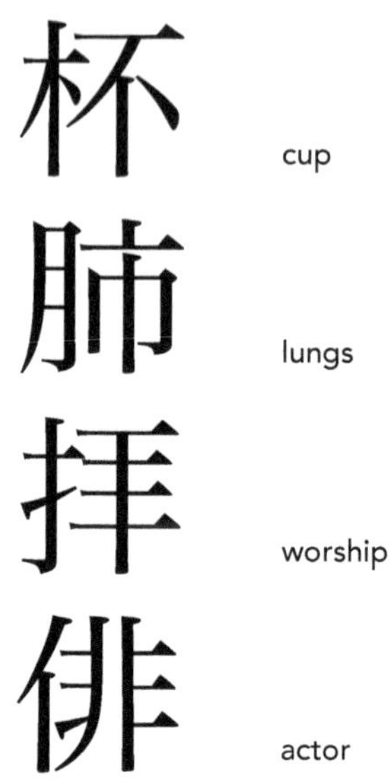

cup

lungs

worship

actor

The comments here refer to the right part of the character – the classical position of the phonetic. In all of these characters, there is a strong sense of balance in the component on the right. In the first three it is composed of a central vertical line with strokes that fan out to the left and right symmetrically. It reminds me of a folding clothes stand. It is similar visually to the inkblot group in the sense that if you were to fold it in half, each side would be roughly the same. In the final character, the central line seems to have split in two so we now have two vertical lines, each with lines fanning out to the left and right. This is the wrong/non- radical 非. This group accounts for a large proportion of the *Joyo Kanji* with the reading HAI.

一杯	IPPAI	full, to capacity
乾杯	KAMPAI	toast, cheers
肺臓	HAIZOU	lungs (medical)
拝啓	HAIKEI	Dear … (formal salutation in a letter)
俳優	HAIYUU	actor
俳句	HAIKU	poem, 17-mora poem with three lines of three, five and seven syllables

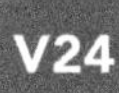

Mirrored sparks KOU

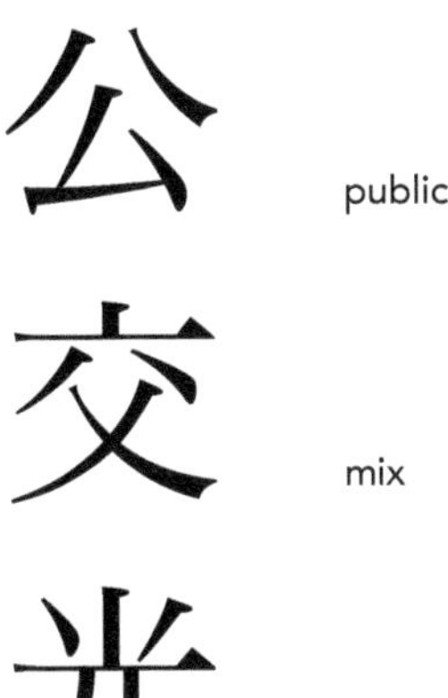

public

mix

light

These characters all have two short strokes placed evenly on the left and right that appear to mirror one another. Between them lines intersect in various configurations: meeting in a point to make a katakana mu ム, crossing neatly in the middle to resemble a cartoon rabbit's snout 父, which is also a neat ideograph of the idea of mixing. In the third character, all the lines seem to emanate outward from the centre like a star – an apt representation of the meaning, light 光.

公園	KOUEN	park
公私	KOUSHI	public and private
交通	KOUTSUU	traffic
郊外	KOUGAI	suburbs
光線	KOUSEN	ray of light, beam
光栄	KOUEI	an honour, privilege
観光	KANKOU	sightseeing

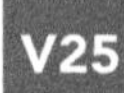

Dissected line KYO

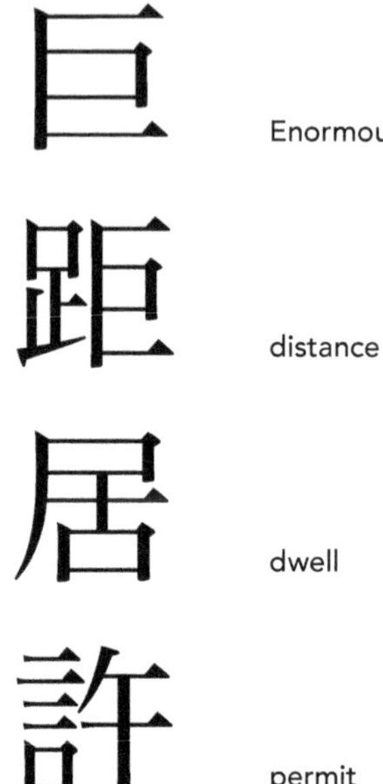

These characters all have one straight, vertical line that is crossed around the middle, which makes me think of dissection. The vertical lines are met at the top by a perpendicular horizontal line, and all but the last have another perpendicular line at the bottom. Some of these horizontal 'lines' are actually rectangles, or thick stripes. The width of the middle stripe in 巨 is an apt representation of the meaning Enormous – which I like to write with a capital E to echo the kanji's shape. The character for dwell 居 looks like a dwelling of some sort. There aren't many kanji with the reading KYO so the idea of a dissected line is a strong association.

巨大	KYODAI	gigantic, enormous
距離	KYORI	distance, range
居住	KYOJUU	residence
穴居	KEKKYO	cave dwelling
免許	MENKYO	licence, permit

Direction

In these groups, the kanji are united by the direction of their lines.

V26

Upward arrow TA/TAKU

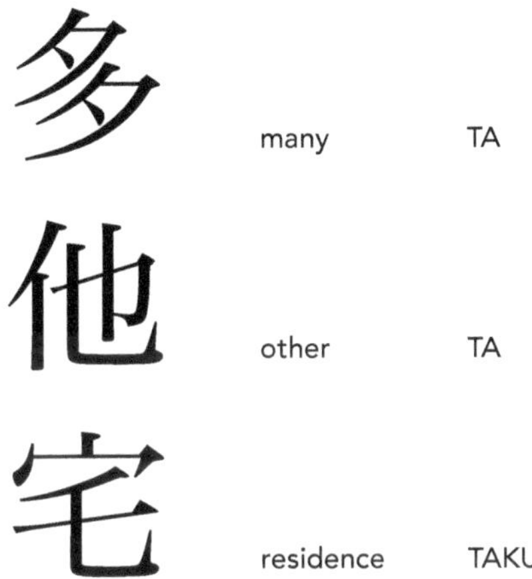

多	many	TA
他	other	TA
宅	residence	TAKU

These characters all contain an arrow-like line that sweeps from the bottom left to the top right. This line suggests movement and appears to be pointing to the top right. There aren't many characters with the reading TA or TAKU, so this is another reliable mnemonic.

多分	TABUN	maybe, a great deal
多数	TASUU	countless, majority
他人	TANIN	another person
他国	TAKOKU	foreign country
宅急便	TAKKYUUBIN	courier service, express home delivery
住宅	JUUTAKU	residence

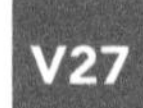

Hook KYOKU

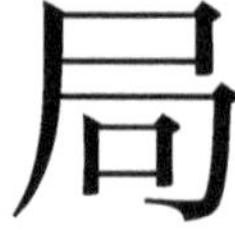

bureau

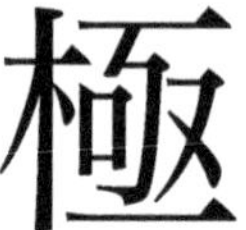

extreme, poles

The characters in this group contain a zigzag line that first extends horizontally to the right, then bends toward the bottom and hooks back to the left. Nestled within this hook is the mouth radical 口. It is similar to the KA phonetic 可, but rather than two perpendicular lines, it contains one line that changes direction mid-flight. This movement to the right and then back to the left reminds me of the nine series, another group with a zigzag look and KY~ sound.

郵便局	YUUBINKYOKU	post office
極端	KYOKUTAN	extreme
極度	KYOKUDO	maximum
極限	KYOKUGEN	utmost limits
積極的	SEKKYOKUTEKI	positive, assertive, proactive

Stripes and sparks

A large number of characters contain multiple parallel lines. They fall under the category of pattern in terms of the principles of art, and I have called them stripes to keep the language simple. The distance between stripes, and whether or not they are crossed, seems to correlate with certain sounds. I use the word sparks to refer to small strokes that emanate from a character.

V28 Stripy oblong SHU

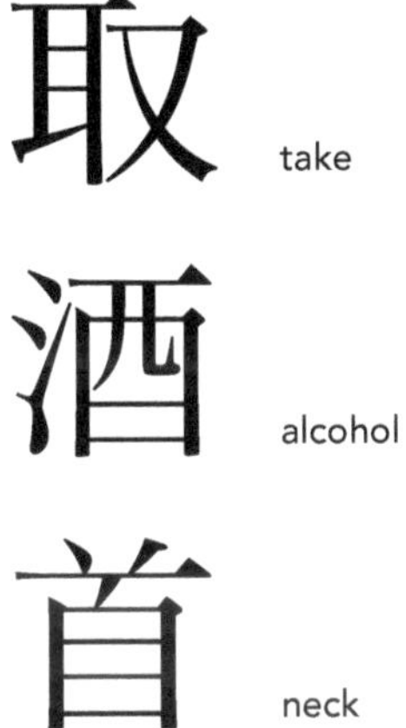

取 take

酒 alcohol

首 neck

The characters in this group all contain an upright oblong that is traversed by one or more stripes. In the case of 酒, the two outward curving lines at the top of the sake jar radical 酉 resemble a third stripe from afar, and give the oblong a similar texture to the others.

取材	SHUZAI	news coverage	飲酒運転	INSHU UNTEN	drink driving
聴取	CHOUSHU	listening	首相	SHUSHOU	Prime Minister
取得	SHUTOKU	obtain, acquire	首尾一貫	SHUBI IKKAN	consistency
梅酒	umeSHU	plum liqueur	首席	SHUSEKI	head, chief, top of the class
酒宴	SHUEN	drinking party, banquet			

V29 Wide stripes with legs KEN/GEN

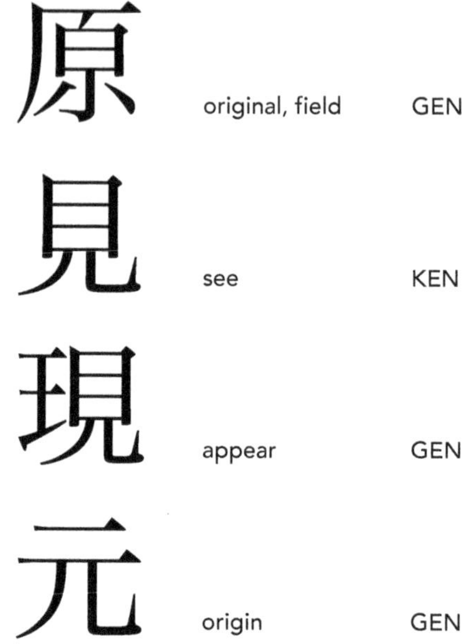

These kanji all contain widely spaced parallel horizontal stripes. In the first three characters, the lines appear within a vertical oblong, either a sun 日 or an eye 目. In the fourth character 元 the lines appear on their own, in the form of the number two, 二. All of these characters have two strokes under the stripy element that flare down and outwards – in most cases the human legs radical 儿.

Connotation: These kanji represent fundamental and miraculous/essential concepts: origin, original, see and appear, so the sound GEN carries these connotations.

源泉	GENSEN	source, origin	現実	GENJITSU	reality
原爆	GENBAKU	atomic bomb	現金	GENKIN	cash
意見	IKEN	opinion	元気	GENKI	in good spirits, energetic
見学	KENGAKU	study by observation	多元	TAGEN	pluralism, multi-
現在	GENZAI	current			

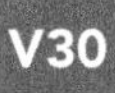

V30 Thin, uncrossed stripes SHIN

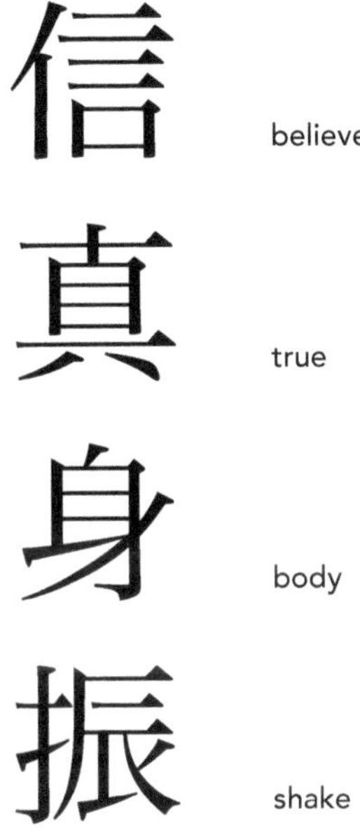

信 believe

真 true

身 body

振 shake

These kanji all feature thinly spaced parallel horizontal lines. The lines are uncrossed, creating a clean visual look. Each stripy element sits on top of another element and therefore occupies the upper or upper right position of the kanji.

信用	SHINYOU	confidence, faith
通信	TSUUSHIN	communication, transmission
自信	JISHIN	self-confidence
写真	SHASHIN	photograph
純真	JUNSHIN	purity, sincerity
身体	SHINTAI	body
自身	JISHIN	by oneself, personally
振動	SHINDOU	vibration
不振	FUSHIN	slump, stagnation

V31 Thin, crossed stripes KEN

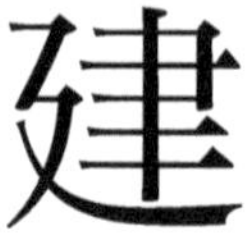
build

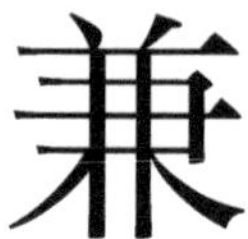
and, concurrently

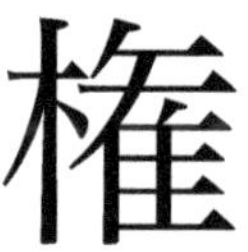
authority, right

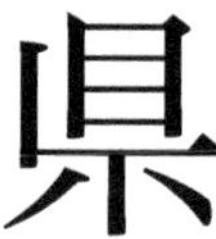
prefecture

These characters all have a square overall shape and multiple horizontal lines spaced close together, or what I like to call 'dense lines'. In the first three characters, these lines are pierced by one or two vertical lines, creating a crosshatch design, which suggests order, detail and busyness. At first glance, they resemble a ledger or a spreadsheet. In the case of 県, the vertical line runs along the side, but the impression of order and detail remains.

建築	KENCHIKU	construction, architecture
兼用	KENYOU	multi-use, multi-purpose
権利	KENRI	right, privilege
大分県	OIITA KEN	Oita Prefecture (Kyushu)

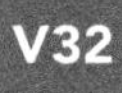

V32 Stripy border KAN

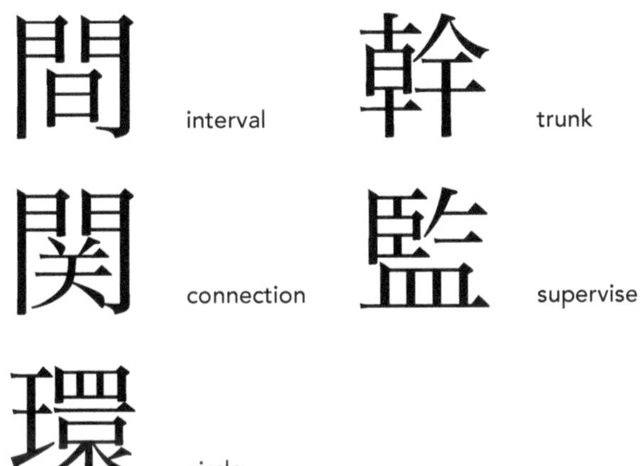

The characters in this group all feature a stripy outer element or enclosure. The first two have the gate radical 門 enclosure; a bold symmetrical border with two stripy oblongs at the top. The next kanji 環 has a stripy rectangle on the top. The character 幹 has a stripy border on the left, while 監 features a stripy element on both the left and the bottom. The tiny squares formed by the stripes give a sense of order and detail.

Connotation: Most of these kanji connote the idea of being in the middle or connection. An interval is the space between time or music, a connection joins two things and a circle connects many points. A supervisor is the intermediary between upper management and the lower echelons of a business. In Buddhist mythology, the trunk of a tree is said to connect heaven and hell, as represented by the Bodhi tree Buddha sat beside.

関係	KANKEI	relationship
時間	JIKAN	time, hour
間奏	KANSOU	musical interlude
環境	KANKYOU	environment, circumstance
新幹線	SHINKANSEN	bullet train
監督	KANTOKU	supervision, director (e.g. film)

V33 Three parallel lines JUN/SHUN

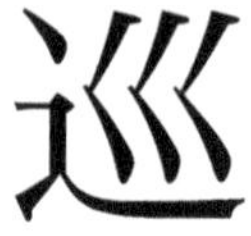

patrol, go around

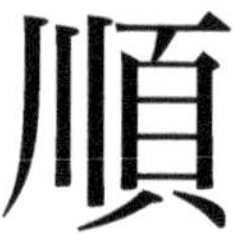

order

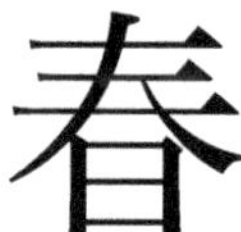

spring

These characters all feature three evenly spaced parallel lines. In the first character 巡, the three lines are vertical and bend in the middle. This is the winding river radical 巛, a visually appealing component with three identical lines that bend in unison, creating a zigzag pattern. The second character 順 also contains three vertical lines that mean river – this time they are straighter, in the form of the river radical 川. In the third character 春, the three lines are horizontal and look like the kanji number three 三 (SAN). There aren't many characters with the reading JUN or SHUN, so it's another strong visual-sound association.

巡回	JUNKAI	go around, patrol
順番	JUNBAN	turn, sequential order
順位	JUN'I	rank, position (in a race)
順序	JUNJO	order, sequence
春季	SHUNKI	spring (rare)
青春	SEISHUN	youth

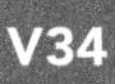

V34 Two vertical stripes TOU

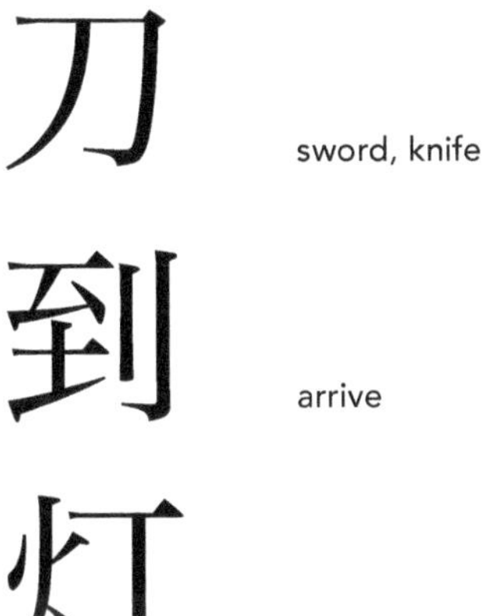

刀 sword, knife

到 arrive

灯 lamp

The first kanji in this group, the sword or katana 刀, is the model for the ones that follow. It has two parallel vertical lines that are widely spaced apart. The next character 到 contains the same sword component in its narrow form on the right. In addition, the overall shape of the left and right components echoes the idea of two parallel vertical elements. In the third character, both the left and right components feature a vertical line 灯 – one is a very narrow version of 火 fire, and the other is a narrow version of the TEI phonetic 丁. Apart from 至, none of the vertical lines in this group are crossed, so visually these kanji suggest length, matching the long sound TOU.

刀剣	TOUKEN	sword
短刀	TANTOU	short sword, dagger
到着	TOUCHAKU	arrival
周到	SHUUTOU	meticulous, careful
電灯	DENTOU	electric light
点灯	TENTOU	lighting, lamp

V35 Sparks on top EI

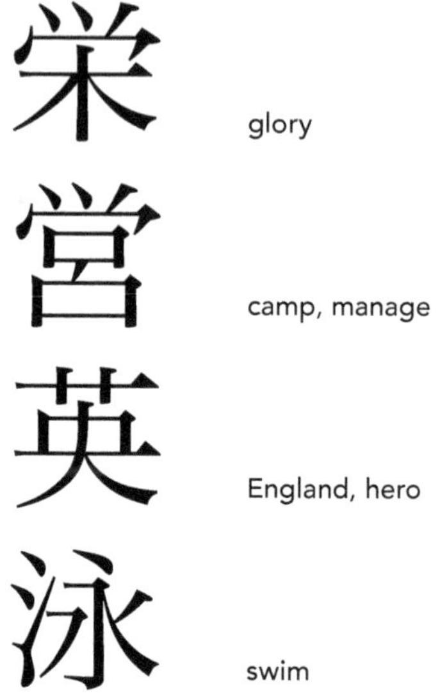

栄	glory
営	camp, manage
英	England, hero
泳	swim

These characters all have two or three short strokes on top – I think of them as sparks. The first two characters are topped with the same combination of the katakana tsu radical ⺍ and the crown radical 冖. The third character has the grass radical 艹 on top, and the fourth has a combination of the top water drop from the water radical and the top dash on the EI phonetic 永. In addition, they all have a square overall shape and are balanced between the left and right. Three of them also feature two strokes that flare down and outwards to the left and right on the bottom. There aren't many characters with the reading EI, so this is a reliable **mnemonic**.

栄養	EIYOU	nutrition
光栄	KOUEI	an honour, privilege
営業	EIGYOU	business, operations
経営	KEIEI	management, (business) operation
英雄	EIYUU	hero
英語	EIGO	English language
水泳	SUIEI	swimming
泳法	EIHOU	swimming style

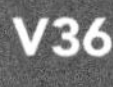

V36 Sparks and stripes SEN/ZEN

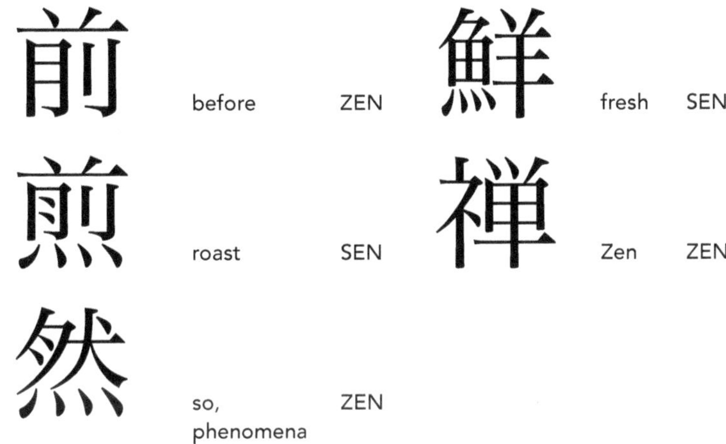

The characters in this group all have a stripy element on one side, and two or more short strokes that seem to emanate like sparks from either the stripy element, or the character as a whole. The combination of stripes and sparks gives them a dynamic, striking appearance. The stripy feature includes the moon radical 月 and a stripy grid in the centre of the fish radical 魚. The sparky element includes the fire radical in its bottom position incarnation 灬 and the katakana tsu radical ッ.

前回	ZENKAI	last time
午前	GOZEN	morning, AM
煎茶	SENCHA	green tea, tea leaves
自然	SHIZEN	nature
突然	TOTSUZEN	abrupt, sudden
偶然	GUUZEN	coincidence
全然	ZENZEN	not at all, no way! (with negative verb), wholly (with positive verb)
新鮮	SHINSEN	fresh
禅	ZEN	dhyana (profound meditation) (Buddhism), Zen
禅宗	ZENSHUU	Zen (Buddhism)

6 Series

In this section, the visual similarities of the characters are easier to see when they are placed side by side. Viewed as a series, one character seems to morph into the next, the elements moving and reshaping while keeping the visual theme going. Since they all have the same or a similar ON reading, it's a helpful way to remember the readings through association.

V37 The wool series MOU/BOU

毛 → 耗 → 網 → 亡 → 盲

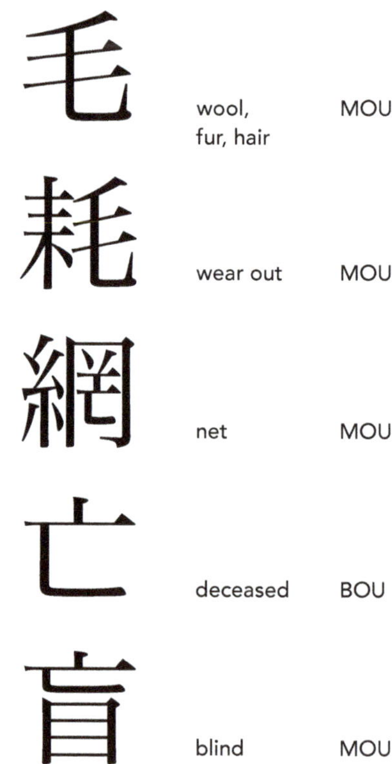

The first two characters in this series contain the wool character 毛 and origin of the katakana mo も. The third one here looks like a variation of that – as if the picture has been cut up into horizontal strips and pushed to the left and right. This truncation results in the dead component 亡, which appears in the final two characters. All of them contain a stroke that moves from the top left to the bottom right and looks like a fish hook.

毛布	MOUFU	blanket
消耗	SHOUMOU	consumption, waste
通信網	TSUUSHINMOU	communications network
漁網	GYOMOU	fishing net
亡者	MOUJA	the dead
盲点	MOUTEN	blind spot (lit. blind dot)
文盲	MONMOU	illiteracy

V38 The five series GO/GOU

五 → 語 → 互 → 呉 → 誤 → 号

五	five	GO
語	language	GO
互	mutual	GO
呉	give, Wu Kingdom	GO
誤	mistake	GO
号	number	GOU

All of the characters in this group contain a square (the mouth radical 口) positioned near at least one horizontal line. The first character in this series contains the character for five 五, which is nestled between two horizontal lines. The next contains a miniature five on the top right. In the third character, the square appears to have lifted up, so it is now suspended halfway between the two horizontal lines. This creates a step-like shape and a symmetrical ideograph that adeptly conveys the concept of mutuality 互. From here, the top line disappears and the square again appears to lift up. The step shape remains, and in the resulting character the square seems to be hovering over a chair 呉. This element appears again on the right side of the next character. Finally, the chair shape seems to sink below the horizontal line, leaving the square hovering above in 号.

五	GO	five
五感	GOKAN	the five senses
日本語	NIHONGO	Japanese language
英語	EIGO	English language
互換	GOKAN	interchange, compatible (e.g. computer operating system)
呉越同舟	GOETSU DOUSHUU	bitter enemies (placed by fate) in the same boat
正誤	SEIGO	right or wrong, correction
誤解	GOKAI	misunderstanding
番号	BANGOU	number
号令	GOUREI	order, command
10号車	JUUGOUSHA	carriage No. 10 (e.g. on a shinkansen ticket)

V39 The boundary series KON

根 → 昆 → 混 → 婚

根	root
昆	elder brother
混	mix, confuse
婚	marriage

The characters in this group are linked by a combination of the sun radical 日 and another component either on top or below. The first character contains the boundary radical and KON phonetic 艮, which is composed of a sun with two 'legs' below it. The left leg is sturdy and has a short stroke that resembles a foot. The right stroke looks like a slightly skew-whiff spoon radical 匕. In the next character, a short horizontal stroke is added to the left leg and the spoon radical is fully formed, resulting in the compare radical 比. The same combination of sun and compare recurs in the third character with the addition of the water radical 氵. In the final character, the sun and legs reverse their positions, and compare morphs into the family radical 氏.

根拠	KONKYO	basis, foundation
昆虫	KONCHUU	insect
昆布	KONBU	kelp
混乱	KONRAN	disorder, chaos
結婚	KEKKON	marriage
結婚式	KEKKONSHIKI	wedding ceremony
婚約	KONYAKU	engagement
婚約者	KONYAKUSHA	fiancé

V40 The nine series KYUU

九 → 灸 → 急 → 級

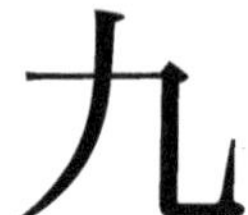
nine

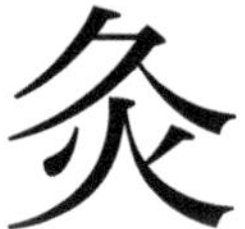
moxibustion

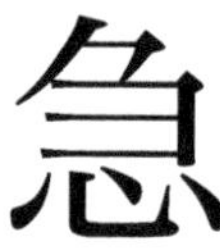
urgent

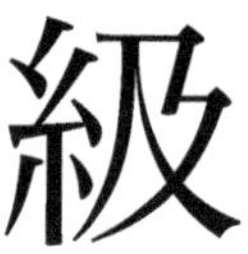
level

This series starts with nine 九 which is KYUU in Japanese and is a character that flouts the standard stroke order rules. Usually the horizontal line goes first, but here the vertical line does. It is crossed by a horizontal line that changes direction midway, creating a zigzag effect. In the next character 灸, a similar shape can be seen on the top, which also looks like a katakana ku ク. In the third character, the same shape is squashed down so it looks like a head – it sits on top of a katakana yo ヨ. In the right part of the final character, the KU shape elongates and not only hooks out to the right, but also doubles back on itself toward the left, creating another zigzag 及 (the KYUU phonetic component).

Connotation: There is a mathematical connotation to the number nine and level. KYUU can also carry a sense of urgency as in the word emergency 救急 (KYUUKYUU).

九百	KYUUHYAKU	900
九州	KYUUSHUU	Kyushu, Southern Japanese island
鍼灸	SHINKYUU	acupuncture and moxibustion
灸治	KYUUJI	treatment with moxa, cupping
急速	KYUUSOKU	rapid
緊急	KINKYUU	urgent, emergency
救急	KYUUKYUU	first-aid, emergency
救急車	KYUUKYUUSHA	ambulance
上級	JOUKYUU	advanced level
二級	NIKYUU	Level 2 (e.g. of the JLPT)

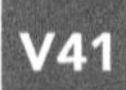

V41 The good series ROU/RYOU

良 → 郎 → 療 → 寮

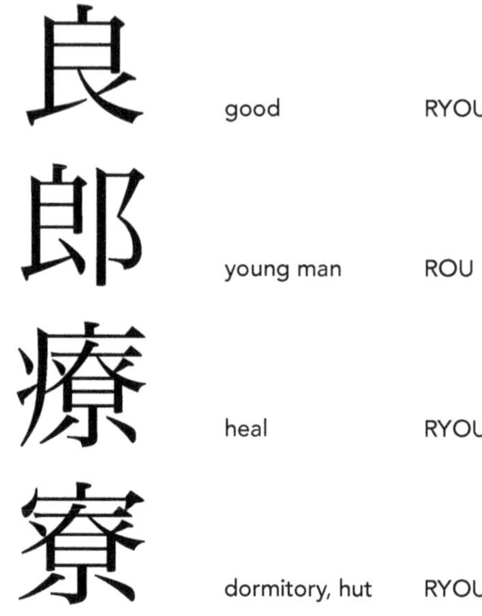

良	good	RYOU
郎	young man	ROU
療	heal	RYOU
寮	dormitory, hut	RYOU

The first two characters in this series contain the good radical. The first is composed of the sun radical 日 hi, with two strokes below moving downward and to the right – the same 'feet' we saw in the KON phonetic 艮. The second character contains a condensed version of the good radical which has only one foot next to the right village radical. The third and fourth characters contain a similar combination of the sun radical 日 with three strokes below it – this time in the form of the small radical 小.

Connotation: All these characters have a positive connotation: good and to heal; a hut would have been a haven in prehistoric times; a young man carries a positive connotation across cultures.

良好	RYOUKOU	favourable
良心	RYOUSHIN	conscience
新郎	SHINROU	bridegroom
医療	IRYOU	medical care, treatment
治療	CHIRYOU	cure, medical treatment
寮母	RYOUBO	housemother, dorm mother

7 Blur your eyes

Kanji that look similar from afar

If you blur your eyes, you will see that these characters all have a similar overall shape, which can be used as a way to remember their ON readings.

V42 Graduate's cap KEI

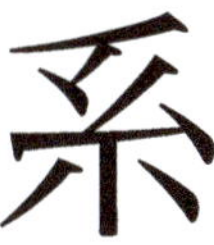

system

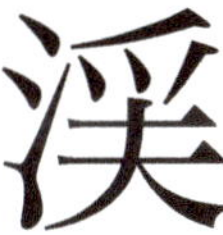

valley

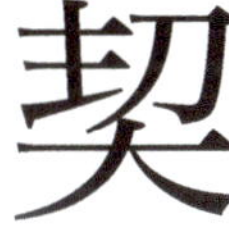

promise

In a sea of parallel horizontal strokes, the gentle gradient of the top line on the first two characters in this group stands out. It reminds me of a graduate's cap. The third character also contains a gentle gradient – the bottom stroke of the top left component 契. In addition, all three characters have a bottom component that flares out, either the big radical 大 or the flanking strokes of 小.

系統	KEITOU	system, lineage
渓流	KEIRYUU	mountain stream
契約	KEIYAKU	contract

V43 Washing SEN

先 previous

洗 wash

染 dye/colour

The first two characters in this series share the previous component 先. The third resembles the others in terms of composition. It has the water radical on the left, a cross in the top section, and the branches of the tree radical 木 flare out in a similar way to the legs in the first two characters. Incidentally, they all come first in these common compounds.

先生	SENSEI	teacher
先日	SENJITSU	the other day
洗顔	SENGAN	face washing
洗濯	SENTAKU	washing, laundry
染料	SENRYOU	dye
染色	SENSHOKU	dyeing, staining

Significance of the number 3

The number 3 三 is pronounced san in Japanese, sān in Mandarin and sāam in Cantonese. The similarity between the sound for 三 and 生, meaning 'life' or 'give birth' in the Chinese language has imbued this number with a lucky connotation. It contrasts with the number four, which is unlucky in both Chinese and Japanese, because it shares an ON reading with 死 SHI meaning death. The number three is also significant for Buddhists who go for refuge to the Three Jewels or Three Treasures: the Buddha, the Dharma (teachings) and the Sangha (spiritual community).

8 Symbolic links

These characters are linked by symbolism, which can be associated with their ON reading to aid with memorisation.

V44 Lucky number three SEN/SAN

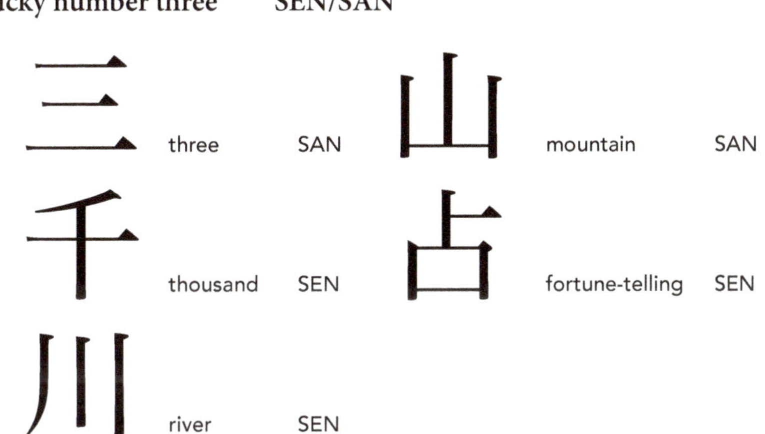

The characters in this group are united by the fact that they each reflect the concept of three. The first character is three 三, which consists of three parallel horizontal lines and in Japanese is SAN. The character 1000 千 is also a number, and is also composed of three strokes – note also the three zeros. The next two kanji are pictographs that feature three parallel vertical lines and represent nature, in river 川 and mountain 山. The final character in the group 占 has five strokes but can be split into three components: two lines and a square. It is also closely connected to the history of kanji, the earliest records of which were found on bones used for fortune-telling.

三	SAN	three
千円	SEN EN	1000 yen
千人力	SENNINRIKI	strength of a thousand men
千差万別	SENSA BANBETSU	extremely varied and wide-ranging
河川	KASEN	river, stream
高山	KOUZAN	high mountain
登山	TOZAN	mountain climbing
八面山	HACHIMENZAN	mountain in Oita
占拠	SENKYO	occupation (of territory)
占星術	SENSEIJUTSU	astrology

V45 The water dragon RYUU

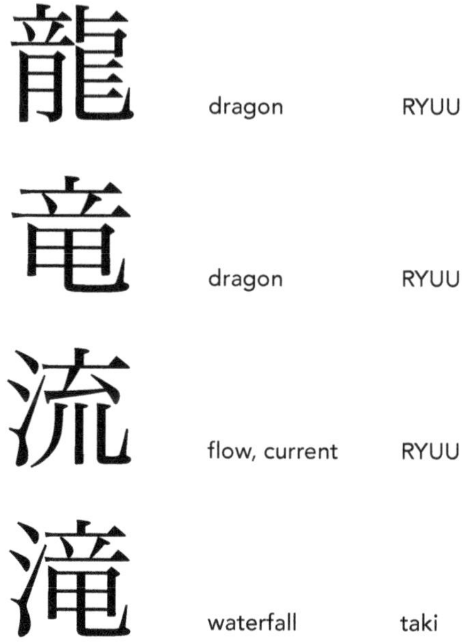

An association with water and dragons connects the characters in this group. In Japanese mythology, dragons are strongly associated with bodies of water and usually live in an ocean or river. The first two characters 龍 and 竜 both mean dragon. The third character 流 visually resembles the simpler dragon. They both have a 'head' element on top and an element on the bottom that flows downward and curves to the right. In dragon it appears to be a tail, in flow it appears to be the curve of a river. The multiple lines of the river radical 川 in 流 seem to embody the idea of water flowing downwards. Teamed with the water radical this character has a strong connotation of water.

I have included the character for waterfall 滝 here, even though it has no ON reading and its kun reading is taki, to emphasise the symbolic connection in the Japanese language between water and dragons. It is composed of the dragon character 竜 and the water radical 氵. Imagine a waterfall as a long, watery dragon.

竜	RYUU	dragon, naga (mythical serpent or cobra creatures that appear in Hindu and Buddhist scriptures)
竜頭蛇尾	RYUUTOU DABI	anticlimax, strong beginning but weak ending (lit. dragon head, snake tail)
龍舟	RYUUSHUU	dragon boat
龍馬	RYUUME	horse (Dragon Horse) (Shogi)
龍太郎	RYUUTAROU	boy's name
流行	RYUUKOU	fashion, fad
流動	RYUUDOU	flow
電流	DENRYUU	electric current
滝	taki	waterfall

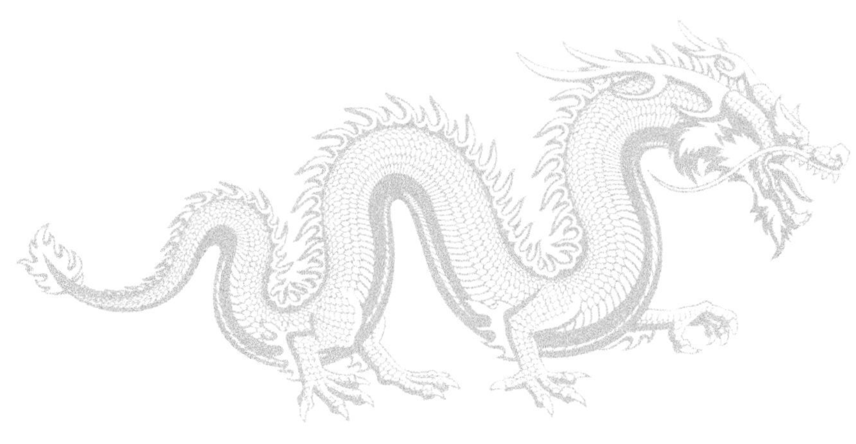

APPENDICES

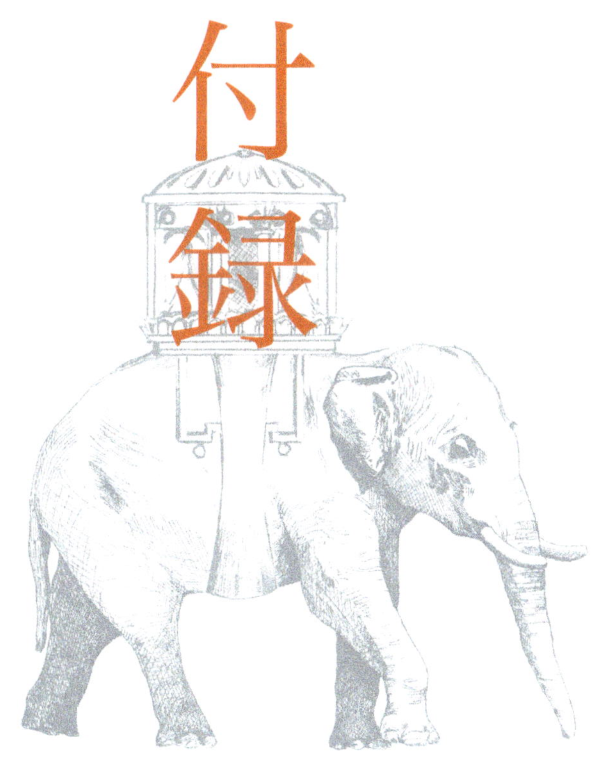

APPENDICES

REFERENCES

Australian Curriculum, Assessment and Reporting Authority. (2013). *Draft F-10 Australian Curriculum: Languages: Japanese.*

Baddeley, A. (1992). Working Memory. *Science, 255* (50440).

Bentley, J. (2001). The Origin of Man'yōgana. *Bulletin of the School of Oriental and African Studies, University of London, 64* (1).

Bernhardt, E. (1991). *Reading development in a second language*: Theoretical, empirical, and classroom perspectives. Norwood, NJ: Ablex.

Boiko, L. (2013). *Testing the power of phonetic components in Japanese kanji.* Retrieved from: http://namakajiri.net

Bourke, B. (1996). *Maximising efficiency in the kanji learning task.* Unpublished doctoral dissertation, The University of Queensland.

Chen, H. (1986). *Peng's Complete Treasury of Chinese Radicals.* Times Books International.

Chikamatsu, N. (1996). The effects of L1 orthography on L2 word recognition: a study of American and Chinese learners of Japanese. *Studies in Second Language Acquisition, 18* (432).

Cole, R. & Pickering, S. (2010). Phonological and visual similarity effects in Chinese and English language users: Implications for the use of cognitive resources in short-term memory. *Bilingualism: Language and Cognition, 13* (4).

Dexter, K. (2017). *On'yomi And Kun'yomi in Kanji: What's the Difference?* Retrieved from www.tofugu.com

Dörnyei, Z. (2005). *The Psychology of the Language Learner: Individual Differences in Second Language Acquisition.* London: Routledge.

Douglas, M. O. (1992). *Development of orthography-related reading/writing strategies by learners of Japanese as a foreign language.* Unpublished doctoral dissertation, University of Illinois at Urbana Campaign, Illinois.

Ehrman, M. (1996). *Understanding Second Language Learning Difficulties.* Thousand Oaks: Sage.

Favorite Japanese English Dictionary. (1999). Tokyo: Shoseki.

Fenollosa, E. (1936). *The Chinese Written Character as a Medium for Poetry.* San Francisco: City Lights.

Flores d'Arcais, G., Saito, H. & Kawakami, M. (1995). Phonological and Semantic Activation in Reading Kanji Characters. *Journal of Experimental Psychology: Learning, Memory and Cognition, 21* (1).

Flower, L. & Hayes, J. (1984). Images, Plans and Prose. *Written Communication, 1.*

Gamage, G. (2003). Perceptions of kanji learning strategies: do they differ among Chinese character and alphabetic background learners? *Australian Review of Applied Linguistics, 26* (2).

Halpern, J. (Ed.) (2001). *Kanji Learner's Dictionary.* Tokyo: Kodansha.

Halpern, J. (2001). Kana and romanization. *Kanji Dictionary Publishing Society*. http://www.kanji.org

Harris, K. (2011). *Bushudo: The way of the radical and kanji pedagogy.* University of Wisconsin.

Heisig, J. (1977). *Remembering the Kanji 1*: a complete course on how not to forget the meaning and writing of Japanese characters. University of Hawaii Press.

Heisig, J. (1986). *Remembering the Kanji 2*: a systematic guide to reading Japanese characters. University of Hawaii Press.

Henshall, K. (1998). *A Guide to Remembering Japanese Characters.* Tokyo: The Charles E. Tuttle Company Co., Inc.

Hiraga, M. (2006). Kanji: The Visual Metaphor. *Style, 40* (1 & 2).

Hulstjn, J.H. (1997). Mnemonic methods in foreign language vocabulary learning. In Coady, J. & Huckin, T. (Eds). *Second Language Vocabulary Acquisition: A rationale for pedagogy.* England: Cambridge U Press.

Hummel, K. & French, L. (2010). Phonological memory and implications for the second language classroom. *The Canadian Modern Language Review / La Revue canadienne des langues vivantes, 66* (3).

Juuyou Kanji Jiten [Daily Use Kanji Dictionary]. (2005). Kyoto: Nippon Kanji Kyoiku Shinkokai.

Kanken Yosou Mondaishuu (Kanji Kentei Practice Test Questions) (2017). Tokyo: Obunsha.

Kato, T. (2005). Learning strategies employed by Chinese-background learners in learning Japanese vocabulary. *Japanese Studies, 25* (3).

Koda, K. (1989). Effects of L1 orthographic representation on L2 phonological coding strategies. *Journal of Psycholinguistic Research, 18* (2).

Kondo-Brown, K. (2006). How do English L1 learners of advanced Japanese infer unknown kanji words in authentic texts? *Language Learning, 56* (1).

Kubota, M. and Toyoda, E. (2001). Learning strategies employed for learning words written in kanji versus kana. *Australian Review of Applied Linguistics, 24* (2).

Kuiper, K (2001). *In celebration of The Tale of Genji, the world's first novel.* Encyclopædia Britannica, Inc.

Kushner, E. (2009). *Crazy for Kanji.* Berkeley: Stone Bridge Press.

Kusk, A. (1998). *Tuttle Kanji Cards II.* Tuttle Publishing.

Lam, A., Perfetti, C. & Bell, L. (1991). Automatic phonetic transfer in bidialectal reading. *Applied Psycholinguistics, 12.*

Leyi, L. (1993). *Tracing the Roots of Chinese Characters: 500 Cases.* Beijing Language and Culture University Press.

Li, S., Gong, D., Jia, S., Zhang, W. & Ma, Y. (2011). Object and spatial visualizers have different object processing patterns: behavioral and ERP evidence. *NeuroReport*, 22.

Lieh-Ting, S. (2008). *Enhancing the effectiveness of kanji learning for the L1 Chinese-background students through a Sino-Japanese phonological correspondence-based strategy*. Indiana: Purdue University Press.

McGovern, J. (English Ed.) (2005). *Kanji Power Handbook for the Japanese Language Proficiency Test*. Tokyo: Aruku.

Machida, S. (2001). Japanese text comprehension by Chinese and non-Chinese background learners. *System, 29* (1).

Mark, E. (2016). *Oracle Bones*. Ancient History Encyclopedia. Retrieved from https://www.ancient.eu/Oracle_Bones/

Mark, E. (2016). *Chinese Writing*. Ancient History Encyclopedia. Retrieved from https://www.ancient.eu/Chinese_Writing/

Matsunaga, S., & Crosby, M. E. (1997). The relationship between spatial ability of native speakers of Japanese and their coding strategy when reading kanji. *Computer Assisted Language Learning, 10* (4).

Matsunaga, S. (1996). The linguistic nature of kanji re-examined: do kanji represent only meanings? *The Journal of the Association of Teachers of Japanese, 30* (2).

Miwa, K. (2012). Semantic radicals in Japanese two-character word recognition. *Language and Cognitive Processes, 27* (1).

Mori, Y. & Mori, J. (2011). Review of recent research (2000–2010) on learning and instruction with specific reference to L2 Japanese. *Language Teaching, 44* (4).

Mori, Y. & Sato, K. (2007). Japanese language students' perceptions on kanji learning and their relationship to novel kanji word learning ability. *Language Learning, 57* (1).

Mori, Y. (1998). Effects of first language and phonological accessibility on kanji recognition. *The Modern Language Journal, 82* (1).

Mori, Y. (2003). The roles of context and word morphology in learning new kanji words. *The Modern Language Journal, 87* (iii).

Mori, Y. and Nagy, W. (1999). Integration of information from context and word elements in interpreting novel kanji compounds. *Reading Research Quarterly, 34* (1).

Mori, Y. and Shimizu, H. (2007). Japanese language students' attitudes toward kanji and their perceptions of kanji learning strategies. *Foreign Language Annals, 40* (3).

Mori, Y. (2012). Five myths about kanji and kanji learning. *Japanese Language and Literature, 46* (1).

Nagy, W., Anderson, R. and Herman, R. (1987). Learning word meanings from context during normal reading. *American Educational Research Journal, 24* (2).

Okita, Y. (1995). *Kanji gakushuu sutoratejii to gakusei no kanji gakushuuni taisuru shinnen [Kanji learning strategies and student beliefs on kanji learning]*. Sekai no Nihongo Kyooiku 5 [Japanese Language Education Around the Globe].

O'Neill, P. (1987). *Essential Kanji.* New York: Weatherhill.

Pye, M. (1971). *A Study of Kanji.* Hokuseido Press.

Reid, J. (Ed.). (1995). *Learning Styles in the ESL/EFL Classroom.* Boston: Heinle & Heinle.

Riding, R. (2000). *Cognitive Styles and Learning Strategies.* London: David Fulton.

Saito, H., Masuda, H. & Kawakami, M. (1998). Form and sound similarity effects in kanji recognition. *Reading and Writing, 10* (3–5).

Scarino, A. (2012). A *rationale for acknowledging the diversity of learner achievements in learning particular languages in school education in Australia.* Research Centre for Languages & Cultures, University of South Australia.

Schwartz, A. C. (2013). *Huayuanzhuang east I: A study and annotated translation of the oracle bone inscriptions.* University of Chicago.

Spahn, M. & Hadamitzki, W. (1996). *The Kanji Dictionary.* Hong Kong: Tuttle Publishing.

Suzuki, T. (1990). *Nihon-go to gaikoku-go [Japanese and foreign languages].* Tokyo: Iwanami Shoten.

Tamaoka, K. & Taft, M. (2010). The sensitivity of native Japanese speakers to On and Kun kanji readings. *Reading and Writing: An Interdisciplinary Journal, 23.*

Townsend, H. (2011). *Phonetic components in Japanese characters.* Linguistics dissertation, San Diego State University.

Toyoda, E. (2000). English-speaking learners' use of component information in processing unfamiliar kanji. *Australian Review of Applied Linguistics, 23* (1).

Toyoda, E., Muhammad Firdaus, A. and Kano, C. (2013). Identifying useful phonetic components of kanji for learners of Japanese. *Japanese Language and Literature, 47.*

Tucker, B. (1995). Minds of Their Own: Visualizers Compose. *The English Journal: National Council of Teachers of English, 84* (8).

Usuki, M. (2000). *Promoting Learner Autonomy*: learning from the Japanese language learners' perspectives. Hokuriku University.

Vance, J. (2001). *Building Word Power in Japanese.* Tokyo: Kodansha International.

Wan, J.F. (1999). Zhongri hanzi de duyin bijiao (The comparative study on the pronunciation of Sino-Japanese words). *Nihongo no gakushu to kenkyu, 1 [Study and Research into Japanese].*

Wang, B.-T. (2004). Guanyu hanyu de yunmu yu riyu hanzi yindu [A study on the vowels of Chinese and Japanese Kanji On-reading]. *Nihongo no gakushu to kenkyu, 3.*

Wang, S. (1998). A study on the learning and teaching of hanzi – Chinese characters. *Working Papers in Educational Linguistics, 69* (101).

Williams, N. (2009). *Kanji Portraits*: Origins, radicals and stories. Retrieved from kanjiportraits.wordpress.com/

ONLINE RESOURCES

The kanji words and kanji characters detailed in *The Kanji Code* were either based on my own knowledge, or looked up and confirmed from multiple dictionaries and online resources. My English translations were checked for accuracy by native Japanese proofreaders. Words and kanji meanings were not taken in any bulk form from any of the following resources, however these resources were referred to during the checking process.

Nichijou Kanji Hyou [Joyo Kanji/Daily-use Kanji], Agency for Cultural Affairs, Government of Japan. http://www.bunka.go.jp

Pop Jisyo Japanese-English Dictionary. www.popjisyo.com

Jim Breen's WWWJDIC http://nihongo.monash.edu/cgi-bin/wwwjdic?1B

Yamasa Online Kanji Dictionary, The Yamasa Institute www.yamasa.org

字源 Jigen [Kanji Origins] https://jigen.net/kanji/20094

Kanji Jiten [Kanji Dictionary] (2018). https://kanji.jitenon.jp/

Sears, R. (2017) Chinese Etymology. Retrieved from hanziyuan.net.

41 phonetics were derived from a list of kanji containing identical phonetic components that appeared in a dissertation by Hiroko Townsend (2011).

過	KA	乍	SAKU	相	SOU	半	HAN
我	GA	次	SHI	燥	SOU	漠	BAKU
牙	GA	伸	SHIN	槽	SOU	皮	HI
各	KAKU	辰	SHIN	則	SOKU	必	HI
肌	KI	借	SHAKU	弟	DAI	福	FUKU
其	KI	殊	SHU	診	CHIN	壁	HEKI
義	GI	旬	JUN	中	CHUU	扁	HEN
圭	KEI	招	SHOU	長	CHOU	包	HOU
径	KEI	成	SEI	通	TSUU	逢	HOU
采	SAI	青	SEI	版	HAN	密	MITSU
才	SAI						

All other phonetics were identified by the author. All visual groups, their descriptions and images are the original work of the author.

ACKNOWLEDGEMENTS

As a non-native speaker of Japanese, I have needed assistance from a number of Japanese people. I am grateful to Hideaki Maruoka for checking my translations of hundreds of example words and kanji; and to Hiroko Uchihara for checking the kana-related words and kanji. They both provided invaluable native-speaker insights. I wish to thank Hiroko Townsend for generously sharing the phonetic components that she identified, and Noriko Williams for kindly giving permission to reference her kanji portraits in the creative component stories. I am grateful to Carly Tenille Slater for her thorough proofreading which noticeably improved the manuscript. I received invaluable advice from friends and family on the visual groups and the component names. Thank you Pat Jameson, Magdalena Ndong Nzue, Rani Ramjan and Hamish Clarke. Thank you to my dissertation supervisor Dr Peter Roger for his advice and suggestions; and to my sub-supervisor Dr Izumi Inoue who not only provided invaluable assistance during the project, but also encouraged me to publish a textbook.

Thank you to the staff and students of Nakatsu Minami High School and Yabakei High School in Oita Prefecture in Japan. Their dedication to their studies inspired me to persist with Japanese when I was struggling, and their greetings and handwritten notes cheered me up when I was homesick. The staff provided a lot of assistance in my daily life and encouraged my kanji study, in particular Yoshiko Norimatsu, Yoshiko Kondo and Kaori Watanabe. Thank you to fellow JET Programme participants: Cynthia Hawkins for being my kanji buddy and for helping to compile the first digital list of ON readings; Lee Sean Huang and Jessica Browning for hosting study sessions; Sarah Dzida for providing invaluable feedback and proofreading of the dissertation, and much practical advice during the publication phase.

I am grateful to Virginia Buckingham for applying her talent to the design of the book and cover. Thank you Pinyo Fordham for creating graceful visual group images; Chantal Smith for her wonderful kana and phonetic images.

I am grateful to my parents Helen Cumming and Lachlan Cumming, who have always encouraged me to follow my dreams. My mother also provided invaluable advice on the publishing process, something that as an Editor she has much experience in. I am grateful to my grandmother Leila Cumming, a lifelong learner who finished her PhD at the age of 70, for inspiring my interest in foreign languages. Special thanks go to Ian Hamilton for keeping me healthy and happy, and for lending his proofreading expertise at various stages of the manuscript. And finally thank you Daniel for inspiring the step ladder component name and for putting up with 'kanji, kanji, kanji'.

GLOSSARY

creative component
A phonetic component that does not have an obvious meaning, so the author has invented one.

cognitive style
An individual's preferred and habitual modes of perceiving, remembering, organising, processing and representing information.

form-sound character ***keisei moji***
Characters made up of a radical and a phonetic. The radical indicates the meaning or meaning category of the character. The phonetic indicates a likely ON reading and may also contribute to the meaning.

hiragana
Phonetic script used for words of Japanese origin and conjunctions, word endings and particles.

Japanese Language Proficiency Test (JLPT)
Exam used to measure Japanese language proficiency.

Joyo Kanji
The 2,136 daily-use kanji characters officially listed by the Japanese Ministry of Education, Culture, Sports, Science and Technology that Japanese students are expected to learn by the end of high school.

kanji
Logographic characters originally imported from China, used in Japanese written language to represent words.

kanji compound
Two or more kanji characters put together to make a word. Also referred to as a kanji word.

katakana
Phonetic script used for loan words, onomatopoeia and as a hint to kanji readings.

kun reading ***kun yomi***
One of two types of pronunciation that can be applied to a kanji character; a word which originated in Japanese and was later applied to an imported kanji character.

learning style
An individual's natural and preferred method for absorbing and retaining new information and skills.

object visualiser (OV)
A sub-category of the visualiser cognitive style; OVs habitually use visual properties (e.g. colour and shape) to construct high-resolution objects and scenes.

ON reading *on yomi*
One of two types of pronunciation that can be applied to a kanji character; a Japanese adaptation of the original Chinese reading.

phonetic component *onpu*
A component that indicates a kanji character's likely ON reading.

phonological activation
The mental process of recognition of the sound represented by a character or word, whether verbally or mentally.

phonological memory (PM)
A sub-component of working memory concerned with recall of sounds. Also known as Phonological Loop.

power phonetic
A phonetic component that appears in five or more kanji characters.

radical *bushu*
The part of a kanji that indicates the meaning or meaning category; also known as a *semantic* or *meaning component*.

spatial visualiser (SV)
A sub-category of the visualiser cognitive style; SVs are more likely to use imagery to represent and transform spatial relations.

subvocalisation
The act of sounding out the phonetic sounds in a written text during reading, whether verbally or mentally.

verbaliser
Category of cognitive style; *verbalisers* are better at working with verbal information.

visualiser
Category of cognitive style; *visualisers* are better at working with visual or spatial information.

working memory (WM)
Memory used to store temporary information and used in language comprehension.

卓 **10 AM** (KAN) Composed of the ten radical 十 and the early character 早, it suggests the idea of '10 early in the day' – that is, 10 AM. The fact that it appears in the morning character 朝 is a bonus association.

其 **step ladder** (KI) This component resembles a ladder, and the two strokes at the bottom could represent two feet stepping onto it.

竟 **nosy neighbour** (KYOU) The stand radical 立 combined with the see radical 見 suggests a person standing up and peeping over their fence to look at the house next door. This fits with the idea of a border 境 (Radical: earth). Standing and looking also fits with a mirror, 鏡 (R: metal).

禺 **fasten together** (GUU) This component resembles a clip that extends from the top grid into the lower box, a visual depiction of the idea of togetherness. Research suggests that the meaning of this component is 'together', which fits with even number 偶 (R: person) and coincidence 偶然, as well as encounter 遇 (R: movement).

乍 **craft letter F** (SAKU) This striking component could be seen as a wonky letter F. Imagine that a school child has been asked to make a craft version of the letter using cardboard and glue, but gets it wrong and puts two horizontal strokes instead of one. Craft fits with the meaning 'to make' 作 (R: person).

㐱 **rash** (SHIN) The three parallel strokes fanning down from the person radical (in its upward arrow incarnation) resemble a rash. This fits with the characters for measles 疹 (R: sickness) and diagnose 診 (R: speech).

戋 **thinly sliced** (SEN) Said to have originally depicted two halberds slicing through a harvest, research suggests this component carries the meaning of thinning*. I've used a modern turn of phrase to express the same meaning. This fits with shallow 浅 (R: water) – a thin layer of water, and coin 銭 (R: metal) – a thin piece of metal.

喿 **Christmas tree/pine cone** (SOU) Composed of a tree radical 木 and three mouth radicals 口 on top, it is easy to imagine that the squares are presents hovering above a Christmas tree. The shape also resembles a pine cone, something that is used as a Christmas ornament.

甬 **pack elephant** (TSUU) Scholars have different views on the origin of this component. It may represent a cylindrical object, with something being passed through*. I prefer to imagine that the bottom component is an elephant – the small hook on the bottom right is the trunk curling inward, and the other vertical strokes are the legs. The katakana MA マ is a box of cargo that the elephant is carrying. This fits with 'passing through' 通 (R: movement) – imagine a procession of pack elephants passing through a village along the Silk Road. It also fits with pain 痛 (R: sickness) – the elephant's hooves ache from the weight of the cargo.

壬 **crying baby** (NIN) This phonetic appears in the character for responsibility 任 (R: person) and pregnancy (R: woman) 妊, so I have dubbed it a 'crying baby'. A person with a crying baby = responsibility, and a woman with a baby = pregnancy. Visually, it could be seen as a baby with its arms outstretched and tipping its head back to cry. Research suggests that this component originally represented a smithy table with a bulge in the middle, and the concepts of 'burden and responsibility'*.

畐 **full box** (FUKU) Imagine that the grid is a box so full of presents that one is bursting out the top and pushing the lid (the top horizontal line) off. This fits with width 幅 (R: turban/scarf) – you measure an object's full width with a tape measure/scarf; good fortune 福 (R: altar/worship) – if you pray, you will be blessed with a box of treasure ('your coffers will overflow'); and deputy 副 (R: sword) – imagine the second in command, charged with guarding a full box of treasures with her sword.

辟 **heckler/punish** (HEKI) The meaning of this kanji is punish, but I have added the word heckler as a mnemonic because it sounds similar to HEKI. Imagine a comedian onstage, being punished by the spicy (辛) words coming out of the mouth (口) of a heckler, and bombing so badly that they feel like they are dying (尸 corpse).

扁 **knitting** (HEN) Imagine that the horizontal rectangle in 戸 is a knitting needle, and the cross hatch element below is knitting hanging down from it. This fits with the character for knit 編 (R: thread), and lean 偏 (R: person) – imagine a person leaning in close to check their knitting handiwork.

甫 **piercing sword/needle** (HO) The intersecting horizontal and vertical strokes that resemble a Christian cross could also been seen as a sword. If you imagine that this is being thrust in the direction of a person (the historical version of a police officer with a gun) it fits catch/seize 捕 (R: hand) and arrest 逮捕. If you substitute the sword for a needle, it fits with the idea of supplement 補 (R: clothing) – imagine a person using a needle to sew a supplementary patch onto a damaged piece of clothing.

夆 **striking needle/bee sting** (HOU) This component is composed of the strike radical 夂 and what could be a needle with thread wound around it 丰. This fits with the meaning of sew 縫 (R: thread) – striking cloth with a needle. If the needle is substituted for a bee sting, it fits with bee 蜂 (R: insect) – an insect that strikes with its sting.

宓 **hidden treasure** (MITSU) Research suggests that 宓 represents a wrapped halberd (spear-axe) within a shrine or house and the concept of 'secret'*. I have adapted this slightly by calling it a hidden treasure. Imagine that the U crown is the lid of a box the weapon has been put in for safe keeping. This fits with the meaning of secret 密 and honey 蜜 (R: insect) – honey is the hidden treasure within a beehive.

莫 **sundown** (BO/~AKU) This component is very similar to the sunset kanji 暮 – the only difference is that it lacks the sun radical on the bottom. And like that kanji, it can be seen to represent the big (大) sun (日) going down, and falling below the grass (艹). I have used the name sundown to distinguish it slightly from sunset.

录 **chisel/tea harvest (catch)** (~OKU) Research suggests that this may represent a cloth bag filled with water, representing the concept of catching (Leyi, 1993). This fits with record 録 (R: metal) – to capture something by carving it onto metal.

Having always found this component visually compelling, I have included a creative component. The top section contains angular, evenly spaced lines that would be at home in a modern font (a katakana ヨ or back-wards letter E). This contrasts with the bottom, a modified water radical 水. Usually the water radical suggests harmony and flow, but these lines do not connect. Instead, there are four small sparks that point in different directions like a disjoined letter X. This mini explosion suggests movement and chaos, contrasting with the order of the top part.

Having learnt this component in the context of record 録, I have come to associate it with the act of chiselling. Imagine that the top is the blade of a chisel, and the sparks below are little dents or etchings carved onto a wood or metal canvas. They could also be seen as small chips of wood or metal flying off during the chiselling process. To apply this concept to the green character 緑 (R: thread), I took a common use (green tea), and reimagined the blade as a harvester cutting and collecting green tea leaves. The bottom part represents the cut leaves as they spray outwards from the blade.

The creative component names and stories are the original work of the author. Sentences marked with an asterisk contain references to etymological content in Noriko Williams' *Kanji Portraits* (2009).

APPENDIX 2: RADICALS LIST

RADICAL	MEANING	JAPANESE NAME
	NATURE	
水 氵	water, 3 water drops	mizu/sanzui
木	tree	ki
土	earth	tsuchi
日	sun	hi
艸 艹	grass	kusa
火 灬	fire	hi
田	field	ta
貝	shell, money	kai
頁	big shell	oogai
月	moon	tsuki
石	stone	ishi
川	river	kawa
山	mountain	yama
雨	rain	ame
气	steam, air	ki gamae
冫	ice, 2 water drops	ni sui
穴	cave	ana
谷	valley	tani
支	branch	shi nyou
	HUMAN BODY	
口	mouth	kuchi
手 扌	hand	te
心 忄	heart	kokoro/ risshinben
肉 月	meat, organ	niku
目	eye	me
儿	legs	nin nyou
欠	yawn, lack	akubi

RADICAL	MEANING	JAPANESE NAME
尸	corpse	shikabane
歹	decay	gatsu hen
足 ⻊	foot	ashi
癶	footsteps	hatsu gashira
首	neck	kubi
身	body	mi
皮	skin	kegawa
彡	hair/3	san dzukuri
血	blood	chi
歯	tooth	ha
	PEOPLE	
人 亻 𠆢	person	hito
女	woman	onna
王 玉	king, ball/jewel	ou, tama
子	child	ko
氏	clan, family name	uji
士	scholar, samurai	samurai
臣	official	shin
自	myself	mizukara
己	oneself	onore
厶	private, katakana MU	mu
老 耂	old age	rou
	ENCLOSURES	
辶	movement	shin nyou
疒	sickness	yamaidare
广	ma border (麻)/ dotted cliff	madare
彳	stepping	gyounin ben
阝	left village	kozato hen

RADICAL	MEANING	JAPANESE NAME
阝	right village	mura
囗	country enclosure	kuni gamae
門	gate	mon
宀	U crown	u kanmuri
亠	pot lid	nabe buta
廴	long stride	in nyou
厂	cliff border	gan dare
勹	wrapping	tsutsumi gamae
凵	inbox	ukebako
匚	C box/ box frame	hako gamae
丶	dot	ten
⺍	katakana TSU	tsu
冖	wa crown	wa kanmuri
丿	bend, katakana NO	no
亅	hook	hanebou

VERBS & LANGUAGE

RADICAL	MEANING	JAPANESE NAME
言	speech	gen
食 飠	eat	shoku
示 礻	worship, altar	shimesu
又	again/ right hand	mata
立	stand	tatsu
止	stop	tomeru
工	work, katakana E	takumi
見	see	miru
走	run	hashiru

RADICAL	MEANING	JAPANESE NAME
干	dry	kan
曰	say	iwaku
比	compare	kuraberu
生	live	umareru
非	wrong, non-	arazu
行	go	gyou

NATURAL MATERIALS

RADICAL	MEANING	JAPANESE NAME
竹	bamboo	take
糸 幺	thread	ito
金	metal	kane
巾	turban, scarf	haba
衣 衤	clothes	koromo
麻	hemp	asa
韋	tanned leather	nameshi gawa
疋 𤴔	bolt of cloth	hiki

MATH & MEASUREMENT

RADICAL	MEANING	JAPANESE NAME
一	one	ichi
二	two	ni
八	eight	hachi gashira
十	ten	juu
寸	inch	sun
大	big	dai
小	small	chiisai
長 镸	long	nagai
高	tall	takai
乙, 乚	second	otsu
片	slice, fragment	kata
釆	divide	nogome

RADICAL	MEANING	JAPANESE NAME
面	surface	men
方	way	hou
西 覀	west	nishi
艮	boundary	kon
斉	even	sei
夂	winter	fuyu gashira
夕	evening	yuube
	FOOD	
米	rice	kome
禾	grain, two-branch tree	nogi
皿	dish	sara
匕	spoon	saji no hi
酉	sake, alcohol	hiyomi no tori
麦	wheat	mugi
豆	bean	mame
	ANIMALS	
馬	horse	uma
虫	insect	mushi
犬 犭	dog	inu
羊	sheep	hitsuji
鳥	bird	tori
隹	old bird	furutori
牛	cow	ushi
魚	fish	uo
毛	fur, wool	ke
牙	tusk/fang	kiba
羽	wings, feathers	hane

RADICAL	MEANING	JAPANESE NAME
	WARFARE	
刀 刂	sword, knife	katana
支 攵	strike, activity	nobun
力	power	chikara
弓	bow	yumi
矢	arrow	ya
戈	halberd (spear-axe)	hoko
斤	axe	ono
丨	stick	bou
	MAN-MADE TOOLS	
戸	door	tobiranoto
罒 罒	net	ami gashira
耒	plow	raisuki
几	desk	tsukue
卩	stamp, seal	fushi dzukuri
車	vehicle	kuruma
	SENSES	
白	white	shiro
青	blue	ao
音	sound	oto
	SUPERNATURAL	
竜 龍	dragon	ryuu
辰	zodiac dragon/ morning	shin no tatsu
鬼	demon	oni
卜	fortune-telling/ katakana TO	boku no to

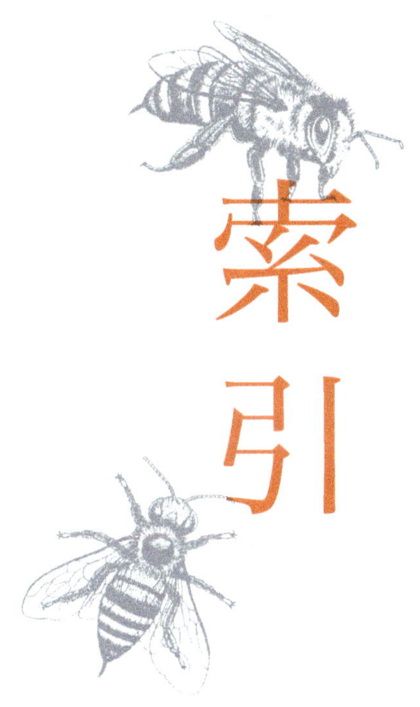

索引

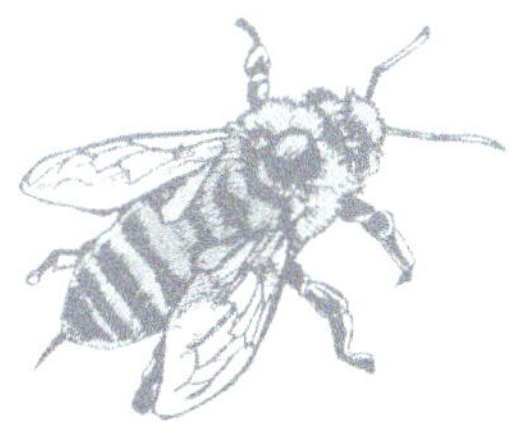

INDEXES

PHONETIC	READING	NAME	TYPE	REFERENCE
永	EI	eternal	**kanji**	**P 1**
可	KA	possible	**kanji**	**P 2**
加	KA	add	**kanji**	**P 3**
化	KA	change	**kanji**	**P 4**
果	KA	fruit	**kanji**	**P 5**
咼	KA	open mouth	**component**	**P 6**
牙	GA	tusk	**radical**	**P 7**
我	GA	myself, obstinate	**kanji**	**P 8**
義	GI	morality	**kanji**	**P 9**
各	KAKU/~AKU	each	**kanji**	**P 10, PR 12**
干	KAN	dry	**radical**	**P 11**
官	KAN	bureaucrat	**kanji**	**P 12**
門	KAN	gate	**radical**	**P 13**
𠦝	KAN	10 AM	**creative component**	**P 14**
几	KI	desk	**radical**	**P 15**
己	KI	oneself	**radical**	**P 16**
其	KI	step ladder	**creative component**	**P 17**
奇	KI	strange	**kanji**	**P 18**
及	KYUU	reach	**kanji**	**P 19**
求	KYUU	want	**kanji**	**P 20**
巨	KYO	Enormous	**kanji**	**P 21**
兄	KYOU	older brother	**kanji**	**P 22**
竟	KYOU	nosy neighbour	**creative component**	**P 23**
共	KYOU	share	**kanji**	**P 24**
夹	KYOU	pinch	**kanji**	**P 25**

PHONETIC	READING	NAME	TYPE	REFERENCE	
区	KU	ward	**kanji**	**P 26**	
禺	GUU	fasten together	**creative component**	**P 27**	
屈	KUTSU	bend	**kanji**	**P 28**	
糸	KEI	thread	**radical**	**P 29**	
圭	KEI	jade	**kanji**	**P 30**	
圣	KEI	straight	**component**	**P 31**	
敬	KEI	respect	**kanji**	**P 32**	
龹	KEN	ticket	**component**	**P 33**	
犬	KEN	dog	**radical**	**P 34**	
㑒	KEN	everyone, all	**component**	**P 35**	
県	KEN	prefecture	kanji	**P 36**	
臤	KEN	solid	**kanji**	**P 37**	
古	KO	old	**kanji**	**P 38**	**Power Phonetic**
五	GO	five	**kanji**	**P 39**	
工	KOU	katakana E, work	**radical**	**P 40**	
耂	KOU	old age	**radical**	**P 41**	
交	KOU	mix	**kanji**	**P 42**	
洪	KOU	flood	**kanji**	**P 43**	
冓	KOU	combine	**component**	**P 44**	
高	KOU	tall	**radical**	**P 45**	
艮	KON	boundary	**radical**	**P 46**	**Power Phonetic**
左	SA	left	**kanji**	**P 47**	
少	SA	a few	**kanji**	**P 48**	
采	SAI	dice	**kanji**	**P 49**	
才	ZAI	talent	**kanji**	**P 50**	

PHONETIC	READING	NAME	TYPE	REFERENCE	
斉	SAI	even	**radical**	**P 51**	
乍	SAKU	craft letter F	**creative component**	**P 52**	
祭	SATSU	festival	**kanji**	**P 53**	
参	SAN	participate	**kanji**	**P 54**	
司	SHI	manage	**kanji**	**P 55**	
士	SHI	scholar	**radical**	**P 56**	**Power Phonetic**
次	SHI	next	**kanji**	**P 57**	
匕	SHI	spoon	**radical**	**P 58**	
直	SHOKU/~OKU	direct	**kanji**	**P 59, PR 17**	
寺	JI	temple	**kanji**	**P 60**	
昔	SHAKU	long ago	**kanji**	**P 61**	
朱	SHU	bright red	**kanji**	**P 62**	
十	JUU	ten	**radical**	**P 63**	
旬	JUN	ten days	**kanji**	**P 64**	
小	SHOU	small	**radical**	**P 65**	
肖	SHOU	similar	**kanji**	**P 66**	
召	SHOU	summon	**kanji (honorific)**	**P 67**	
申	SHIN	say	**kanji (honorific)**	**P 68**	
辰	SHIN	zodiac dragon	**radical**	**P 69**	
㐱	SHIN	rash	**creative component**	**P 70**	
亲	SHIN	relative	**component**	**P 71**	
生	SEI	life	**radical**	**P 72**	
正	SEI	correct	**kanji**	**P 73**	
青	SEI	blue	**radical**	**P 74**	**Power Phonetic**
成	SEI	become	**kanji**	**P 75**	

PHONETIC	READING	NAME	TYPE	REFERENCE
泉	SEN	fountain	**kanji**	**P 76**
戔	SEN	thinly sliced	**creative component**	**P 77**
善	ZEN	kind	**kanji**	**P 78**
且	SO	moreover	**kanji (formal)**	**P 79**
相	SOU	mutual	**kanji**	**P 80**
曽	SOU	great grandma	**kanji**	**P 81**
曹	SOU	sergeant	**kanji**	**P 82**
喿	SOU	Christmas tree/ pine cone	**creative component**	**P 83**
則	SOKU	rule	**kanji**	**P 84**
弟	DAI	younger brother	**kanji**	**P 85**
旦	TAN	dawn	**kanji**	**P 86**
単	TAN/~AN	single	**kanji**	**P 87, PR 4**
知	CHI	wisdom	**kanji**	**P 88**
竹	CHIKU	bamboo	**radical**	**P 89**
中	CHUU	centre	**kanji**	**P 90**
主	CHUU	main	**kanji**	**P 91**
長	CHOU	long	**radical**	**P 92**
兆	CHOU	omen	**kanji**	**P 93**
甬	TSUU	pack elephant	**creative component**	**P 94**
丁	TEI	nail	**kanji**	**P 95**
疋	TEI	bolt of cloth	**radical**	**P 96**
氏	TEI	ancient tribe	**kanji (rare)**	**P 97**
廷	TEI	court	**kanji**	**P 98**
啇	TEKI	stem	**component**	**P 99**

PHONETIC	READING	NAME	TYPE	REFERENCE	
同	DOU	same	**kanji**	**P 100**	
童	DOU	child	**kanji**	**P 101**	
壬	NIN	crying baby	**creative component**	**P 102**	
忍	NIN	endure	**kanji**	**P 103**	
白	HAKU	white	**radical**	**P 104**	
半	HAN	half	**kanji**	**P 105**	
反	HAN	opposite	**kanji**	**P 106**	**Power Phonetic**
必	HI	certainly, must	**kanji**	**P 107**	
皮	HI	skin	**radical**	**P 108**	**Power Phonetic**
非	HI	non-	**kanji**	**P 109**	
付	FU	attach	**kanji**	**P 110**	
畐	FUKU	full box	**creative component**	**P 111**	
复	FUKU	lathe/repeat	**component**	**P 112**	
分	FUN	minute	**kanji**	**P 113**	
辟	HEKI	heckler/ punish	**kanji/ creative component**	**P 114**	
扁	HEN	knitting	**creative component**	**P 115**	
甫	HO	piercing sword/ needle	**creative component**	**P 116**	
莫	BO/~AKU	sundown	**creative component**	**P 117, PR 13**	**Power Phonetic**
包	HOU	wrapping	**kanji**	**P 118**	**Power Phonetic**
夆	HOU	sewing needle/ bee sting	**creative component**	**P 119**	
亡	BOU	dead	**kanji**	**P 120**	
麻	MA	hemp	**radical**	**P 121**	
未	MI	not yet	**kanji**	**P 122**	

PHONETIC	READING	NAME	TYPE	REFERENCE	
宓	MITSU	hidden treasure	**creative component**	**P 123**	
名	MEI	name	**kanji**	**P 124**	
明	MEI	bright	**kanji**	**P 125**	
面	MEN	surface	**kanji**	**P 126**	
令	REI	order	**kanji**	**P 127**	**Power Phonetic**
良	ROU	good	**kanji**	**P 128**	
予	YO	look ahead	**kanji**	**P 129**	
羊	YOU	sheep	**radical**	**P 130**	
辶	~OU	movement	**radical**	**PR 1**	
方	~OU	way	**radical**	**PR 2**	
米	~AI/EI	rice	**radical**	**PR 3**	
品	~IN	goods	**kanji**	**PR 5**	
占	~EN	fortune-telling	**kanji**	**PR 6**	
免	~EN	evade	**kanji**	**PR 7**	
亦	~EN	also	**kanji**	**PR 8**	
因	~IN/ON	cause	**kanji**	**PR 9**	
元	~AN/EN	origin	**kanji**	**PR 10**	
番	~N	number	**kanji**	**PR 11**	
楽	~AKU	fun	**kanji**	**PR 14**	
出	~UTSU	exit	**kanji**	**PR 15**	
谷	~OKU	valley	**radical**	**PR 16**	
录	~OKU	chisel, tea harvest (catch)	**creative component**	**PR 18**	
刀	~ATSU/ETSU	sword	**radical**	**PR 19**	
斤	~ITSU/ETSU	axe	**radical**	**PR 20**	

ON READING	KANJI	MEANING	ADDITIONAL ON READING	KUN READING
AN	安	relax, cheap	n	yasu(i)
I	以	by means of, includes	n	n
I	伊	phonetic I	n	n
IN	因	cause	n	yo(ru)
IN	咽	throat, choked	n	n
IN	員	member, employee	n	n
IN	韻	rhyme, tone	n	n
IN	隠	hide, conceal	n	kaku(su), kaku(reru)
IN	院	institution	n	n
U	宇	universe	n	n
EI	永	eternal	n	naga(i)
EI	泳	swim	n	oyo(gu)
EI	詠	compose, recite	n	yo(mu)
EI	栄	glory, honour, prosper	n	saka(eru), ha(eru), ha (e)
EI	営	camp, run (a business)	n	itona(mu)
EI	英	England, hero	n	n
ON	恩	kindness, mercy	n	n
KA	加	add	n	kuwa(eru), kuwa(waru)
KA	火	fire	n	hi
KA	可	can, passable	n	n
KA	河	river	n	kawa
KA	歌	song	n	uta, uta(u)
KA	架	hang up, stand	n	ka(keru), ka(karu)
KA	嘉	excellent, auspicious	n	yo(i), yomi
KA	化	change, convert	KE	ba(keru), ba(kasu)
KA	花	flower	n	hana
KA	果	fruit, result	n	ha(tasu), ha(teru), ha(te)
KA	課	lesson, section	n	n
KA	菓	sweets	n	n

KANJI	RADICAL	RADICAL NAME	GRADE	REFERENCE
安	宀	U crown	3	**K 1**
以	亻	person	4	**K 2**
伊	亻	person	9	**K 3**
因	囗	mouth	5	**PR 9**
咽	口	mouth	8	**PR 9**
員	口	mouth	3	**V 14**
韻	音	sound	8	**V 14**
隠	阝	left village	8	**V 14**
院	阝	left village	3	**V 14**
宇	宀	U crown	6	**K 4**
永	水	water	5	**P 1**
泳	水	water	3	**V 35, P 1**
詠	言	speech	8	**P 1**
栄	木	tree	4	**V 35**
営	⺍	katakana tsu	5	**V 35**
英	艹	grass	4	**V 35**
恩	心	heart	5	**PR 9**
加	力	power	4	**K 5, P 3, V 18**
火	火	fire	1	**KL 16**
可	口	mouth	5	**P 2, V 18**
河	氵	water	5	**P 2**
歌	欠	lack, yawn	2	**P 2**
架	木	tree	8	**P 3**
嘉	口	mouth	N/A	**P 3**
化	匕	spoon	3	**P 4, V 18**
花	艹	grass	1	**P 4**
果	木	tree	4	**P 5, V 9**
課	言	speech	4	**P 5**
菓	艹	grass	8	**P 5**

ON READING	KANJI	MEANING	ADDITIONAL ON READING	KUN READING
KA	過	pass through	n	su(giru), su(gosu), ayama(tsu), ayama(chi)
KA	渦	whirlpool	n	uzu
KA	禍	misfortune, disaster	n	n
KA	価	price, value	n	atai
KA	下	down, below, descend, inferior	GE	shita, shimo, moto, sa(geru), kuda(ru), o(riru), o(rosu)
GA	賀	congratulate	n	n
GA	牙	tusk, fang	GE	kiba
GA	雅	elegant	n	n
GA	芽	bud, sprout	n	me
GA	我	self	n	ware, wa
GA	蛾	moth	GI	himushi
GA	餓	starve	n	u(eru)
KAI	介	mediate, shellfish	n	n
KAI	界	world, boundary	n	n
KAI	会	meet, meeting	E	a(u)
KAKU	各	each, every	n	ono-ono
KAKU	格	status	KOU	n
KAKU	閣	tall building, (government) cabinet	n	n
KAN	干	dry	n	ho(su), hi(ru)
KAN	汗	sweat	n	ase
KAN	肝	liver, courage	n	kimo
KAN	刊	publish	n	n
KAN	官	government, bureaucrat	n	n
KAN	館	(large) building	n	yakata
KAN	管	pipe, control	n	kuda
KAN	間	space between, interval	KEN	aida, ma
KAN	閑	leisure, quietness	n	n

KANJI	RADICAL	RADICAL NAME	GRADE	REFERENCE
過	辶	movement	5	P 6
渦	氵	water	8	P 6
禍	ネ	worship	8	P 6
価	イ	person	5	V 9
下	一	one	1	V 18
賀	貝	shell	5	P 3
牙	牙	tusk	8	P 7
雅	隹	old bird	8	P 7
芽	艹	grass	4	P 7
我	戈	halberd (spear-axe)	6	P 8
蛾	虫	insect	N/A	P 8
餓	食	eat	8	P 8
介	人	person	8	V 6
界	田	field	3	V 6
会	人	person	2	V 6
各	口	mouth	4	P 10, PR 12
格	木	tree	5	P 10, PR 12
閣	門	gate	6	P 10
干	干	dry	6	P 11
汗	氵	water	8	P 11
肝	肉 月	meat, organ	8	P 11
刊	リ	sword	5	P 11
官	宀	U crown	4	P 12, V 4
館	食	eat	3	P 12
管	竹	bamboo	4	P 12
間	門	gate	2	P 13, V 32
閑	門	gate	8	P 13

ON READING	KANJI	MEANING	ADDITIONAL ON READING	KUN READING
KAN	関	connection, barrier	n	seki
KAN	簡	simple	n	n
KAN	乾	dry	n	kawa(ku), kawa(kasu)
KAN	幹	trunk	n	miki
KAN	韓	Korea	n	n
KAN	完	complete, perfect	n	n
KAN	冠	crown	n	kanmuri
KAN	寒	cold	n	samu(i)
KAN	環	ring, circle	n	wa
KAN	監	supervise, direct	n	n
GAN	玩	play with, enjoy	n	n
GAN	頑	stubborn	n	n
KI	機	mechanism, chance	n	hata
KI	気	spirit, air	KE	n
KI	机	desk	n	tsukue
KI	飢	hunger, starve	n	u(eru)
KI	記	write down, account	n	shiru(su)
KI	起	get up, occur	n	o(kiru), o(koru), o(kosu)
KI	棋	Japanese chess, shogi	n	n
KI	期	time period	GO	n
KI	旗	flag, banner	n	hata
KI	基	foundation, base	n	moto, motoi
KI	奇	strange, unusual	n	n
KI	騎	ride horses	n	n
KI	寄	draw near	n	yo(ru), yo(seru)
GI	義	righteousnous, morality	n	n
GI	儀	ceremony	n	n
GI	犠	sacrifice	n	n
KYUU	及	extend, reach	n	oyo(bu), oyo(bi), oyo(bosu)

KANJI	RADICAL	RADICAL NAME	GRADE	REFERENCE
関	門	gate	4	P 13, V 32
簡	竹	bamboo	6	P 13
乾	乙	second	8	P 14
幹	干	dry	5	P 14, V 32
韓	韋	tanned leather	8	P 14
完	宀	U crown	4	PR 10, V 4
冠	冖	wa crown	8	PR 10, V 4
寒	宀	U crown	3	V 4
環	王	king, jewel	8	V 32
監	皿	dish	8	V 32
玩	王	king, jewel	8	PR 10
頑	頁	big shell	8	PR 10
機	木	tree	4	K 6
気	气	steam	1	KL 1
机	木	tree	6	P 15
飢	食	eat	8	P 15
記	言	speech	2	P 16
起	走	run	3	P 16
棋	木	tree	8	P 17
期	月	moon	3	P 17
旗	方	way	4	P 17
基	土	earth	5	P 17
奇	大	big	8	P 18
騎	馬	horse	8	P 18
寄	宀	U crown	5	P 18
義	羊	sheep	5	P 9
儀	亻	person	8	P 9
犠	牛	cow	8	P 9
及	丿	bend, katakana no	8	P 19

ON READING	KANJI	MEANING	ADDITIONAL ON READING	KUN READING
KYUU	吸	breathe in, inhale, smoke	n	su(u)
KYUU	級	level, grade	n	n
KYUU	求	want, request	n	moto(meru)
KYUU	球	ball, sphere	n	tama
KYUU	救	save, rescue	n	suku(u)
KYUU	九	nine	KU	kokono(tsu)
KYUU	灸	moxibustion (traditional Chinese therapy)	KU	yaito
KYUU	急	urgent, emergency	n	iso(gu)
KYO	巨	Enormous, great	n	n
KYO	拒	refuse	n	koba(mu)
KYO	距	distance	n	n
KYO	居	dwell, live	n	i(ru)
KYO	許	permit	n	yuru(su)
KYOU	兄	older brother	KEI	ani
KYOU	況	condition, situation	n	n
KYOU	競	compete	KEI	kiso(u), se(ru)
KYOU	境	border, boundary	KEI	sakai
KYOU	鏡	mirror, lens	n	kagami
KYOU	共	share, together with	n	tomo
KYOU	供	offer, present	KU	sona(eru), tomo
KYOU	狭	narrow	n	sema(i), seba(meru), seba(maru)
KYOU	挟	pinch, hold between	n	hasa(mu), hasa(maru)
KYOKU	局	bureau	n	n
KYOKU	極	extreme, poles	GOKU	kiwa(meru), kiwa(maru), kiwa(mi)
KU	久	a long time	KYUU	hisa(shii)
KU	句	phrase	n	n
KU	区	ward, district	n	n
KU	駆	drive	n	ka(keru), ka(ru)

KANJI	RADICAL	RADICAL NAME	GRADE	REFERENCE
吸	口	mouth	6	P 19
級	糸	thread	3	P 19, V 40
求	水	water	4	P 20
球	王	king, jewel	3	P 20
救	攵	strike	4	P 20
九	乙	second	1	V 40
灸	火	fire	9	V 40
急	心	heart	3	V 40
巨	二	two	8	P 21, V 25
拒	扌	hand	8	P 21, V 25
距	足	foot	8	P 21
居	尸	corpse	5	V 25
許	言	speech	5	V 25
兄	儿	legs	2	P 22
況	氵	water	8	P 22
競	立	stand	4	P 22
境	土	earth	5	P 23
鏡	金	metal	4	P 23
共	八	eight	4	P 24
供	亻	person	6	P 24
狭	犭	dog	8	P 25
挟	扌	hand	8	P 25
局	尸	corpse	3	V 27
極	木	tree	4	V 27
久	丿	bend, katakana no	5	K 7
句	口	mouth	5	KL 2
区	匚	C box	3	KL 3, P 26
駆	馬	horse	8	P 26

ON READING	KANJI	MEANING	ADDITIONAL ON READING	KUN READING
GUU	偶	by chance, even number	n	n
GUU	遇	encounter	n	n
GUU	隅	corner	n	sumi
KUTSU	屈	bend, yield	n	kaga(mu)
KUTSU	掘	dig	n	ho(ru)
KUTSU	窟	cavern	n	n
KEI	計	plan, measure	n	haka(ru)
KEI	系	system	n	n
KEI	係	duty, person in charge	n	kaka(ru), kakari
KEI	圭	square jewel, jade	n	n
KEI	桂	Japanese Judas tree	n	katsura
KEI	径	diameter	n	n
KEI	経	longitude, pass through	KYOU	he(ru)
KEI	茎	stem	n	kuki
KEI	敬	respect, reverence	n	uyama(u)
KEI	警	guard, warn	n	n
KEI	型	type, model	n	kata
KEI	契	pledge, promise	n	chigi(ru)
KEI	啓	open, enlighten	n	n
KEI	渓	valley	n	n
KETSU	穴	cave, hole	n	ana
KETSU	決	decide, fix	n	ki(meru), ki(maru)
KETSU	欠	lack, deficiency	n	ka(keru), ka(ku)
KETSU	血	blood	n	chi
KEN	券	ticket	n	n
KEN	拳	fist	n	kobushi
KEN	圏	sphere	n	n
KEN	犬	dog	n	inu
KEN	献	present, offering	KON	n

KANJI	RADICAL	RADICAL NAME	GRADE	REFERENCE
偶	亻	person	8	**P 27**
遇	辶	movement	8	**P 27**
隅	阝	left village	8	**P 27**
屈	尸	corpse	8	**P 28, PR 15**
掘	扌	hand	8	**P 28**
窟	穴	cave	8	**P 28**
計	言	speech	2	**K 8**
系	糸	thread	6	**P 29, V 42**
係	亻	person	3	**P 29**
圭	土	earth	9	**P 30**
桂	木	tree	9	**P 30**
径	彳	stepping	4	**P 31**
経	糸	thread	5	**P 31**
茎	艹	grass	8	**P 31**
敬	攵	strike	6	**P 32**
警	言	speech	6	**P 32, V 12**
型	土	earth	4	**V 12**
契	大	big	8	**V 12, V 42**
啓	口	mouth	8	**V 12**
渓	氵	water	N/A	**V 42**
穴	穴	cave	6	**V 5**
決	氵	water	3	**V 5**
欠	欠	lack, yawn	4	**V 5**
血	血	blood	3	**V 5**
券	刀	sword	5	**P 33**
拳	手	hand	8	**P 33**
圏	囗	country enclosure	8	**P 33**
犬	犬	dog	1	**P 34**
献	犬	dog	8	**P 34**

ON READING	KANJI	MEANING	ADDITIONAL ON READING	KUN READING
KEN	検	check, examine	n	n
KEN	険	precipitous, danger	n	kewa(shii)
KEN	験	test, verify	GEN	n
KEN	県	prefecture	n	n
KEN	懸	hang, suspend	KE	ka(keru), ka(karu)
KEN	堅	firm, strict	n	kata(i)
KEN	賢	wisdom, clever	n	kashiko(i)
KEN	見	look, see	n	mi(ru), mi(eru), mi(seru)
KEN	建	build	KON	ta(teru), ta(tsu)
KEN	兼	and, concurrently	n	ka(neru)
KEN	権	authority, right	GON	n
GEN	元	origin	GAN	moto
GEN	原	original, field	n	hara
GEN	現	appear, actual	n	arawa(reru), arawa(su)
KO	己	self	KI	onore
KO	古	old	n	furu(i)
KO	枯	wither, die	n	ka(reru), ka(rasu)
KO	故	reason, happenstance	n	yue
KO	固	solidify, set	n	kata(meru), kata(maru), kata(i)
KO	個	individual, counter for articles	KA	n
KO	錮	confine, tie	n	n
KO	呼	call, exhale	n	yo(bu)
GO	五	five	n	itsu, itsu(tsu)
GO	悟	become enlightened, realise, perceive	n	sato(ru)
GO	語	language, say	n	kata(ru), kata(rau)
GO	互	mutual, reciprocal	n	taga(i)
GO	呉	Wu kingdom of China, give	n	n
GO	誤	mistake, error	n	ayama(ru)

KANJI	RADICAL	RADICAL NAME	GRADE	REFERENCE
検	木	tree	5	P 35
険	阝	left village	5	P 35
験	馬	horse	10	P 35
県	目	eye	3	P 36, V 31
懸	心	heart	8	P 36, V 13
堅	土	earth	8	P 37, V 13
賢	貝	shell	8	P 37, V 13
見	見	see	1	V 29
建	廴	long stride	4	V 31
兼	八	eight	8	V 31
権	木	tree	6	V 31
元	儿	legs	2	PR 10, V 29
原	厂	cliff border	2	V 29
現	王	king, jewel	5	V 29
己	己	oneself	6	K 9
古	口	mouth	2	KL 4, P 38, V 7
枯	木	tree	8	P 38
故	攵	strike	5	P 38, V 7
固	囗	country enclosure	4	P 38
個	亻	person	5	P 38
鋼	金	metal	8	P 38
呼	口	mouth	6	V 7
五	二	two	1	P 39, V 38
悟	忄	heart	8	P 39
語	言	speech	2	P 39, V 38
互	二	two	8	V 38
呉	口	mouth	8	V 38
誤	言	speech	6	V 38

ON READING	KANJI	MEANING	ADDITIONAL ON READING	KUN READING
KOU	工	construct, manufacture	KU	n
KOU	紅	crimson, deep red	KU	beni, kurenai
KOU	孝	filial piety, parental respect	n	n
KOU	考	think	n	kanga(eru), kanga(e)
KOU	交	interchange, mix	n	ma(jiru), ma(zeru), maji(waru), maji(eru), ma(zaru), ma(zeru)
KOU	校	school	n	n
KOU	洪	flood, deluge	n	n
KOU	港	port, harbour	n	minato
KOU	講	lecture	n	n
KOU	構	build, construct	n	kama(eru), kama(u)
KOU	高	tall, high	n	taka(i), taka(meru), taka(maru)
KOU	稿	manuscript, draft	n	n
KOU	口	mouth	KU	kuchi
KOU	向	face toward, over there	n	mu(ku), mu(keru), mu(kau), mu(kou)
KOU	甲	shell, first, instep	KAN	kinoe
KOU	公	public, official	n	ooyake
KOU	光	light, ray	n	hika(ru), hikari
GOU	号	number	n	n
KOKU	谷	valley	n	tani
KON	恨	bear a grudge, malice	n	ura(mu), ura(meshii)
KON	根	root	n	ne
KON	墾	cultivate, reclaim	n	n
KON	懇	kind, cordial	n	nengo(ro)
KON	痕	scar, trace	n	ato
KON	昆	insect, elder brother	n	n
KON	混	mix, blend, confusion	n	ma(jiru), ma(zeru)
KON	婚	marriage	n	n
SA	左	left, progressive	n	hidari

KANJI	RADICAL	RADICAL NAME	GRADE	REFERENCE
工	工	work	2	P 40, V 8
紅	糸	thread	6	P 40
孝	子	child	6	P 41
考	耂	old age	2	P 41
交	亠	pot lid	2	P 42, V 24
校	木	tree	1	P 42
洪	氵	water	8	P 43
港	氵	water	3	P 43
講	言	speech	5	P 44
構	木	tree	5	P 44
高	高	tall	2	P 45, V 8
稿	禾	grain	8	P 45
口	口	mouth	1	V 8
向	口	mouth	3	V 8
甲	田	field	8	V 9
公	八	eight	2	V 24
光	儿	legs	2	V 24
号	口	mouth	3	V 38
谷	谷	valley	2	PR 16
恨	忄	heart	8	P 46
根	木	tree	3	P 46, V 39
墾	土	earth	8	P 46
懇	心	heart	8	P 46
痕	疒	sickness	8	P 46
昆	日	sun	8	V 39
混	氵	water	5	V 39
婚	女	woman	8	V 39
左	工	work	1	K 10, P 47

ON READING	KANJI	MEANING	ADDITIONAL ON READING	KUN READING
SA	沙	sand	SHA	suna
SA	佐	assist, help	n	n
SA	差	difference	n	sa(su)
SA	砂	sand	SHA	suna
SAI	采	dice	n	n
SAI	彩	colouring	n	irodo(ru)
SAI	才	talent	n	n
SAI	財	wealth, assets	ZAI	n
ZAI	剤	medicine	n	n
ZAI	材	timber, materials	n	n
SAI	斎	abstinence, purification, Buddhist vegetarian diet	n	toki
SAI	済	settle (debt), relieve (burden)	n	su(mu), su(masu)
ZAI	在	exist	n	a(ru)
SAKU	作	make, produce	SA	tsuku(ru)
SAKU	昨	yesterday, past	n	n
SAKU	搾	squeeze	n	shibo(ru)
SATSU	察	investigate, judge	n	n
SATSU	擦	rub	n	su(ru), su(reru)
SATSU	刷	print, brush	n	su(ru)
SATSU	刹	temple	SETSU	n
SAN	散	scatter	n	chi(ru), chi(rasu), chi(rakasu)
SAN	参	participate	n	mai(ru)
SAN	惨	disaster, wretched	ZAN	miji(me)
SAN	三	three	n	mi(tsu), mi
SAN	山	mountain	n	yama
SHI	止	to stop	n	to(maru), to(meru)
SHI	司	officiate, administrate, manage	n	n

KANJI	RADICAL	RADICAL NAME	GRADE	REFERENCE
沙	氵	water	8	KL 5, P 48
佐	亻	person	8	P 47
差	工	work	4	P 47
砂	石	stone	6	P 48
采	釆	divide	8	P 49
彩	彡	hair	8	P 49
才	扌	hand	2	P 50, V 3
財	貝	shell	5	P 50, V 3
剤	刂	sword	8	P 51
材	木	tree	4	P 50, V 3
斎	齊	even	8	P 51
済	氵	water	6	P 51
在	土	earth	5	V 3
作	亻	person	2	P 52
昨	日	sun	4	P 52
搾	扌	hand	8	P 52
察	宀	U crown	4	P 53
擦	扌	hand	8	P 53
刷	刂	sword	4	PR 19
刹	刂	sword	8	PR 19
散	攵	strike	4	K 11
参	ム	private	4	P 54
惨	忄	heart	8	P 54
三	一	one	1	V 44
山	山	mountain	1	V 44
止	止	stop	2	K 19, V 16
司	口	mouth	4	KL 6, P 55

ON READING	KANJI	MEANING	ADDITIONAL ON READING	KUN READING
SHI	伺	enquire, visit	n	ukaga(u)
SHI	詞	part of speech, words	n	n
SHI	嗣	succeed, heir	n	n
SHI	飼	raise animals	n	ka(u)
SHI	士	scholar, samurai	n	n
SHI	仕	official, serve	JI	tsuka(eru)
SHI	志	intention	n	kokoroza(su), kokorozashi
SHI	誌	document, magazine	n	n
SHI	支	support, branch	n	sasa(eru)
SHI	枝	branch, limb	n	eda
SHI	肢	limbs (arm, leg)	n	n
SHI	姿	figure, appearance	n	sugata
SHI	資	assets, capital	n	n
SHI	恣	selfish, arbitrary	n	n
SHI	諮	consult	n	haka(ru)
SHI	死	death	n	shi(nu)
SHI	脂	fat	n	abura
SHI	指	finger, indicate	n	yubi, sa(su)
SHI	市	market, city	n	ichi
SHI	子	child	SU	ko
SHI	史	history, chronical	n	n
SHI	氏	clan, family name	n	uji
JI	寺	Buddhist temple	n	tera
JI	侍	warrior, attendant	n	samurai
JI	時	time, hour	n	toki
SHITSU	質	substance, quality	SHICHI, CHI	n
SHAKU	昔	old times	SEKI	mukashi
SHAKU	借	borrow, rent	n	ka(riru)
SHU	朱	vermilion, bright red	n	ake

KANJI	RADICAL	RADICAL NAME	GRADE	REFERENCE
伺	亻	person	8	P 55
詞	言	speech	6	P 55
嗣	口	mouth	8	P 55
飼	食	eat	5	P 55
士	士	scholar	4	P 56, V 16
仕	亻	person	3	P 56
志	心	heart	5	P 56
誌	言	speech	6	P 56
支	支	branch	5	P 56
枝	木	tree	5	P 56
肢	肉 月	meat, organ	8	P 56
姿	女	woman	6	P 57
資	貝	shell	5	P 57
恣	心	heart	8	P 57
諮	言	speech	8	P 57
死	歹	decay	3	P 58
脂	肉 月	meat, organ	8	P 58
指	扌	hand	3	P 58
市	巾	turban	2	V 16
子	子	child	1	V 16
史	口	mouth	4	V 16
氏	氏	clan	4	V 16
寺	寸	inch	2	P 60
侍	亻	person	8	P 60
時	日	sun	2	P 60
質	貝	shell	5	PR 20
昔	日	sun	3	P 61
借	亻	person	4	P 61
朱	木	tree	8	P 62

ON READING	KANJI	MEANING	ADDITIONAL ON READING	KUN READING
SHU	殊	special, particularly	n	koto
SHU	主	chief, main, principal	SU	nushi, omo
SHU	手	hand	n	te
SHU	守	protect	SU	mamo(ru), mori
SHU	取	take, obtain	n	to(ru)
SHU	酒	alcohol, sake	n	sake
SHU	首	neck	n	kubi
SHUU	収	income, obtain	n	osa(meru), osa(maru)
SHUU	秋	autumn, fall	n	aki
SHUU	臭	bad smell, stink	n	kusai, nio(u)
SHUU	囚	prisoner	n	n
SHUU	州	state	n	su
SHUU	修	practice, study	SHU	osa(meru), osa(maru)
JUU	十	ten	n	too, to
JUU	汁	juice, soup	n	shiru
SHUTSU	出	exit, go out	SUI	de(ru), da(su)
SHUN	春	spring	n	haru
JUN	旬	ten day period	SHUN	n
JUN	殉	martyrdom	n	n
JUN	巡	patrol, go around	n	megu(ru)
JUN	順	order, obey	n	n
SHOU	小	small	n	chii(sai), ko, o
SHOU	少	a few	n	suku(nai), suko(shi)
SHOU	省	ministry	SEI	kaeri(miru), habu(ku)
SHOU	肖	resemblance, look like	n	n
SHOU	消	extinguish, cancel	n	ki(eru), ke(su)
SHOU	硝	saltpeter, nitrate	n	n
SHOU	招	summon, invite	n	mane(ku)
SHOU	紹	introduce	n	n

KANJI	RADICAL	RADICAL NAME	GRADE	REFERENCE
殊	歹	decay	8	**P 62**
主	丶	dot	3	**V 17**
手	手	hand	1	**V 17**
守	宀	U crown	3	**V 17**
取	又	again	3	**V 28**
酒	酉	sake, alcohol	3	**V 28**
首	首	neck	2	**V 28**
収	又	again	6	**V 2, V 20**
秋	禾	grain	2	**V 2, V 20**
臭	自	myself	8	**V 2**
囚	囗	country enclosure	8	**V 2**
州	川	river	3	**V 20**
修	亻	person	5	**V 20**
十	十	ten	1	**P 63**
汁	氵	water	8	**P 63**
出	凵	inbox	1	**PR 15**
春	日	sun	2	**V 33**
旬	日	sun	8	**P 64**
殉	歹	decay	8	**P 64**
巡	巛	river	8	**V 33**
順	頁	big shell	4	**V 33**
小	小	small	1	**P 65, V 19**
少	小	small	2	**P 65**
省	目	eye	4	**P 65, V 19**
肖	肉 月	meat, organ	8	**P 66**
消	氵	water	3	**P 66**
硝	石	stone	8	**P 66**
招	扌	hand	5	**P 67**
紹	糸	thread	8	**P 67**

ON READING	KANJI	MEANING	ADDITIONAL ON READING	KUN READING
SHOU	照	illuminate, lighting	n	te(ru), te(rasu), te(reru)
SHOU	賞	prize, reward	n	n
SHOU	章	chapter, section	n	n
JOU	上	up, above	SHOU	ue, uwa, kami, a(geru), a(garu), nobo(ru), nobo(su)
JOU	状	status, condition	n	n
JOU	情	feelings, emotion	SEI	nasa(ke)
SHOKU	植	plant, grow	n	u(eru), u(waru)
SHOKU	殖	increase, multiply	n	fu(eru), fu(yasu)
SHIN	新	new	n	atara(shii), ara(ta)
SHIN	親	parent, intimacy	n	oya, shita(shii), shita(shimu)
SHIN	申	say (humbly)	n	mou(su)
SHIN	伸	extend, stretch	n	no(biru), no(basu), no(beru)
SHIN	神	god, mind	JIN	kami
SHIN	唇	lips	n	kuchibiru
SHIN	娠	pregnancy	n	n
SHIN	震	shake, quake	n	furu(u), furu(eru)
SHIN	診	diagnose, examine	n	mi(ru)
SHIN	疹	measles, sickness	CHIN	hashika
SHIN	審	investigation, hearing	n	n
SHIN	信	believe, trust	n	n
SHIN	身	body, person	n	mi
SHIN	振	shake, wave	n	fu(ru), fu(ri), bu(ru)
SU	寿	longevity, congratulations	JU	kotobuki
SUN	寸	measurement, tiny	n	n
SE	世	world, generation	SEI	yo
SEI	生	birth, life, student	SHOU	nama, u(mareru), u(mu), i(kiru)
SEI	性	character, gender	SHOU	n
SEI	正	correct, justice	SHOU	tada(shii), tada(su), masa

KANJI	RADICAL	RADICAL NAME	GRADE	REFERENCE
照	灬	fire	4	**P 67**
賞	貝	shell	4	**V 19**
章	立	stand	3	**V 19**
上	一	one	1	**V 21**
状	犬	dog	5	**V 21**
情	忄	heart	5	**V 21**
植	木	tree	3	**P 59, PR 17**
殖	歹	decay	8	**P 59, PR 17**
新	斤	axe	2	**P 71**
親	見	see	2	**P 71**
申	田	field	3	**P 68**
伸	亻	person	8	**P 68**
神	礻	worship	3	**P 68**
唇	口	mouth	8	**P 69**
娠	女	woman	8	**P 69**
震	雨	rain	8	**P 69**
診	言	speech	8	**P 70**
疹	疒	sickness	N/A	**P 70**
審	宀	U crown	8	**PR 11**
信	亻	person	4	**V 30**
身	身	body	3	**V 30**
振	扌	hand	8	**V 30**
寿	寸	inch	8	**KL 7**
寸	寸	inch	6	**K 12**
世	一	one	3	**K 13**
生	生	live	1	**P 72**
性	忄	heart	5	**P 72**
正	止	stop	1	**P 73**

ON READING	KANJI	MEANING	ADDITIONAL ON READING	KUN READING
SEI	政	government, politics	SHOU	matsurigoto
SEI	青	blue, green	SHOU	ao, ao(i)
SEI	清	clear, pure	SHOU	kiyo(meru), kiyo(maru), kiyo(i)
SEI	請	ask, request	SHIN	ko(u), u(keru)
SEI	精	spirit, energy	SHOU	n
SEI	静	quiet	JOU shizu(meru)	shizu, shizu(ka), shizu(maru),
SEI	成	become, reach	JOU	na(ru), na(su)
SEI	誠	sincerity	n	makoto
SEI	盛	prosper, flourish	JOU	mo(ru), saka(n), saka(ru)
SETSU	切	cut	SAI	ki(ru), ki(reru)
SETSU	折	fold, bend	n	o(ru), ori, o(reru)
SEN	泉	spring, fountain	n	izumi
SEN	線	line, track	n	n
SEN	浅	shallow, superficial	n	asa(i)
SEN	銭	money, coin	n	zeni
SEN	占	fortune-telling, occupy	n	shi(meru), urana(u)
SEN	煎	roast, boil	n	i(ru)
SEN	鮮	fresh, vivid	n	aza(yaka)
SEN	先	before, previous	n	saki
SEN	洗	wash	n	ara(u)
SEN	染	dye, colour	n	so(meru), so(maru), hi(miru), shi(mi)
SEN	千	thousand	n	chi
SEN	川	river	n	kawa
ZEN	善	good, virtuous	n	yo(i)
ZEN	膳	meals, table	n	n
ZEN	前	before, in front	n	mae
ZEN	然	so, phenomena, thing	NEN	n
ZEN	禅	Zen (Buddhism)	n	n

KANJI	RADICAL	RADICAL NAME	GRADE	REFERENCE
政	攵	strike	5	P 73
青	青	blue	1	P 74
清	氵	water	4	P 74
請	言	speech	8	P 74
精	米	rice	5	P 74
静	青	blue	4	P 74
成	戈	halberd (spear-axe)	4	P 75
誠	言	speech	6	P 75
盛	皿	dish	6	P 75
切	刀	sword	2	PR 19
折	扌	hand	4	PR 20
泉	水	water	6	P 76
線	糸	thread	2	P 76
浅	氵	water	4	P 77
銭	金	metal	5	P 77
占	卜	fortune-telling	8	PR 6, V 44
煎	灬	fire	8	V 36
鮮	魚	fish	8	V 36
先	儿	legs	1	V 43
洗	氵	water	6	V 43
染	木	tree	6	V 43
千	十	ten	1	V 44
川	川	river	1	V 44
善	口	mouth	6	P 78
膳	肉 月	meat, organ	8	P 78
前	刂	sword	2	V 36
然	灬	fire	4	V 36
禅	礻	worship	8	V 36

ON READING	KANJI	MEANING	ADDITIONAL ON READING	KUN READING
SO	祖	ancestor	n	n
SO	租	crop tax, tariff	n	n
SO	組	organise, assemble	n	ku(mu), kumi
SO	粗	rough, course	n	ara(i)
SOU	曽	great- (grandmother, etc.), formerly	ZOU	n
SOU	相	mutual, reciprocal	SHOU	ai
SOU	想	think, idea	SO	n
SOU	僧	Buddhist priest, monk	n	n
SOU	層	layer, class	n	n
SOU	曹	official, sergeant	n	n
SOU	漕	rowing, canal transportation	n	n
SOU	槽	vat, tank	n	n
SOU	操	manipulate, operate	n	ayatsu(ru), misao
SOU	燥	drying, dehydration	n	n
SOU	送	send	n	oku(ru)
SOKU	則	rule	n	n
SOKU	側	side	n	gawa
SOKU	測	measure	n	haka(ru)
ZOKU	俗	common, vulgar	n	n
TA	太	thick, plump	TAI	futo(i), futo(ru)
TA	多	many	n	oo(i)
TA	他	other, another	n	hoka
DAI	弟	younger brother	TEI, DE	otouto
DAI	第	No., prefix for numbers	n	n
TAKU	宅	house, residence	n	n
TAN	旦	dawn	DAN	n
TAN	担	carry, bear	n	katsu(gu), nina(u)
TAN	胆	gallbladder, courage	n	kimo

KANJI	RADICAL	RADICAL NAME	GRADE	REFERENCE
祖	ネ	worship	5	KL 8, P 79
租	禾	grain	8	P 79
組	糸	thread	2	P 79
粗	米	rice	8	P 79
曽	曰	say	8	K 14, P 81
相	木	tree	3	P 80
想	心	heart	3	P 80
僧	亻	person	8	P 81
層	尸	corpse	6	P 81
曹	曰	say	8	P 82
漕	氵	water	9	P 82
槽	木	tree	8	P 82
操	扌	hand	6	P 83
燥	火	fire	8	P 83
送	辶	movement	3	PR 1
則	刂	sword	5	P 84
側	亻	person	4	P 84
測	氵	water	5	P 84
俗	亻	person	8	PR 16
太	大	big	2	K 15
多	夕	evening	2	K 16, V 26
他	亻	person	3	V 26
弟	弓	bow	2	P 85
第	竹	bamboo	3	P 85
宅	宀	U crown	6	V 26
旦	日	sun	8	P 86
担	扌	hand	6	P 86
胆	肉 月	meat, organ	8	P 86

ON READING	KANJI	MEANING	ADDITIONAL ON READING	KUN READING
TAN	単	single	n	n
TAN	箪	bamboo basket	n	hako
DAN	弾	bullet	n	hi(ku), hazu(mu), tama
CHI	知	wisdom, knowledge	n	shi(ru)
CHI	地	ground, earth	JI	n
CHI	智	wisdom, intellect	n	n
CHIKU	竹	bamboo	n	take
CHIKU	築	build	n	kizu(ku)
CHUU	中	centre, middle	JUU	naka
CHUU	仲	go-between, mediator	n	naka
CHUU	虫	insect	n	mushi
CHUU	忠	loyalty, devotion	n	n
CHUU	注	pour	n	soso(gu)
CHUU	駐	stationed, stopover	n	n
CHOU	長	long, leader	n	naga(i)
CHOU	帳	notebook	n	n
CHOU	張	stretch, spread	n	ha(ru)
CHOU	兆	omen, trillion	n	kiza(su), kiza(shi)
CHOU	挑	challenge	n	ido(mu)
CHOU	眺	look, gaze	n	naga(meru)
CHOU	跳	leap, prance	n	ha(neru), to(bu)
CHOKU	直	straight, direct, frank	JIKI	tada(chi ni), nao(su), nao(ru)
TSUU	通	pass through, traffic	TSU	too(ru), too(su), too(ri), kayo(u)
TSUU	痛	pain	n	ita(i), ita(mu), ita(meru)
TEI	訂	revise, correct	n	n
TEI	定	decide, fix	JOU	sada(meru), sada(maru), sada(ka)
TEI	低	low	n	hiku(i), hiku(meru)
TEI	亭	pavilion, restaurant	n	n

KANJI	RADICAL	RADICAL NAME	GRADE	REFERENCE
単	⺍	katakana tsu	4	**P 87, PR 4**
箪	竹	bamboo	N/A	**P 87**
弾	弓	bow	8	**PR 4**
知	矢	arrow	2	**K 17, P 88**
地	土	earth	2	**KL 9**
智	日	sun	9	**P 88**
竹	竹	bamboo	1	**P 89**
築	竹	bamboo	5	**P 89**
中	丨	stick	1	**P 90**
仲	亻	person	4	**P 90**
虫	虫	insect	1	**P 90**
忠	心	heart	6	**P 90**
注	氵	water	3	**P 91**
駐	馬	horse	8	**P 91**
長	長	long	2	**P 92**
帳	巾	turban	3	**P 92**
張	弓	bow	5	**P 92**
兆	儿	legs	4	**P 93**
挑	扌	hand	8	**P 93**
眺	目	eye	8	**P 93**
跳	足	foot	8	**P 93**
直	目	eye	2	**PR 17**
通	辶	movement	2	**P 94**
痛	疒	sickness	6	**P 94**
訂	言	speech	8	**KL 10, P 95**
定	宀	U crown	3	**KL 11, P 96**
低	亻	person	4	**KL 12, P 97**
亭	亠	pot lid	8	**P 95**

ON READING	KANJI	MEANING	ADDITIONAL ON READING	KUN READING
TEI	停	stop, halt	n	n
TEI	堤	embankment	n	tsutsu(mi)
TEI	抵	resist	n	n
TEI	邸	residence	n	yashiki
TEI	底	bottom	n	soko
TEI	廷	court	n	n
TEI	庭	courtyard, garden	n	niwa
TEKI	滴	drop, drip	n	shizuku, shitata(ru)
TEKI	摘	pick, pluck	n	tsu(mu)
TEKI	適	suitable	n	n
TEKI	敵	enemy	n	kataki
TEN	天	heavens, natural	n	ame,ama
TEN	店	shop	n	mise
TEN	点	dot, point, mark, grade	n	n
DEN	伝	transmit	n	tsuta(waru), tsuta(eru), tsuta(u)
TO	都	metropolis, capital	TSU	miyako
TO	徒	disciple, follower	n	n
TO	途	way, road	n	n
TO	塗	paint (v.), coat (v.)	n	nu(ru)
DO	土	earth, soil, ground	TO	tsuchi
TOU	等	etc., equal, (first) class	n	hito(shii)
TOU	答	answer, solution	n	kota(eru), kota(e)
TOU	登	climb, ascend	TO	nobo(ru)
TOU	刀	sword, knife	n	katana
TOU	到	arrive, reach	n	n
TOU	灯	lamp, light	n	hi
DOU	同	same	n	ona(ji)
DOU	洞	cave	n	hora

KANJI	RADICAL	RADICAL NAME	GRADE	REFERENCE
停	亻	person	4	**P 95**
堤	土	earth	8	**P 96**
抵	扌	hand	8	**P 97**
邸	阝	right village	8	**P 97**
底	广	ma border	4	**P 97**
廷	廴	long stride	8	**P 98**
庭	广	ma border	3	**P 98**
滴	氵	water	8	**P 99**
摘	扌	hand	8	**P 99**
適	辶	movement	5	**P 99**
敵	攵	strike	5	P **99**
天	一	one	1	**K 18**
店	广	ma border	2	**PR 6**
点	灬	fire	2	**PR 6**
伝	亻	person	4	**KL 13**
都	阝	right village	3	**V 10**
徒	彳	stepping	4	**V 10**
途	辶	movement	8	**V 11**
塗	土	earth	8	**V 11**
土	土	earth	1	**V 10**
等	竹	bamboo	3	**V 10**
答	竹	bamboo	2	**V 11**
登	癶	footsteps	3	**V 11**
刀	刀	sword	2	**V 34**
到	刀	sword	8	**V 34**
灯	火	fire	4	V 34
同	口	mouth	2	**P 100**
洞	氵	water	8	**P 100**

ON READING	KANJI	MEANING	ADDITIONAL ON READING	KUN READING
DOU	胴	trunk, torso	n	n
DOU	童	child	n	warabe
DOU	撞	clash	TOU, SHU	tsu(ku)
DOU	瞳	pupil (of eye)	TOU	hitomi
DOU	道	road, way, teachings	TOU	michi
DOU	導	guide, lead	n	michibi(ku)
NA	奈	phonetic NA	n	n
NIN	任	responsibility	n	maka(seru), maka(su)
NIN	妊	pregnancy	n	n
NIN	忍	endure, bear	n	shino(bu), shino(baseru)
NIN	認	recognise	n	mito(meru)
NEN	粘	sticky	n	neba(ru)
HA	波	wave	n	nami
HAI	杯	cup, glass, counter for glasses	n	sakazuki
HAI	肺	lungs	n	n
HAI	拝	worship	n	oga(mu)
HAI	俳	actor, haiku	n	n
HAKU	白	white	BYAKU	shiro, shiro(i)
HAKU	泊	stay overnight	n	to(maru), to(meru)
HAKU	拍	beat, clap	HYOU	n
BAKU	漠	desert, obscure	n	n
BATSU	罰	penalty, punishment	BACHI	n
HAN	半	half	n	naka(ba)
HAN	伴	accompany, companion	BAN	tomona(u)
HAN	反	opposite, anti-	HON, TAN	so(ru), so(rasu)
HAN	坂	slope, hill	n	saka
HAN	阪	heights, slope	n	saka
HAN	版	printing block, publishing	n	n

KANJI	RADICAL	RADICAL NAME	GRADE	REFERENCE
胴	肉 月	meat, organ	8	P 100
童	立	stand	3	P 101
撞	扌	hand	9	P 101
瞳	目	eye	8	P 101
道	辶	movement	2	PR 1
導	寸	inch	5	PR 1
奈	大	big	8	K 20
任	亻	person	5	P 102
妊	女	woman	8	P 102
忍	心	heart	8	P 103
認	言	speech	6	P 103
粘	米	rice	8	PR 6
波	氵	water	3	K 21
杯	木	tree	8	V 23
肺	肉 月	meat, organ	6	V 23
拝	扌	hand	6	V 23
俳	亻	person	6	V 23
白	白	white	1	P 104
泊	氵	water	8	P 104
拍	扌	hand	8	P 104
漠	氵	water	8	PR 13
罰	罒	net	8	PR 19
半	十	ten	2	P 105
伴	亻	person	8	P 105
反	又	again	3	P 106
坂	土	earth	3	P 106
阪	阝	left village	8	P 106
版	片	slice, fragment	5	P 106

ON READING	KANJI	MEANING	ADDITIONAL ON READING	KUN READING
HAN	販	sell, trade	n	n
HAN	飯	cooked rice, meal	n	meshi
BAN	番	number, turn	n	n
HI	比	compare	n	kura(beru)
HI	秘	secret	n	hi(meru)
HI	非	wrong, non-	n	arazu
HI	泌	seep out, ooze, secrete	HITSU	n
HI	皮	skin, cover	n	kawa
HI	披	reveal, expose	n	n
HI	彼	he, that	n	kare, kano
HI	被	subject of an activity, receive	n	koumu(ro)
HI	疲	tired	n	tsuka(reru)
HI	緋	scarlet	n	aka, ake
HI	悲	sad, grief	n	kana(shii), kana(shimu)
HI	扉	door	n	tobira
BI	美	beautiful	n	utsuku(shii)
HIN	品	goods, article	n	shina
FU	不	not, un-	BU	n
FU	付	attach	n	tsu(keru), tsu(ku)
FU	布	cloth	n	nuno
FU	附	attach, append	n	n
FU	符	sign, symbol	n	n
FU	府	urban prefecture	n	n
FUKU	幅	width	n	haba
FUKU	福	luck, (good) fortune	n	n
FUKU	副	deputy, vice-	n	n
FUKU	復	return, repeat	n	n
FUKU	腹	stomach, abdomen	n	hara

KANJI	RADICAL	RADICAL NAME	GRADE	REFERENCE
販	貝	shell	8	P 106
飯	食	eat	4	P 106
番	田	field	2	PR 11
比	比	compare	5	K 22
秘	禾	grain	6	KL 14, P 107
非	非	wrong	5	KL 15, P 109
泌	氵	water	8	P 107
皮	皮	skin	3	P 108
披	扌	hand	8	P 108
彼	彳	stepping	8	P 108
被	衤	clothes	8	P 108
疲	疒	sickness	8	P 108
緋	糸	thread	9	P 109
悲	心	heart	3	P 109
扉	戸	door	8	P 109
美	羊	sheep	3	V 22
品	口	mouth	3	PR 5
不	一	one	4	K 23
付	亻	person	4	KL 17, P 110
布	巾	turban	5	KL 18
附	阝	left village	8	P 110
符	竹	bamboo	8	P 110
府	广	ma border	4	P 110
幅	巾	turban	8	P 111
福	ネ	worship	3	P 111
副	刂	sword	4	P 111
復	彳	stepping	5	P 112
腹	肉 月	meat, organ	6	P 112

ON READING	KANJI	MEANING	ADDITIONAL ON READING	KUN READING
FUKU	複	duplicate, compound	n	n
FUKU	覆	cover, capsize	n	oo(u), kutsugae(ru), kutsugae(su)
FUN	分	minute, part	BUN, BU	wa(keru), wa(kareru), wa(karu), wa(ke)
FUN	粉	powder	n	ko, kona
HEI	丙	third in ranking	n	n
BEI	米	rice, United States	MAI	kome
HEKI	壁	wall	n	kabe
HEKI	癖	bad habit, weakness	n	kuse
HEN	偏	incline, lean	n	katayo(ru)
HEN	遍	everywhere	n	n
HEN	編	knit, edit	n	a(mu)
HEN	変	change, strange	n	ka(waru), ka(eru)
BEN	勉	study, make an effort	n	n
HO	保	preserve, protect	n	tamo(tsu)
HO	捕	catch, seize	n	to(raeru), to(ru), tsuka(maeru), tsuka(maru)
HO	補	supplement, compensate	n	ogina(u)
BO	募	gather, recruit	n	tsuno(ru)
BO	墓	grave, tomb	n	haka
BO	暮	sunset, spend time	n	ku(reru), ku(rasu)
BO	慕	long for, admire	n	shita(u)
BO	模	model, pattern	MO	n
HOU	包	wrap, package	n	tsutsu(mu), tsutsu(mi)
HOU	泡	bubble	n	awa
HOU	抱	hug, embrace	b	da(ku), ida(ku), kaka(eru)
HOU	胞	sac surrounding foetus, in utero	n	n
HOU	砲	gun, cannon	n	n

KANJI	RADICAL	RADICAL NAME	GRADE	REFERENCE
複	衤	clothes	5	**P 112**
覆	襾	west	8	**P 112**
分	刀	sword	2	**P 113**
粉	米	rice	4	**P 113**
丙	一	one	8	**KL 19**
米	米	rice	2	**PR 3**
壁	土	earth	8	**P 114**
癖	疒	sickness	8	**P 114**
偏	亻	person	8	**P 115**
遍	辶	movement	8	**P 115**
編	糸	thread	5	**P 115**
変	夂	winter	4	**PR 8**
勉	力	power	3	**PR 7**
保	亻	person	5	**K 24**
捕	扌	hand	8	**P 116**
補	衤	clothes	6	**P 116**
募	力	power	8	**P 117**
墓	土	earth	5	**P 117**
暮	日	sun	6	**P 117**
慕	心	heart	8	**P 117**
模	木	tree	6	**P 117**
包	勹	wrapping	4	**P 118**
泡	氵	water	8	**P 118**
抱	扌	hand	8	**P 118**
胞	肉 月	meat, organ	8	**P 118**
砲	石	stone	8	**P 118**

ON READING	KANJI	MEANING	ADDITIONAL ON READING	KUN READING
HOU	飽	tire of, satiate	n	a(kiru), a(kasu)
HOU	縫	sew	n	nu(u)
HOU	蜂	bee, wasp	n	hachi
HOU	方	direction, person	n	kata
HOU	訪	visit	n	otozu(reru), tazu(neru)
HOU	放	release, liberate	n	hana(su), hana(reru), hana(tsu)
HOU	芳	fragrant	n	kanba(shii)
BOU	亡	deceased, dying	MOU	na(i)
BOU	忙	busy	n	isoga(shii)
BOU	忘	forget	n	wasu(reru)
BOU	望	hope, expect	MOU	nozo(mu)
BOU	房	tassel, house	n	fusa
BOU	防	protect, defend	n	fuse(gu)
BOU	肪	fat	n	n
HON	翻	turn over, waver	n	hirugae(ru), hirugae(su)
MA	麻	hemp, numb	n	asa
MA	摩	rub, polish	n	n
MA	磨	grind, polish, brush (teeth)	n	miga(ku)
MA	魔	demon, witch	n	n
MAKU	膜	membrane	n	n
MAKU	幕	curtain	BAKU	n
MATSU	末	end, last part	BATSU	sue
MI	未	not yet (reached, achieved)	n	n
MI	味	taste, flavour	n	aji, aji(wau)
MI	魅	charm, bewitch	n	n
MITSU	密	secret	n	n
MITSU	蜜	honey	n	n
MU	武	military	BU	n
MEI	名	name	MYOU	na

KANJI	RADICAL	RADICAL NAME	GRADE	REFERENCE
飽	食	eat	8	**P 118**
縫	糸	thread	8	**P 119**
蜂	虫	insect	8	**P 119**
方	方	way	2	**PR 2**
訪	言	speech	6	**PR 2**
放	攵	strike	3	**PR 2**
芳	艹	grass	8	**PR 2**
亡	亠	pot lid	6	**P 120, V 37**
忙	忄	heart	6	**P 120**
忘	心	heart	8	**P 120**
望	月	moon	4	**P 120**
房	戸	door	8	**PR 2**
防	阝	left village	5	**PR 2**
肪	肉 月	meat, organ	8	**PR 2**
翻	羽	wings	8	**PR 11**
麻	麻	hemp	8	**KL 20, P 121**
摩	手	hand	8	**P 121**
磨	石	stone	8	**P 121**
魔	鬼	demon	8	**P 121**
膜	肉 月	meat, organ	8	**PR 13**
幕	巾	turban	6	**PR 13**
末	木	tree	4	**K 25**
未	木	tree	4	**P 122, V 22**
味	口	mouth	3	**P 122**
魅	鬼	demon	8	**P 122**
密	山	mountain	6	**P 123**
蜜	虫	insect	8	**P 123**
武	止	stop	5	**K 26**
名	口	mouth	1	**P 124, V 15**

ON READING	KANJI	MEANING	ADDITIONAL ON READING	KUN READING
MEI	銘	inscription	n	n
MEI	明	bright	MYOU	aka(rui), aka(rumu), aki(raka), a(keru), a(ku)
MEI	盟	alliance	n	n
MEI	迷	be confused, lead astray	MAI	mayo(u)
MEI	命	life, destiny, order	MYOU	inochi
MEI	鳴	cry (of bird or animal)	n	na(ku), na(ru), na(rasu)
MEN	面	face, surface	n	omo, omote, tsura
MEN	麺	noodles	n	n
MEN	免	evade, dismiss	n	manuka(reru)
MOU	毛	hair, fur	n	ke
MOU	耗	wear out	KOU	n
MOU	網	net, network	n	ami
MOU	盲	blind	n	n
RAKU	落	fall	n	o(chiru), o(tosu)
RAKU	絡	entwine	n	kara(mu), kara(maru), kara(meru)
RAKU	楽	fun, music, comfort	GAKU	tano(shimu), tano(shii)
RI	利	profit, advantage	n	ki(ku)
RI	理	logic, science	n	n
RYUU	龍	dragon	RYOU	tatsu
RYUU	竜	dragon, imperial	RYOU	tatsu
RYOU	良	good	n	yo(i)
RYOU	療	heal, cure	n	n
RYOU	寮	dormitory, hostel	n	n
RYOKU	緑	green	ROKU	midori
RIN	臨	attend, meet	n	nozo(mu)
RU	流	flow, current	RYUU	naga(reru), naga(su)
REI	礼	etiquette, bow	RAI	n
REI	令	order, command	n	n

KANJI	RADICAL	RADICAL NAME	GRADE	REFERENCE
銘	金	metal	8	P 124
明	日	sun	2	P 125, V 15
盟	皿	dish	6	P 125
迷	辶	movement	5	PR 3
命	口	mouth	3	V 15
鳴	鳥	bird	2	V 15
面	面	surface	3	P 126
麺	麦	wheat	8	P 126
免	儿	legs	8	PR 7
毛	毛	fur	2	K 27, V 37
耗	耒	plow	8	V 37
網	糸	thread	8	V 37
盲	目	eye	8	V 37
落	艹	grass	3	PR 12
絡	糸	thread	8	PR 12
楽	木	tree	2	PR 14
利	刂	sword	4	K 30
理	玉	king, jewel	2	KL 21
龍	龍	dragon	10	V 45
竜	龍	dragon	8	V 45
良	艮	boundary	4	V 41
療	疒	sickness	8	V 41
寮	宀	U crown	8	V 41
緑	糸	thread	3	PR 18
臨	臣	official	6	PR 5
流	氵	water	3	K 31, V 45
礼	礻	worship	3	K 32
令	人	person	4	KL 22, P 127

ON READING	KANJI	MEANING	ADDITIONAL ON READING	KUN READING
REI	冷	cold, cool	n	tsume(tai), hi(eru), hi(yasu), sa(meru)
REI	鈴	bell	RIN	suzu
REI	齢	age	n	n
REI	零	zero, nothing	n	n
REN	恋	love	n	koi, ko(u), koi(shii)
RO	呂	phonetic RO	n	n
ROU	浪	wave, reckless	n	n
ROU	郎	young man	n	n
ROU	朗	clear, bright	n	hoga(raka)
ROU	廊	corridor	n	n
ROKU	録	record	n	n
YAKU	薬	drug, medicine	n	kusuri
YU	由	origin, reason	YUU, YUI	yoshi
YUU	友	friend	n	tomo
YUU	有	have, possess, exist	U	a(ru)
YUU	雄	male, hero	n	o, osu
YO	与	give	n	ata(eru)
YO	予	prior, forecast	n	n
YO	預	deposit, custody	n	azu(keru), azu(karu)
YOU	羊	sheep	n	hitsuji
YOU	洋	ocean, foreign, Western	n	n
YOU	養	raise, nurture	n	yashina(u)
YOKU	欲	desire, crave	n	hossuru (ほっ(する)), ho(shii)
YOKU	浴	bathe	n	a(biru), a(biseru)
WA	和	harmony, peace, Japanese style	O	yawa(ragu), yawa(rageru), nago, nago(mu)
–	滝	waterfall	n	taki

KANJI	RADICAL	RADICAL NAME	GRADE	REFERENCE
冷	冫	ice	4	**P 127**
鈴	金	metal	8	**P 127**
齢	歯	tooth	8	**P 127**
零	雨	rain	8	**P 127**
恋	心	heart	8	**PR 8**
呂	口	mouth	8	**K 33**
浪	氵	water	8	**P 128**
郎	阝	right village	8	**P 128, V 41**
朗	月	moon	6	**P 128**
廊	广	ma border	8	**P 128**
録	金	metal	4	**PR 18**
薬	艹	grass	3	**PR 14**
由	田	field	3	**K 28**
友	又	again	2	**V 1**
有	月	moon	3	**V 1**
雄	隹	old bird	8	**V 1**
与	一	one	8	**K 29**
予	亅	hook	3	**KL 23, P 129**
預	頁	big shell	5	**P 129**
羊	羊	sheep	3	**P 130**
洋	氵	water	3	**P 130**
養	食	eat	4	**P 130**
欲	欠	lack, yawn	6	**PR 16**
浴	氵	water	4	**PR 16**
和	口	mouth	3	**K 34**
滝	氵	water	8	**V 45**

abstinence, purification 斎 P 51
accompany, companion 伴 P 105
account, write down 記 P 16
actor, haiku 俳 V 23
add 加 K 5, P 3, V 18
age 齢 P 127
alcohol, sake 酒 V 28
alliance 盟 P 125
ancestor 祖 KL 8, P 79
and, concurrently 兼 V 31
answer, solution 答 V 11
anti-, opposite 反 P 106
appear, actual 現 V 29
arrive, reach 到 V 34
ask, request 請 P 74
assets, capital 資 P 57
assist, help 佐 P 47
attach 付 KL 17, P 110
attach, append 附 P 110
attend, meet 臨 PR 5
authority, right 権 V 31
autumn, fall 秋 V 2, V 20
bad habit, weakness 癖 P 114
bad smell, stink 臭 V 2
ball, sphere 球 P 20
bamboo 竹 P 89
bamboo basket 箪 P 87
bathe 浴 PR 16
bear a grudge, malice 恨 P 46
beat, clap 拍 P 104
beautiful 美 V 22
become, reach 成 P 75
bee, wasp 蜂 P 119
before, in front 前 V 36
before, previous 先 V 43
believe, trust 信 V 30
bell 鈴 P 127
bend, yield 屈 P 28, PR 15
blind 盲 V 37
blood 血 V 5
blue, green 青 P 74
body, person 身 V 30
border, boundary 境 P 23
borrow, rent 借 P 61
bottom 底 P 97
branch, limb 枝 P 56
breathe in, inhale, smoke 吸 P 19
bright 明 P 125, V 15
bubble 泡 P 118
bud, sprout 芽 P 7
build 建 V 31
build 築 P 89
build, construct 構 P 44
bullet 弾 PR 4
bureau 局 V 27
bureaucrat, government 官 P 12, V 4
busy 忙 P 120
by chance, even number 偶 P 27
by means of, includes 以 K 2
cabinet (government) 閣 P 10
call, exhale 呼 V 7
camp, run (a business) 営 V 35
can, passable 可 P 2, V 18
capital, metropolis 都 V 10
carry, bear 担 P 86
catch, seize 捕 P 116
cause 因 PR 9
cave 洞 P 100
cave, hole 穴 V 5
cavern 窟 P 28
centre, middle 中 P 90
ceremony 儀 P 9
challenge 挑 P 93
change, convert 化 P 4, V 18

change, strange	変	PR 8
chapter, section	章	V 19
character, gender	性	P 72
charge (person in charge)	係	P 29
charm, bewitch	魅	P 122
check, examine	検	P 35
chief, main, principal	主	V 17
child	子	V 16
child	童	P 101
clan, family name	氏	V 16
clash	撞	P 101
clear, bright	朗	P 128
clear, pure	清	P 74
climb, ascend	登	V 11
cloth	布	KL 18
coin, money	銭	P 77
cold	寒	V 4
cold, cool	冷	P 127
colouring	彩	P 49
common, vulgar	俗	PR 16
compare	比	K 22
compete	競	P 22
complete, perfect	完	PR 10, V 4
compose, recite	詠	P 1
condition, situation	況	P 22
confine, tie	錮	P 38
confused, lead astray	迷	PR 3
congratulate	賀	P 3
connection, barrier	関	P 13, V 32
construct, manufacture	工	P 40, V 8
consult	諮	P 57
cooked rice, meal	飯	P 106
corner	隅	P 27
correct, justice	正	P 73
corridor	廊	P 128
court	廷	P 98
courtyard, garden	庭	P 98
cover, capsize	覆	P 112
crimson, deep red	紅	P 40
crop tax, tariff	租	P 79
crown	冠	PR 10, V 4
cry (of bird or animal)	鳴	V 15
cultivate, reclaim	墾	P 46
cup, counter for glasses	杯	V 23
curtain	幕	PR 13
cut	切	PR 19
danger, precipitous	険	P 35
dawn	旦	P 86
death	死	P 58
deceased, dying	亡	P 120, V 37
decide, fix	決	V 5
decide, fix	定	KL 11, P 96
demon, witch	魔	P 121
deposit, custody	預	P 129
deputy, vice-	副	P 111
desert, obscure	漠	PR 13
desire, crave	欲	PR 16
desk	机	P 15
destiny, life	命	V 15
diagnose, examine	診	P 70
diameter	径	P 31
dice	采	P 49
difference	差	P 47
dig	掘	P 28
direction, person	方	PR 2
disaster, misfortune	禍	P 6
disaster, wretched	惨	P 54
disciple, follower	徒	V 10
distance	距	P 21
dog	犬	P 34
door	扉	P 109
dormitory, hostel	寮	V 41
dot, grade	点	PR 6
down, descend	下	V 18
dragon	龍	V 45

dragon, imperial	竜	V 45
draw near	寄	P 18
drive	駆	P 26
drop, drip	滴	P 99
dry	干	P 11
dry	乾	P 14
drying, dehydration	燥	P 83
duplicate, compound	複	P 112
dwell, live	居	V 25
dye, colour	染	V 43
each, every	各	P 10, PR 12
earth, soil, ground	土	V 10
elegant	雅	P 7
embankment	堤	P 96
encounter	遇	P 27
end, last part	末	K 25
endure, bear	忍	P 103
enemy	敵	P 99
England, hero	英	V 35
enlighten, open	啓	V 12
enlightened (become), realise, perceive	悟	P 39
Enormous, great	巨	P 21, V 25
enquire, visit	伺	P 55
entwine	絡	PR 12
error, mistake	誤	V 38
etc., equal, (first) class	等	V 10
eternal	永	P 1
etiquette, bow	礼	K 32
evade, dismiss	免	PR 7
everywhere	遍	P 115
excellent, auspicious	嘉	P 3
exist	在	V 3
exit, go out	出	PR 15
extend, stretch	伸	P 68
extinguish, cancel	消	P 66
extreme, poles	極	V 27
face toward, over there	向	V 8
face, surface	面	P 126
fall	落	PR 12
fat	脂	P 58
fat	肪	PR 2
feelings, emotion	情	V 21
few	少	P 65
figure, appearance	姿	P 57
filial piety, parental respect	孝	P 41
finger, indicate	指	P 58
fire	火	KL 16
firm, strict	堅	P 37, V 13
fist	拳	P 33
five	五	P 39, V 38
flag, banner	旗	P 17
flood, deluge	洪	P 43
flow, current	流	K 31, V 45
flower	花	P 4
fold, bend	折	PR 20
forecast, prior	予	KL 23, P 129
forget	忘	P 120
fortune-telling, occupy	占	PR 6, V 44
foundation, base	基	P 17
fragrant	芳	PR 2
fresh, vivid	鮮	V 36
friend	友	V 1
fruit, result	果	P 5, V 9
fun, music, comfort	楽	PR 14
gallbladder, courage	胆	P 86
gather, recruit	募	P 117
get up, occur	起	P 16
give	与	K 29
glory, prosper	栄	V 35
go around, patrol	巡	V 33
god, mind	神	P 68
good	良	V 41
good, virtuous	善	P 78
goods, article	品	PR 5

government, politics	政	P 73
grave, tomb	墓	P 117
great-(grandmother, etc.), formerly	曽	K 14, P 81
green	緑	PR 18
ground, earth	地	KL 9
guard, warn	警	P 32, V 12
guide, lead	導	PR 1
gun, cannon	砲	P 118
hair, fur	毛	K 27, V 37
half	半	P 105
hand	手	V 17
hang up, stand	架	P 3
hang, suspend	懸	P 36, V 13
harbour, port	港	P 43
have, possess, exist	有	V 1
he, that	彼	P 108
heal, cure	療	V 41
heavens, natural	天	K 18
heir, succeed	嗣	P 55
hemp, numb	麻	KL 20, P 121
hide, conceal	隠	V 14
hill, slope	坂	P 106
history, chronical	史	V 16
honey	蜜	P 123
hope, expect	望	P 120
house, residence	宅	V 26
hug, embrace	抱	P 118
hunger, starve	飢	P 15
illuminate, lighting	照	P 67
increase, multiply	殖	P 59, PR 17
individual, counter for articles	個	P 38
inscription	銘	P 124
insect	虫	P 90
insect, elder brother	昆	V 39
institution	院	V 14
intention	志	P 56
introduce	紹	P 67
investigate, judge	察	P 53
investigation, hearing	審	PR 11
Japanese chess, shogi	棋	P 17
Japanese Judas tree	桂	P 30
juice, soup	汁	P 63
kind, cordial	懇	P 46
kindness, mercy	恩	PR 9
knit, edit	編	P 115
Korea	韓	P 14
lack, deficiency	欠	V 5
lamp, light	灯	V 34
language, say	語	P 39, V 38
large building	館	P 12
layer, class	層	P 81
lean, incline	偏	P 115
leap, prance	跳	P 93
lecture	講	P 44
left, progressive	左	K 10, P 47
leisure, quietness	閑	P 13
lesson, section	課	P 5
level, grade	級	P 19, V 40
life,birth, student	生	P 72
light, ray	光	V 24
limbs (arm, leg)	肢	P 56
line, track	線	P 76
lips	唇	P 69
liver, courage	肝	P 11
logic, science	理	KL 21
long for, admire	慕	P 117
long time	久	K 7
long, leader	長	P 92
longevity, congratulations	寿	KL 7
longitude, pass through	経	P 31
look, gaze	眺	P 93
look, see	見	V 29

love	恋	PR 8
low	低	KL 12, P 97
loyalty, devotion	忠	P 90
luck, (good) fortune	福	P 111
lungs	肺	V 23
magazine, document	誌	P 56
make, produce	作	P 52
male, hero	雄	V 1
manuscript, draft	稿	P 45
many	多	K 16, V 26
market, city	市	V 16
marriage	婚	V 39
martyrdom	殉	P 64
meals, table	膳	P 78
measles, sickness	疹	P 70
measure	測	P 84
measure, plan	計	K 8
measurement, tiny	寸	K 12
mechanism, chance	機	K 6
mediate, shellfish	介	V 6
mediator, go-between	仲	P 90
medicine	剤	P 51
medicine, drug	薬	PR 14
meet, meeting	会	V 6
member, employee	員	V 14
membrane	膜	PR 13
military	武	K 26
ministry	省	P 65, V 19
minute, part	分	P 113
mirror, lens	鏡	P 23
mix, blend, confusion	混	V 39
mix, interchange	交	P 42, V 24
model, pattern	模	P 117
moth	蛾	P 8
mountain	山	V 44
mouth	口	V 8
moxibustion (Chinese therapy)	灸	V 40
mutual, reciprocal	相	P 80
mutual, reciprocal	互	V 38
name	名	P 124, V 15
narrow	狭	P 25
neck	首	V 28
net, network	網	V 37
new	新	P 71
nine	九	V 40
nitrate, saltpeter	硝	P 66
No., prefix for numbers	第	P 85
noodles	麺	P 126
not yet (achieved)	未	P 122, V 22
not, un-	不	K 23
notebook	帳	P 92
number	号	V 38
number, turn	番	PR 11
obtain, income	収	V 2, V 20
ocean, foreign, Western	洋	P 130
offer, present	供	P 24
official, sergeant	曹	P 82
official, serve	仕	P 56
officiate, manage	司	KL 6, P 55
old	古	KL 4, P 38, V 7
old times	昔	P 61
older brother	兄	P 22
omen, trillion	兆	P 93
operate, manipulate	操	P 83
order, command	令	KL 22, P 127
order, obey	順	V 33
organise, assemble	組	P 79
origin	元	PR 10, V 29
origin, reason	由	K 28
original, field	原	V 29
other, another	他	V 26
pain	痛	P 94
paint (v.), coat (v.)	塗	V 11

parent, intimacy	親	P 71
part of speech, words	詞	P 55
participate	参	P 54
pass through	過	P 6
pass through, traffic	通	P 94
pavilion, restaurant	亭	P 95
peace, Japanese style	和	K 34
penalty, punishment	罰	PR 19
permit	許	V 25
phenomena, thing, so	然	V 36
phonetic I	伊	K 3
phonetic NA	奈	K 20
phonetic RO	呂	K 33
phrase	句	KL 2
pick, pluck	摘	P 99
pinch, hold between	挟	P 25
pipe, control	管	P 12
plant, grow	植	P 59, PR 17
play with, enjoy	玩	PR 10
pledge, promise	契	V 12, V 42
polish, brush (teeth)	磨	P 121
pour	注	P 91
powder	粉	P 113
practice, study	修	V 20
prefecture	県	P 36, V 31
pregnancy	娠	P 69
pregnancy	妊	P 102
present, offering	献	P 34
price, value	価	V 9
priest (Buddhist), monk	僧	P 81
print, brush	刷	PR 19
prisoner	囚	V 2
prize, reward	賞	V 19
profit, advantage	利	K 30
prosper, flourish	盛	P 75
protect	守	V 17
protect, defend	防	PR 2
protect, preserve	保	K 24
public, official	公	V 24
publish	刊	P 11
publishing, printing block	版	P 106
pupil (of eye)	瞳	P 101
quality, substance	質	PR 20
quiet	静	P 74
raise animals	飼	P 55
raise, nurture	養	P 130
reach, extend	及	P 19
reason, happenstance	故	P 38, V 7
recognise	認	P 103
record	録	PR 18
refuse	拒	P 21, V 25
relax, cheap	安	K 1
release, liberate	放	PR 2
resemblance, look like	肖	P 66
residence	邸	P 97
resist	抵	P 97
respect, reverence	敬	P 32
responsibility	任	P 102
return, repeat	復	P 112
reveal, expose	披	P 108
revise, correct	訂	KL 10, P 95
rhyme, tone	韻	V 14
rice, United States	米	PR 3
ride horses	騎	P 18
righteousness, morality	義	P 9
ring, circle	環	V 32
river	河	P 2
river	川	V 44
road, way, teachings	道	PR 1
roast, boil	煎	V 36
root	根	P 46, V 39
rough, course	粗	P 79
rowing, canal transport	漕	P 82

rub	擦	P 53
rub, polish	摩	P 121
rule	則	P 84
sac surrounding foetus	胞	P 118
sacrifice	犠	P 9
sad, grief	悲	P 109
same	同	P 100
sand	沙	KL 5, P 48
sand	砂	P 48
save, rescue	救	P 20
say (humbly)	申	P 68
scar, trace	痕	P 46
scarlet	緋	P 109
scatter	散	K 11
scholar, samurai	士	P 56, V 16
school	校	P 42
secret	密	P 123
secret	秘	KL 14, P 107
seep out, ooze	泌	P 107
self	己	K 9
self	我	P 8
selfish, arbitrary	恣	P 57
sell, trade	販	P 106
send	送	PR 1
settle (debt)	済	P 51
sew	縫	P 119
shake, quake	震	P 69
shake, wave	振	V 30
shallow, superficial	浅	P 77
share, together with	共	P 24
sheep	羊	P 130
shell, first, instep	甲	V 9
shop	店	PR 6
side	側	P 84
sign, symbol	符	P 110
simple	簡	P 13
sincerity	誠	P 75
single	単	P 87, PR 4
skin, cover	皮	P 108
slope, heights	阪	P 106
small	小	P 65, V 19
solidify, set	固	P 38
song	歌	P 2
space between, interval	間	P 13, V 32
special, particularly	殊	P 62
sphere	圏	P 33
spirit, air	気	KL 1
spirit, energy	精	P 74
spring (season)	春	V 33
spring, fountain	泉	P 76
square jewel, jade	圭	P 30
squeeze	搾	P 52
starve	餓	P 8
state	州	V 20
stationed, stopover	駐	P 91
status	格	P 10, PR 12
status, condition	状	V 21
stay overnight	泊	P 104
stem	茎	P 31
sticky	粘	PR 6
stomach, abdomen	腹	P 112
stop	止	K 19, V 16
stop, halt	停	P 95
straight, direct, frank	直	PR 17
strange, unusual	奇	P 18
stretch, spread	張	P 92
stubborn	頑	PR 10
study, make an effort	勉	PR 7
subject of an activity	被	P 108
suitable	適	P 99
summon, invite	招	P 67
sunset, spend time	暮	P 117
supervise, direct	監	V 32
supplement, compensate	補	P 116
support, branch	支	P 56

sweat	汗	P 11
sweets	菓	P 5
swim	泳	V 35, P 1
sword, knife	刀	V 34
system	系	P 29, V 42
take, obtain	取	V 28
talent	才	P 50, V 3
tall, high	高	P 45, V 8
tassel, house	房	PR 2
taste, flavour	味	P 122
temple	刹	PR 19
temple (Buddhist)	寺	P 60
ten	十	P 63
ten day period	旬	P 64
test, verify	験	P 35
thick, plump	太	K 15
think	考	P 41
think, idea	想	P 80
third in ranking	丙	KL 19
thousand	千	V 44
three	三	V 44
throat, choked	咽	PR 9
ticket	券	P 33
timber, materials	材	P 50, V 3
time period	期	P 17
time, hour	時	P 60
tire of, satiate	飽	P 118
tired	疲	P 108
transmit	伝	KL 13
true, reality	真	V 30
trunk	幹	P 14, V 32
trunk, torso	胴	P 100
turn over, waver	翻	PR 11
tusk, fang	牙	P 7
type, model	型	V 12
universe	宇	K 4
up, above	上	V 21
urban prefecture	府	P 110
urgent, emergency	急	V 40
valley	渓	V 42
valley	谷	PR 16
vat, tank	槽	P 82
vermilion, bright red	朱	P 62
visit	訪	PR 2
wall	壁	P 114
want, request	求	P 20
ward, district	区	KL 3, P 26
warrior, attendant	侍	P 60
wash	洗	V 43
waterfall	滝	V 45
wave	波	K 21
wave, reckless	浪	P 128
way, road	途	V 11
wealth, assets	財	P 50, V 3
wear out	耗	V 37
whirlpool	渦	P 6
white	白	P 104
width	幅	P 111
wisdom, clever	賢	P 37, V 13
wisdom, intellect	智	P 88
wisdom, knowledge	知	K 17, P 88
wither, die	枯	P 38
world, boundary	界	V 6
world, generation	世	K 13
worship	拝	V 23
wrap, package	包	P 118
wrong, non-	非	KL 15, P 109
Wu kingdom of China	呉	V 38
yesterday, past	昨	P 52
young man	郎	P 128, V 41
younger brother	弟	P 85
Zen (Buddhism)	禅	V 36
zero, nothing	零	P 127

RADICAL NAME	RADICAL	KANJI	REFERENCE
NATURE			
	water	水氵	
		泳	V 35, P 1
		永	P 1
		河	P 2
		渦	P 6
		汗	P 11
		求	P 20
		況	P 22
		渓	V 42
		決	V 5
		港	P 43
		洪	P 43
		混	V 39
		沙	KL 5, P 48
		済	P 51
		汁	P 63
		消	P 66
		清	P 74
		浅	P 77
		泉	P 76
		洗	V 43
		漕	P 82
		測	P 84
		注	P 91
		滴	P 99
		洞	P 100
		波	K 21
		泊	P 104
		漠	PR 13
		泌	P 107
		泡	P 118
		洋	P 130
		浴	PR 16
		流	K 31, V 45
		浪	P 128
		滝	V 45
	tree	木	
		栄	V 35
		果	P 5, V 9
		架	P 3
		格	P 10, PR 12
		機	K 6
		机	P 15
		棋	P 17
		極	V 27
		桂	P 30
		検	P 35
		権	V 31
		枯	P 38
		校	P 42
		構	P 44
		根	P 46, V 39
		材	P 50, V 3
		枝	P 56
		朱	P 62
		植	P 59, PR 17
		染	V 43
		相	P 80
		槽	P 82
		杯	V 23
		模	P 117
		末	K 25
		未	P 122, V 22
		楽	PR 14

RADICAL NAME	RADICAL	KANJI	REFERENCE
earth	土		
		基	P 17
		境	P 23
		型	V 12
		圭	P 30
		堅	P 37, V 13
		墾	P 46
		在	V 3
		地	KL 9
		堤	P 96
		塗	V 11
		土	V 10
		坂	P 106
		壁	P 114
		墓	P 117
sun	日		
		昆	V 39
		昨	P 52
		時	P 60
		昔	P 61
		春	V 33
		旬	P 64
		旦	P 86
		智	P 88
		暮	P 117
		明	P 125, V 15
grass	艹		
		英	V 35
		花	P 4
		菓	P 5
		芽	P 7
		茎	P 31
		芳	PR 2
		薬	PR 14
		落	PR 12
fire	火 灬		
		火	KL 16
		灸	V 40
		照	P 67
		煎	V 36
		然	V 36
		燥	P 83
		点	PR 6
field	田		
		界	V 6
		甲	V 9
		申	P 68
		番	PR 11
		由	K 28
shell	貝		
		賀	P 3
		賢	P 37, V 13
		財	P 50, V 3
		資	P 57
		質	PR 20
		賞	V 19
		販	P 106
big shell	頁		
		頑	PR 10
		順	V 33
		預	P 129

RADICAL NAME	RADICAL	KANJI	REFERENCE
		moon	月
		期	P 17
		望	P 120
		有	V 1
		朗	P 128
		stone	石
		砂	P 48
		硝	P 66
		砲	P 118
		磨	P 121
		river	川 巛
		州	V 20
		巡	V 33
		川	V 44
mountain	山	山	V 44
mountain	山	密	P 123
rain	雨	震	P 69
rain	雨	零	P 127
steam	气	気	KL 1
ice	冫	冷	P 127
cave	穴	窟	P 28
cave	穴	穴	V 5
valley	谷	谷	PR 16
branch	支	支	P 56

RADICAL NAME	RADICAL	KANJI	REFERENCE
HUMAN BODY			
		mouth	口
		員	V 14
		因	PR 9
		咽	PR 9
		可	P 2, V 18
		嘉	P 3
		各	P 10, PR 12
		吸	P 19
		句	KL 2
		啓	V 12
		古	KL 4, P 38, V 7
		呼	V 7
		呉	V 38
		口	V 8
		向	V 8
		号	V 38
		司	KL 6, P 55
		史	V 16
		嗣	P 55
		唇	P 69
		善	P 78
		同	P 100
		品	PR 5
		味	P 122
		名	P 124, V 15
		命	V 15
		呂	K 33
		和	K 34

RADICAL NAME	RADICAL	KANJI	REFERENCE
hand	手 扌		
		拒	P 21, V 25
		挟	P 25
		掘	P 28
		拳	P 33
		才	P 50, V 3
		搾	P 52
		擦	P 53
		指	P 58
		手	V 17
		招	P 67
		振	V 30
		折	PR 20
		操	P 83
		担	P 86
		抵	P 97
		摘	P 99
		撞	P 101
		拝	V 23
		拍	P 104
		披	P 108
		捕	P 116
		抱	P 118
		摩	P 121
heart	心 忄		
		恩	PR 9
		急	V 40
		懸	P 36, V 13
		悟	P 39
		恨	P 46
		懇	P 46
		惨	P 54
		志	P 56
		恣	P 57
		情	V 21
		性	P 72
		想	P 80
		忠	P 90
		忍	P 103
		悲	P 109
		慕	P 117
		忙	P 120
		忘	P 120
		恋	PR 8
meat, organ	肉 月		
		肝	P 11
		肢	P 56
		脂	P 58
		肖	P 66
		膳	P 78
		胆	P 86
		胴	P 100
		肺	V 23
		腹	P 112
		胞	P 118
		肪	PR 2
		膜	PR 13
eye	目		
		県	P 36, V 31
		省	P 65, V 19
		真	V 30
		眺	P 93
		直	PR 17
		瞳	P 101
		盲	V 37

RADICAL NAME	RADICAL	KANJI	REFERENCE
		legs	儿
		兄	P 22
		元	PR 10, V 29
		光	V 24
		先	V 43
		兆	P 93
		免	PR 7
		yawn, lack	欠
		歌	P 2
		欠	V 5
		欲	PR 16
		corpse	尸
		居	V 25
		局	V 27
		屈	P 28, PR 15
		層	P 81
		decay	歹
		死	P 58
		殊	P 62
		殉	P 64
		殖	P 59, PR 17
foot	足	距	P 21
foot	足	跳	P 93
footsteps	癶	登	V 11
neck	首	首	V 28
body	身	身	V 30
skin	皮	皮	P 108

RADICAL NAME	RADICAL	KANJI	REFERENCE
hair	彡	彩	P 49
blood	血	血	V 5
tooth	歯	齢	P 127
PEOPLE			
		person	亻 人
		以	K 2
		伊	K 3
		価	V 9
		会	V 6
		介	V 6
		儀	P 9
		供	P 24
		偶	P 27
		係	P 29
		個	P 38
		佐	P 47
		作	P 52
		仕	P 56
		伺	P 55
		借	P 61
		修	V 20
		信	V 30
		伸	P 68
		僧	P 81
		側	P 84
		俗	PR 16
		他	V 26
		仲	P 90
		低	KL 12, P 97
		停	P 95
		伝	KL 13

RADICAL NAME	RADICAL	KANJI	REFERENCE
		任	P 102
		俳	V 23
		伴	P 105
		付	KL 17, P 110
		偏	P 115
		保	K 24
		令	KL 22, P 127
		woman	女
		婚	V 39
		姿	P 57
		娠	P 69
		妊	P 102
		king, jewel	王 玉
		環	V 32
		玩	PR 10
		球	P 20
		現	V 29
		理	KL 21
child	子	孝	P 41
child	子	子	V 16
clan	氏	氏	V 16
scholar	士	士	P 56, V 16
official	臣	臨	PR 5
myself	自	臭	V 2
oneself	己	己	K 9
private	ム	参	P 54

RADICAL NAME	RADICAL	KANJI	REFERENCE
old age	耂	考	P 41
ENCLOSURES			
		movement	辶
		過	P 6
		遇	P 27
		送	PR 1
		通	P 94
		適	P 99
		途	V 11
		道	PR 1
		遍	P 115
		迷	PR 3
		sickness	疒
		痕	P 46
		疹	P 70
		痛	P 94
		疲	P 108
		癖	P 114
		療	V 41
		ma border	(麻) 广
		庭	P 98
		底	P 97
		店	PR 6
		府	P 110
		廊	P 128
		stepping	彳
		径	P 31
		徒	V 10
		彼	P 108
		復	P 112

RADICAL NAME	RADICAL	KANJI	REFERENCE
		left village	阝
		院	V 14
		隠	V 14
		隅	P 27
		険	P 35
		阪	P 106
		附	P 110
		防	PR 2
		right village	阝
		邸	P 97
		都	V 10
		郎	P 128, V 41
		country enclosure	囗
		圏	P 33
		固	P 38
		囚	V 2
		gate	門
		閣	P 10
		間	P 13, V 32
		関	P 13, V 32
		閑	P 13
		U crown	宀
		安	K 1
		宇	K 4
		寒	V 4
		官	P 12, V 4
		完	PR 10, V 4
		寄	P 18
		察	P 53
		守	V 17
		審	PR 11
		宅	V 26
		定	KL 11, P 96
		寮	V 41
		pot lid	亠
		交	P 42, V 24
		亭	P 95
		亡	P 120, V 37
long stride	廴	建	V 31
long stride	廴	廷	P 98
cliff border	厂	原	V 29
wrapping	勹	包	P 118
inbox	凵	出	PR 15
C box	匚	区	KL 3, P 26
dot	丶	主	V 17
katakana tsu	⺍	営	V 35
katakana tsu	⺍	単	P 87, PR 4
wa crown	冖	冠	PR 10, V 4
bend, katakana no	丿	及	P 19
bend, katakana no	丿	久	K 7

RADICAL NAME	RADICAL	KANJI	REFERENCE
hook	亅	予	KL 23, P 129

VERBS & LANGUAGE

RADICAL NAME	RADICAL	KANJI	REFERENCE
		speech	言
		詠	P 1
		課	P 5
		記	P 16
		許	V 25
		計	K 8
		警	P 32, V 12
		語	P 39, V 38
		誤	V 38
		講	P 44
		詞	P 55
		誌	P 56
		諮	P 57
		診	P 70
		誠	P 75
		請	P 74
		訂	KL 10, P 95
		認	P 103
		訪	PR 2
		eat	食
		餓	P 8
		館	P 12
		飢	P 15
		飼	P 55
		飯	P 106
		飽	P 118
		養	P 130

RADICAL NAME	RADICAL	KANJI	REFERENCE
		worship	ネ
		禍	P 6
		神	P 68
		禅	V 36
		祖	KL 8, P 79
		福	P 111
		礼	K 32
		again	又
		取	V 28
		収	V 2, V 20
		反	P 106
		友	V 1
		stand	立
		競	P 22
		章	V 19
		童	P 101
		stop	止
		止	K 19, V 16
		正	P 73
		武	K 26
		work	工
		工	P 40, V 8
		左	K 10, P 47
		差	P 47
see	見	見	V 29
see	見	親	P 71
run	走	起	P 16

RADICAL NAME	RADICAL	KANJI	REFERENCE
dry	干	幹	P 14, V 32
dry	干	干	P 11
say	曰	曽	K 14, P 81
say	曰	曹	P 82
compare	比	比	K 22
live	生	生	P 72
wrong	非	非	KL 15, P 109

NATURAL MATERIALS

RADICAL NAME	RADICAL	KANJI	REFERENCE
bamboo	竹		
		管	P 12
		簡	P 13
		第	P 85
		箪	P 87
		竹	P 89
		築	P 89
		答	V 11
		等	V 10
		符	P 110
thread	糸		
		級	P 19, V 40
		経	P 31
		系	P 29, V 42
		紅	P 40
		紹	P 67
		線	P 76
		組	P 79
		緋	P 109
		編	P 115
		縫	P 119
		網	V 37
		絡	PR 12
		緑	PR 18
metal	金		
		鏡	P 23
		錮	P 38
		銭	P 77
		銘	P 124
		鈴	P 127
		録	PR 18
turban	巾		
		市	V 16
		帳	P 92
		布	KL 18
		幅	P 111
		幕	PR 13
clothes	衤		
		被	P 108
		複	P 112
		補	P 116
hemp	麻	麻	KL 20, P 121
tanned leather	韋	韓	P 14

RADICAL NAME	RADICAL	KANJI	REFERENCE
MATH & MEASUREMENT			
		one	一
		下	V 18
		三	V 44
		上	V 21
		世	K 13
		天	K 18
		不	K 23
		丙	KL 19
		与	K 29
		two	二
		巨	P 21, V 25
		五	P 39, V 38
		互	V 38
		eight	八
		共	P 24
		兼	V 31
		公	V 24
		ten	十
		十	P 63
		千	V 44
		半	P 105
		inch	寸
		寺	P 60
		寿	KL 7
		寸	K 12
		導	PR 1

RADICAL NAME	RADICAL	KANJI	REFERENCE
		big	大
		奇	P 18
		契	V 12, V 42
		太	K 15
		奈	K 20
small	小	小	P 65, V 19
small	小	少	P 65
long	長	長	P 92
tall	高	高	P 45, V 8
second	乙	乾	P 14
second	乙	九	V 40
slice, fragment	片	版	P 106
divide	釆	采	P 49
surface	面	面	P 126
way	方	旗	P 17
way	方	方	PR 2
west	襾	覆	P 112
boundary	艮	良	V 41
even	齊	斎	P 51
winter	夂	変	PR 8
evening	夕	多	K 16, V 26

RADICAL NAME	RADICAL	KANJI	REFERENCE
FOOD			
		rice	米
		精	P 74
		粗	P 79
		粘	PR 6
		粉	P 113
		米	PR 3
		grain	禾
		稿	P 45
		秋	V 2, V 20
		租	P 79
		秘	KL 14, P 107
		dish	皿
		監	V 32
		盛	P 75
		盟	P 125
spoon	匕	化	P 4, V 18
sake, alcohol	酉	酒	V 28
wheat	麦	麺	P 126
ANIMALS			
		horse	馬
		騎	P 18
		駆	P 26
		験	P 35
		駐	P 91

RADICAL NAME	RADICAL	KANJI	REFERENCE
		insect	虫
		蛾	P 8
		虫	P 90
		蜂	P 119
		蜜	P 123
		dog	犬　犭
		狭	P 25
		犬	P 34
		献	P 34
		状	V 21
		sheep	羊
		義	P 9
		美	V 22
		羊	P 130
bird	鳥	鳴	V 15
old bird	隹	雅	P 7
old bird	隹	雄	V 1
cow	牛	犠	P 9
fish	魚	鮮	V 36
fur	毛	毛	K 27, V 37
tusk	牙	牙	P 7
wings	羽	翻	PR 11

RADICAL NAME	RADICAL	KANJI	REFERENCE
WARFARE			
		sword	刀 刂
		刊	P 11
		券	P 33
		剤	P 51
		刷	PR 19
		刹	PR 19
		切	PR 19
		前	V 36
		則	P 84
		刀	V 34
		到	V 34
		副	P 111
		分	P 113
		利	K 30
		strike	攵
		救	P 20
		敬	P 32
		故	P 38, V 7
		散	K 11
		政	P 73
		敵	P 99
		放	PR 2
		power	力
		加	K 5, P 3, V 18
		勉	PR 7
		募	P 117
		bow	弓
		弟	P 85
		弾	PR 4
		張	P 92

RADICAL NAME	RADICAL	KANJI	REFERENCE
arrow	矢	知	K 17, P 88
halberd (spear-axe)	戈	我	P 8
halberd (spear-axe)	戈	成	P 75
axe	斤	新	P 71
stick	丨	中	P 90
MAN-MADE TOOLS			
door	戸	扉	P 109
door	戸	房	PR 2
net	罒	罰	PR 19
plow	耒	耗	V 37
SENSES			
white	白	白	P 104
blue	青	青	P 74
blue	青	静	P 74
sound	音	韻	V 14
SUPERNATURAL			
dragon	龍	龍	V 45
dragon	龍	竜	V 45
demon	鬼	魔	P 121
demon	鬼	魅	P 122
fortune-telling	卜	占	PR 6, V 44

www.ingramcontent.com/pod-product-compliance
Ingram Content Group UK Ltd.
Pitfield, Milton Keynes, MK11 3LW, UK
UKHW062307290726
14090UKWH00018B/925